Praise for
Our Fathers' Footsteps

"Even oral histories rarely capture the mundane daily experiences of individuals in combat. Beginning with his own father, Levers recreates the stories of four veterans, deftly weaving family memorabilia together with historical accounts of the Normandy invasion in 1944. Throughout, he reflects on the "What if?" possibilities that shaped the trajectories of their lives back then, just as our own lives are shaped by such experiences today. A thought-provoking and interesting book."

Peter Denton, Associate Professor of History
(Adjunct), Royal Military College of Canada

The author has blended some genuinely harrowing and thought-provoking veteran accounts with an insightful narrative to transport the reader back to the Second World War. In doing so, he poses intriguing questions about the randomness of combat and why some participants survive to tell the tale and others don't. Our Fathers' Footsteps *tells the story from the point of view of the participants. The extra level of information provided makes this book a good read for people like myself. For example, you mention the villages by name, how far away they are and in what direction. That's the kind of detail that is often missing from accounts taken from veterans. They knew what they were doing, but not necessarily where and against whom.*

Paul Woodadge - Author and Historian.
Host of You tube's WW2TV

What a great reading adventure into the history of war! Our Fathers' Footsteps is well written and should be on every bookshelf.

Myra Miller, PhD,
Footsteps Researchers

With meticulous attention to atmosphere and detail, Don Levers has created a ground-level portrait that brings to life the hopes, fears, everyday joys and frustrations of those who went off to fight in the Second World War on behalf of Canada – and democracy. Our Fathers' Footsteps *is a loving, highly readable tribute to the men and women of that period, what they lived through – and what we still owe them.*

Anthony Wilson Smith
(President and C.E.O) Historica Canada

Don Levers details the lives of three Canadians and a Brit. They faced the extraordinary events on D-Day in WWII. Combining the personal with the historical, the author captures the essence of what it was like for these men to leave their families and participate in the dramatic Normandy landings beginning on June 6, 1944. Using letters and diaries never before published, Don Levers has provided an intimate glimpse into the thoughts and emotions of men facing their first combat, the weight of their nation's very existence on their shoulders.

Beginning with his father's story, a veteran of the Royal Winnipeg Rifles, the reader is immediately transported into 1940's Manitoba. Impeccably researched, there is plenty here for both the historian and the WWII buff. The photographs alone are worth the purchase of this book. As well, the narration illuminates and brings to life what it was like to answer the call of duty, which motivated these men to face the most defining event of their generation.

James Ballard Author, Poisoned Jungle
Winner of the Independent Book Publishers
Associations' Ben Franklin Silver Award

This is a worthy topic, and your writing is strong and accessible; I read the sample you provided of your father's experiences with interest and felt that it clipped along at an engaging pace.

Michelle Lobkowicz
University of Alberta Press

One of the most passionate storytellers I have known in my career.

Ryan Jespersen
Real Talk Podcast

I have just finished the first reading of Our Fathers' Footsteps. *As I was involved in many of the circumstances described, I kept wishing it would go on and on. You wrote it almost as if you were there.*

Jim Parks
Surviving veteran, The Royal Winnipeg Rifles

Our Fathers' Footsteps *is a poignant chronicle. Don's book is unique. It examines history from a different perspective, as the author states: What if? Immensely readable and thoroughly researched, Don's pursuit of Veteran's next of kin in Normandy during the 75th Anniversary of D-Day is what makes this chronicle diverse.*

Lieutenant-Colonel (Retired) J. Brian Batter
M.M.M., C.D. The Royal Winnipeg Rifles

Having met Don by chance in Normandy in 2019, I feel privileged to read this fascinating book. Personal memories and photos of participants in the stark reality of war allow the reader to become engaged with each individual and their experiences. A fine example of my favourite kind of history.

Dolores Hatch
Royal Regina Rifles Association member,
Director and regimental researcher

From the families of the men whose stories are told in this book.

You have such a creative ability to get to the nub of people's character and set it to paper. It is a skill I admire greatly. You have done a fantastic job in writing a story to bring to life an era, on the other side of the world, of people and families you never knew. Indeed a way of life entirely different from your own.

Marie Brown
Daughter of Sapper Harry Hildyard. Royal Engineers

Quite a significant project you have completed, Don! I want to thank you for all your interest in my Dad's story. Your time and literary prowess have resulted in the culmination of this book.

Patt Nearingburg
Daughter of Lieutenant Johnny Nearingburg.
Highland Light Infantry of Canada.

I spent an enjoyable evening reading my dad's story as written by you. It evoked a range of emotions. It was eerie reading about places we have so recently been to, including the account of the Carpiquet airport. It was sad to read the fate of those killed in action. You have done a remarkable job of telling the story. Your account of dad's life before, during & after the war fits with who he was, how I think of him. I believe he would be very pleased with your handling of his material. I'm wondering if, perhaps, his record-keeping, writing & retelling were all therapy, a catharsis for him. To have his story retold & to live on is heart-warming. Thank you for what you have researched, imagined & told.

Anne Hamilton
Daughter of Jack Hamilton, The Royal Winnipeg Rifles

Also by Don Levers

Ogopogo: The Misunderstood Lake Monster (1985)

Loot for the Taking: [Inspired by the actual events of the Vancouver Safety Deposit Vault Robbery in 1977] (2017)

Sophie's Map of Time – All Mapped Out: [The Fourth Anthology by the Edmonton Writers Group] (2020)

Ogopogo: The Mysterious Stranger (2022)

Our Fathers' Footsteps

Stories of World War II Veterans' "What If" Moments

May we never forget them .

Don Levers

Don Levers

Foreword by Gord Steinke

OUR FATHER'S FOOTSTEPS
Stories of World War II Veterans' "What If" Moments

Edited by: Brad Talbot

Jacket design: M. Lea Kulmatycki

Jacket image: Don Levers/Photographs courtesy (Library Archives Canada) LAC/DND fonds/a132651 and a/135889.

Every reasonable effort has been made to locate copyright holders of material found in this book. In the event that any material has not been correctly sourced, the publisher will gladly receive correspondence in efforts to rectify the citation in future printings.

Published by Hillsborough Publishing – Sturgeon County, Alberta, Canada

ISBN
Hardcover   978-1-7776802-0-6
Paperback   978-1-7776802-1-3
eBook   978-1-7776802-2-0

Publication assistance and digital printing in Canada by

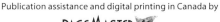

PUBLISHING
PageMaster.ca

For my father Gerry Levers and other extraordinary men and women who served their country with distinction, whose stories have never been told. And to those who helped turn our countries into Nations.

Foreword

By Gord Steinke

Our Fathers' Footsteps is an amazing collection of family war stories compiled from letters, photos, military documents and medal citations, many of which were tucked away for years in drawers and old trunks in attics. Author Don Levers' exhaustive research involved interviewing families of veterans involved in one of the bloodiest and most pivotal battles our nation has ever seen.

On June 6, 1944, the Allies launched the largest seaborne invasion in history on the beaches of Normandy, France. It was known as Operation Overlord. Over 14,000 Canadians were amongst the 150,000 who took part in the D-Day invasion against the fortified defences of Hitler's Atlantic Wall.

Through Don's intense attention to detail, battle logistics, dates, times and places, the reader is taken on a spine-tingling journey through the horror, chaos, and confusion of D-Day. One can almost smell the gunpowder and hear the cries of the wounded and dying.

These profoundly personal recollections paint a picture of the young and not-so-young. Canadian and British soldiers going off to war and ending up in one of the most horrific and critical battles in history. Don tells the gripping story of his father, Gerry, who was wounded during the invasion. He then goes on to recount the horrific story of the men in his father's company being brutally executed by the 12th Waffen SS at Le Chateau d'Audrieu.

The book's various stories tell of the experiences of other soldiers' "What If" moments. Throughout the book, Don asks the question "What If" of his reader. What if his father wasn't wounded? Would he have been with his comrades who were murdered at the hands of the Germans? Don threads these "What If" moments throughout the stories, giving us all something to reflect on.

Our Fathers' Footsteps is filled with heart-touching stories from proud family members about the sacrifices their loved ones made for Canada. Don portrays with great sensitivity the sorrow, the loneliness, and the extreme hardships not only for the soldiers, but also for their families waiting at home for them on farms, in towns, and in cities. The stories of these men also tell who these men were before the war and who they became after doing their duty. Did the war change who these men were?

We, as a nation, are indebted to Don Levers' hard work and dedication for gathering these stories that are such a significant part of not only Canadian history but also the history of England.

Our Fathers' Footsteps will not only keep our veterans' stories alive but also inspire generations of young Canadians to learn about the incredibly brave men and women who fought for our freedom. And for that, I'd like to say thank you, Don.

Honorary Lt. Col. Gord Steinke (author, journalist)

Acknowledgements

I would like to thank the families of the men who helped make this book possible. For the trust they put in me to tell their fathers' stories: Patt Nearingburg, Anne Hamilton, and Marie Brown. Thank you for allowing me to share memories of your fathers. I am indebted to you for your time helping make your fathers sound like the men you remember.

I would also like to thank two members of The Royal Winnipeg Rifles Association, who arranged a trip that I will remember for the rest of my life. Thanks to Brian Batter, a former Lt. Colonel with The Royal Winnipeg Rifles. His knowledge of what happened with the Little Black Devils, during and after the landings, was instrumental in putting Jack Hamilton's and my father's story to paper. Brian did most of the driving as we wound our way through France. His navigational skills helped us reach each of our destinations right on time. Thanks also to Gerry Woodman, who arranged for me to get the nominal roll of the regiment. Seeing the regimental rolls and finding out what happened to the men who were with my father on D-Day inspired me to write these stories. Gerry's contacts with the incredible people of Graye-sur-Mer and Bethonsart helped make our trip so memorable.

I want to acknowledge the other members of our group who helped make our trip to the 75th anniversary of D-Day unforgettable. To Carol Scott, her sister Pat Hunt, and Chris Carmichael, all three of whom ensured there was always food on the table for our group. To Louis-Phillipe Bujold, the only member of our group who spoke French and acted as our intrepid interpreter. To the nieces of Rifleman Fred Marych of The Royal Winnipeg Rifles, who lost his life in Normandy, Pat Nolan, Debra McDonald, Lovey Marych, and Audrey Gibson. You made travelling the roads of France an experience I will always remember. To Anne Hamilton, who sat back with a quiet reserve while absorbing everything going on. These people put up with me as I continued to ask total strangers at any location we stopped at about stories their family might have locked away.

To Gord Steinke, thanks for planting the seed that started me on the journey of writing the book to honour my father and the other men in this book. I also appreciate your taking the time to write the foreword. Thanks for believing in this book and generously agreeing to write the foreword.

It is impossible to recognize everyone who helped me complete this book. To authors and historians Ted Barris and David O'Keefe, thank you for allowing me to use passages from your books and taking the time to respond to my technical questions.

I want to thank my lifelong friend Brad Talbot, MEd, for the countless hours he spent editing this project. His attention to detail helped to make this book complete.

My friend James Ballard, the award-winning author of Poisoned Jungle, encouraged me to complete this book. His observations, suggestions, and assistance were invaluable. Without the help of Brad and James, this book would not be complete.

Special thanks to Lea Kulmatycki for creating the incredible cover for *Our Fathers' Footsteps*.

Thanks to the people of France, Belgium, and Holland, who made us realize that our parents', grandparents', and great-grandparents' contributions have not been forgotten. The warm welcome of your towns and homes while attending the 75th Anniversary of the D- Day landings was overwhelming. Thank you for helping us understand that our families' sacrifices are still appreciated and were not in vain.

Finally, to my wife Deb for her support, love and encouragement on this project. The questions you asked about places and times helped me ensure my facts were accurate. Thank you for your patience as I spent countless hours sitting in front of the computer.

Contents

The Nelson Brothers

John (Jack) Hedley Hamilton
"A" Company 7th Platoon,

Reflections and Conclusion

Introduction

The inspiration for this project began with a few words from Gord Steinke. I met with Gord after learning we shared a historical connection to a small Saskatchewan town. My grandparents and one of his aunts were married in the same stone church in Wapella, Saskatchewan, in the early 1900s. What is most impressive is that this stone-walled church is still standing. During my trip to Wapella several years ago, I took pictures inside the church, including images of the organ my grandmother would play for the congregation and local weddings. After hearing about Gord's connection to Wapella and the small stone church, I reached out to him and shared the pictures. Gord and I wondered what the chances were of my grandmother playing the organ for his aunt's wedding.

During our conversation about rural, small-town Saskatchewan, Gord told me about his book, *Mobsters and Rumrunners of Canada: Crossing the Line*. It includes a section about the Bronfman brothers, who spent time in Wapella during the prohibition years. Gord also told me that he inserted fictionalized dialogue to enhance the reader's enjoyment. It worked: Gord's book is a fascinating look into the Canadian underworld during the prohibition era.

I knew that Gord was interested in the history of Canada's military and the wars we have fought as a nation. I told him I was heading to France for the Normandy landings' 75th anniversary and gave him the short version of my dad's story. After telling me he was envious of the trip on which I was embarking, he commented, "It will be great to walk in your dad's footsteps."

I knew the pilgrimage would be memorable. Still, I didn't understand how powerful an impact it would have on me. My dad was just a small part of something big. He took part in something so enormous that it helped change the course of history. I grew up fascinated with what my father did during the war, but this would be my first trip to see the places he spoke about first-hand.

Gord's comment about walking in my dad's footsteps remained in my head for days. Finally, I pulled out the family history book and looked at my father's letter. It was sent from England on June 16, 1944. I would soon be on my first journey to the shores of Normandy. I knew the significant milestone of the 75th anniversary could be the last for most of the veterans who were still alive. I wondered who would tell their stories after they were gone. In recent years, many veterans have granted interviews so that they could tell their stories before they died. What about the men or women whose stories have never been told and never would be?

Thinking of my dad's story about his experiences based on his correspondence, I realized there might be thousands of these documents, untold stories sitting in a drawer or family history book or in letters left unread for seventy-five years.

I put aside my research on the true story behind a famous Vancouver vault heist to see if I could find more stories like my father's. I would soon be walking in my father's footsteps, as well as those of the hundreds of thousands of men and women who crossed the Normandy beaches. From the shores of France, they battled their way to Germany to help with Europe's liberation. I would thus be walking in "Our Fathers' Footsteps."

Seventy-five years ago, my father was one of the three thousand Canadians in the first assault waves on Juno Beach in Normandy on D-Day, June 6, 1944. More than 14,000 Canadians landed on Juno Beach that day. In addition, over 500 soldiers of the 1st Canadian Parachute Battalion dropped nearby, over five hours before the beach assault. These numbers do not include the thousands of sailors in the Royal Canadian Navy who manned all manner of ships supporting the landings. There were also airmen of the Royal Canadian Air Force, who flew sorties in bombers and fighter planes. Thousands of hours were spent in the air, before and during the actual assault. In the months to follow, many more missions would be flown.

Many historians believe D-Day, code-named Operation Overlord, was one of the most significant amphibious landings in history. However, it was only the beginning of the battle, culminating at the end of the war in Europe. Eleven months and one day after the invasion, Germany signed an unconditional surrender in Reims, France, ending a war that began on September 1, 1939.[1]

Over the years, I have thought about my dad's contributions to the war. What might have happened if the invasion of Europe had failed? As we approached the 75th anniversary, I spent hours contemplating and wondering about the children who would never be born. The men who lost their lives on D-Day on a beach code-named "Juno" on the coast of Normandy during Operation Overlord would never become fathers. In the days, weeks, and months after that day seventy-five years ago, until VE day on May 8, 1945, and finally on September 2, when the Japanese officially surrendered, thousands more potential fathers died in the service of their countries. Like other fathers from across the country, my dad did survive, making other baby boomers and me the lucky ones. I was born in 1954, ten years after my dad survived that longest of days.

Was it luck, fate, or something predetermined? Does everything happen for a reason? What about the soldier who was beside him as they jumped off the landing craft into chest-high cold water? Together they waded through cold, choppy waves onto the beach as artillery and mortar shells dropped around them, and machine-gun fire ricocheted off the sides of the landing craft. He was only an arm's length or two away from another Canadian from Manitoba as they hopscotched their way across the sand. After a few paces on shore, the other soldier was struck down and fell to the beach. *"He was hit pretty badly,"* wrote my father in the letter he sent home. If he and my father altered their paths as they worked their way up from the water, would it have been him lying on the beach?

The stories of the men in this book are related only by circumstances. The stories tell about going to war and surviving their "What If" moments. In many cases, soldiers in combat experience "What If" moments each and every day. Does being shot at throughout a war constitute a "What If" moment? Or is it at the point that the bullet hits the bone? What about close calls, or just surviving when those around them are dying? I'm sure soldiers in every war experienced their own moments.

Two of these stories are about men from The Royal Winnipeg Rifles. They would have known each other. Both were in A company, but their stories before and after the war are different. The men's situations and the names of those in their company are taken from the regiment's nominal rolls, personal memoirs, and letters. The locations and actions of their units were extracted from the official war diaries of each regiment. These stories are not first-hand accounts of the men who were there, but their experiences are based on what the families learned about their fathers as they grew up.

In 2019, all the contributors to this book travelled to Normandy and walked in their fathers' footsteps. Like me, they had the opportunity to wonder, "What If?"

If you have never had the chance to walk in the footsteps of your family, I encourage you to do so. I believe this incredible journey will give you a deep appreciation and a better understanding of what they endured during some of the darkest days the world has ever known.

Thousands of Canadians who are the children of men who assaulted Normandy's beaches or fought in World War II are here today because their parents survived. These are stories about their parents. We are proud to walk in their footsteps.

The personal reflections in these men's stories are taken directly from letters, journals and memoirs. They are italicized to highlight their thoughts and feelings at the time they were written. There is no corresponding endnote for these items. Permission to use the passages was granted by the family members of these men. In addition, quotes from the regimental war diaries are highlighted to reinforce the events recorded by the adjutants regarding daily events. These excerpts are included in the references at the end of this book.

Gerald Wallace (Gerry) Levers
"A" COMPANY, THE ROYAL WINNIPEG RIFLES
Inspired by the letters and journals of Gerry Levers

Part One

Born in Saskatoon, Saskatchewan, Gerry was only seven when the Armistice was signed on November 11, 1918, ending the Great War. Neither of his older brothers — Harold, who was fifteen, or Bert, who was thirteen — really understood what the whole fuss was about any more than Gerry did. The war to end all wars went on for four long years. Before it was over, the family moved again, this time from Saskatoon to Winnipeg. Following Harold's birth in Huntington, Quebec, in 1903, Gerry's dad, Charles Victor, moved his family back and forth across the country, searching for a better job. It seemed that he was never out of work but never found the right one.

Charles, a skilled carpenter, sometimes worked for himself, other times taking any job to help keep his family fed. His problem was his perfectionism. It meant that, after getting the go-ahead on a quoted task, he would end up spending twice the amount of time on the project as he'd allowed. The staircases he built in homes around Saskatoon were meticulously crafted works of art, and his customers were happy. However, spending twice the amount of time on a project didn't put more food on the table for his wife and four children because he always stuck to his original price. In 1916 the family moved again. This time to Manitoba. Charles built their first home on Winnipeg's outskirts, in the area known as Sturgeon Creek, seven miles west of Winnipeg. Shortly after arriving in Manitoba, they became a family with five children.

After the war ended in 1918, it took ten years for the country to get back on a path to some sense of normalcy. Many returning veterans were out of work. Some patriotic companies held jobs for the men who went off to serve their country, while other men returned to farms. Many were wounded physically, and others suffered mental scars they would carry with them for the rest of their lives.

Although unemployment was high, Charles managed to stay busy as a finishing carpenter for some of Winnipeg's most elegant homes. The Levers family avoided the ravages of the Spanish Flu, which killed over twelve hundred people in Winnipeg between 1918 and 1920.[2]

Gerry's first job was measuring out bags of sugar in a corner store. Consistent hard work earned him a promotion to delivery boy. His new position was to deliver groceries by horse and wagon until the weather changed. When winter came, and the snow piled up, it became difficult to make deliveries by anything but a sleigh.

The prospects for better jobs started to pick up. Still, there weren't many opportunities for a kid who never graduated from high school. In 1928, he finally found steady employment as a clerk at the Winnipeg Grain Exchange. Then came September 1929.

The worldwide stock market crash culminated on October 29, 1929, which became known as Black Tuesday. The stock market was in turmoil since September. In the US, record numbers of sales took place in the days before the crash. October 18 seemed to be the beginning of the end. Panic gripped the nation. Five days before the 29th, so many shares were traded that brokers, investment companies, and a portion of the country's most profitable banks tried to stop the panic. They purchased thousands of shares of stocks in an attempt to keep the economy rolling. Unfortunately, the rally their buys triggered on Friday was short-lived. On Monday, the flood gates opened again, and the stock market dropped. The following day, the market completely collapsed when over sixteen million shares were traded. The Dow Jones Industrial Average fell by thirty points, twelve percent of its value. The slide would continue until 1932, as the stock market dropped a full eighty-nine percent in value. Billions of dollars were lost, wiping out the fortunes of thousands of investors.[3]

In Canada, the wheat glut of 1928 threw the Winnipeg Grain exchange into a spiral, triggering a depression in Canada's economy that also began on the 24th. The headlines from the *Toronto Globe* read "Stock Speculators Shaken in Wild Day of Panic." In Toronto and Montréal, liquidation records were set. Horrified investors clogged the financial districts, while employees in the exchanges and brokerage houses worked themselves to near-collapse in an attempt to corral the paperwork. The *Canadian Annual Review of Public Affairs* reckoned, "Never before the 1929 crash had amounts running into billions of dollars been lost on the Canadian Stock Exchanges in so brief a period." In Montréal, some 500,000 shares were sold (5 times the usual amount); in Toronto, 330,000 were sold (13 times more than usual).[4]

In America, there were rumours of investors standing in line on Black Tuesday to jump out of the buildings' windows overlooking Wall Street. Despite those rumours, in the end, there were no confirmed suicides by people leaping from buildings. Over the following months, the suicide rate did begin to increase, but not all of these incidents were related to Black Tuesday.[5]

Living in Winnipeg became difficult for many people, but life in the Levers' household remained stable. Harold, who was now twenty-six, had worked for the Canadian National Railway since turning sixteen. He married before the crash, and he and his new bride were now living on their own. In the early 1920s, his younger brother, Bert, also found a job with the railroad.

During those uncertain times, many men were laid off from companies across the country, including the railroad. However, Bert and Harold managed to continue working throughout the depression. Gerry's older sister Lee had been working for the Hudson's Bay Company since 1926. She maintained her job throughout the dark days of the 1930s and continued working there for the next forty years.

The world went from the Roaring '20s to the Dirty '30s. As the 1930s dragged on, Germany was making headlines around the world. By late 1938, it seemed the world was once again heading down a dark road towards war. Despite the near-collapse, Gerry continued working as a clerk at the Winnipeg Grain Exchange. It was a job, but not a fulfilling or exciting one. He loved to play golf, hockey, and baseball on his days off, but he knew that he would be among the first to volunteer if there was a war.

With the hint of fall in the air, the headlines in the Winnipeg Free Press became more ominous each day. The prospect of another war concerned everyone. Then, on September 30, 1938, the British Prime Minister announced, "Peace for our time." He was hailed as a hero when he returned from Munich after signing a non-aggression pact with the German Fuhrer, Adolf Hitler.[6] People in the Commonwealth, including Canada, breathed a sigh of relief, having no appetite for another world conflict. The respite was short-lived, as, within months, Hitler took over all of Czechoslovakia. Britain began to re-arm the Polish Military and assured Poland they would come to their aid should Germany decide to attack. In late August 1939, tensions increased worldwide when it became known that the Soviet Union and Germany had signed a non-aggression pact.[7]

Using fabricated excuses, Germany invaded Poland on September 1.[8] Two days later, on September 3, Britain and France declared war on Germany. On that day, the Prime Minister of

Winnipeg Tribune Front Page, September 3, 1939.

Canada, William Lyon Mackenzie King, addressed the Canadian people on CBC radio. In a broadcast heard by people around the world, he spoke about the declaration of war against Germany by France and England. He declared that Canada was mobilizing its military reserves to active service in defence of England.

On Sunday, September 3, the *Winnipeg Tribune*'s Extra edition headlines read "IT'S WAR And Britain's In It."

The words were spread across the top of the front page as though painted by a brush.

On September 7, 1939, Parliament met in a special session. Two days later, the House of Commons and the Senate authorized a declaration of war. The following day, King George was asked to declare war on Germany on behalf of Canada.[9]

In large bold print, the *Globe and Mail* newspaper headline for September 11 read:

CANADA DECLARES WAR!

Covering the newspaper's entire front page were stories of the new war on which Canada was about to embark. The centre of the page was taken up with a copy of the announcement in old English script:

Proclamation of War

This was followed by stories about Nazi counter-offensives. One such lengthy piece read, "Dominion Committed To Stand With Britain In Fight Against Hitler."[10]

Since September 1, the thoughts of men and women at the grain exchange were conflicted between news of impending war and their job running one of the world's largest agricultural commodities. The Grain Exchange was housed in one of Winnipeg's most significant buildings. It was a cornerstone of the Canadian grain business. Even during the darkest days of the depression, they carried on with daily operations.

Across the country, offices and businesses came to a standstill, while each person voiced an opinion as to what this new war meant.

Part Two

"Hey, Gerry, you going to join up?" asked one of the clerks. "Just as soon as I can find a recruiting office," affirmed Gerry, who continued, "Want to come with me, Smitty? You're just the kind of kid from the farm they need. You're tall and strong as an ox. I think you have more than enough qualifications. With all that going for you, they'll probably make you an officer."

"Not me," scoffed Smitty. "I got two uncles who were in the great one. They have no spark. It's like the lights have gone out in the attic. Quite the drinkers, though. They were both with the infantry. My dad told me I should have known them before they went over — says they were both good men."

"Yeah, I've seen some guys like them. My uncle Basil lost an arm in Ypres. But you know, he can do the work of any man with two good arms. Still looks after his farm out in Saskatchewan," remarked Gerry.

"My uncles managed to live through battles in the Somme, Vimy Ridge, and Passchendaele without getting wounded, but their heads are not on right anymore. It's like they're both a little off, if you know what I mean," said Smitty. "As for me, I plan to hold off as long as possible," he continued, "if they bring out conscription this time, I'll go home and work on the farm."

"Not me, Smitty. I've been waiting for this day since I was a kid," admitted Gerry.

From Victoria to Halifax, able-bodied men were ready to head off to war. The horrors of what happened to their fathers and uncles only twenty years earlier were forgotten by thousands of young men as they signed up to do their duty. There were many reasons for wanting to join. Jobs were still not plentiful. Many

Canadian men, young and old, were unemployed or underemployed. The outlook was bleak. They headed to the recruitment offices, like their fathers and uncles before them. Men wanted the opportunity to earn a living, give some purpose to their lives, head out on a great adventure, and see the world while serving their country. Like their forefathers who fought in the Great War, they never thought it would last as long as it did.

On Thursday night, after the declaration of war, Gerry prepared to head out early the following morning. His years as a cadet with Winnipeg's Queen's Own Cameron Highlanders, Cadet Corps in his teens prepared him somewhat for what to expect. Using his safety razor with a new blade, Gerry gave himself a close shave and trimmed his mustache. In the morning, he would head to the Robinson, Little and Company building in Winnipeg. He heard the headquarters and recruiting station for a Canadian armoured regiment, the Fort Garry Horse, was in the process of setting up.[11] He felt sure that driving a tank or armoured vehicle would be right up his alley.

Gerry loved to drive his car. On Sundays, there was nothing he liked better than a road trip. It wasn't uncommon for him and his friends to head out to West Hawk Lake in his 1936 Chevrolet two-door, flat back sedan. They would leave early for the one-hundred-mile trip just west of the Ontario border, have a picnic, then be back home before dark. He saved for two years before he bought the car for $625.

He woke before dawn, excited about his prospects. For years Gerry enjoyed steady employment. It didn't pay a lot, only $150 a month. The low wage meant he was still living at home. His mom rose early to prepare a good breakfast. Like mothers across the country in the fall of 1939, Agatha Levers was concerned about the prospect of her son heading off to war. Even though Gerry was twenty-eight, he was still her youngest son.

Gerry's dad and the rest of the family joined him for breakfast. Even during the depression, there was food on the table and a roof over their heads. The talk around the table centred on what another war meant. Holding back her tears, Gerry's mom asked, "How many young men from Winnipeg are going to die this time?"

The conversation around the table ceased as each family member thought about families they knew who lost family members during the last war. When his brother Bert told the family he was thinking about joining the air force, his mother left the kitchen in tears. Before leaving, Gerry went to the parlour and gave his mom an encompassing hug, and his sisters began to cry. His dad and brother both gave him a hearty handshake, then with a deep sigh, his father offered a simple, "Good luck, son, we'll see you tonight."

"Give 'em hell, little brother," piped up Bert.

Gerry left the house at seven. It wouldn't be long until the fall season was upon them, and the day was supposed to be pleasant, the temperature forecasted to rise to the high sixties. Still, it was a little chilly as he walked below the overhanging branches of the elm trees. Leaves beginning to change colours were falling from the trees, floating lazily to the sidewalk. Above him, the gold and orange canopy was gorgeous.

The chilly morning was just right for a one-mile walk to catch the streetcar on Portage Avenue. Trolley buses were beginning to replace streetcars in many areas of Winnipeg. If he'd headed north from the house instead of south, he could have caught one of the trolleys on Sargent Avenue. Today, however, as on every other working day, he headed to the streetcar stop on Portage.

His destination for the recruitment centre was 54 Arthur Street, only a few blocks away from where he worked at the grain exchange. In a little over an hour, his sister Lee would be on the same streetcar. She would get off at Portage and Memorial, ready to begin another day at the six-story flagship store of the Hudson's Bay Company. This iconic store was only twelve blocks from where Gerry worked at the Grain Exchange.

Fort Garry Horse Recruiting Centre, 1939.

Even in the dead of winter, when temperatures dipped well below zero, Gerry would often walk three-quarters of a mile to where Lee worked. In the evening, they would ride home together.

Heading up the stairs, Gerry was confident the Canadian Army would be happy to have such a fine specimen of a man volunteering so quickly. He liked to consider himself stocky at five feet five and one-hundred thirty-five pounds and was by no means overweight. Playing sports like hockey and baseball kept him in shape.

He showed up at the recruitment office dressed in his best grey three-piece worsted wool suit. His toe-capped Oxfords were highly polished. On his head, he wore a fine Craft-Shire Brummel-style fedora. Respect and good manners dictated he remove his hat as soon as he stepped inside the recruiting office. The only thing he figured might go against him was his age. He certainly wasn't too young. In the days since the doors to recruiting centres around the city opened, local newspapers reported that the army had turned away dozens of boys claiming to be eighteen years old. Some of those boys were not yet sixteen. No, Gerry was afraid they might think he was too old. Like his older brothers, his hairline was already receding and becoming thinner with each passing year, making him look older still.

Inside the makeshift recruiting centre, men were already standing in line before him. He waited patiently as those ahead stepped forward, stating to the man in uniform they were there to volunteer.

When his turn came, he hurried to the desk, where a sergeant gave him a quick once-over. Gerry stood to attention before the recruiter. The training he learned from his cadet years was going to pay off, he figured. He was sure the sergeant was taking note of his posture.

"Here to volunteer?" asked the sergeant.

"Yes, sir," affirmed Gerry. He watched as the NCO (Non-Commissioned Officer) before him pulled out the Attestation forms, then carefully inserted carbon paper between each of the pages. After lining them up, the sergeant held them loosely between his fingers, gently tapping them on the desk. The next part of the ritual would be performed hundreds of times in the months to come. He inserted the paper precisely between the rollers of the hefty-looking Royal typewriter, then advanced the sheet to the exact position at which he would begin to type.

Gerry was a patient guy. The sergeant seemed as meticulous with his paperwork as Gerry was at his work. However, he began feeling that the man at the desk took too long to load his typewriter. If this pace continued, the war might be over before the guys behind him even signed up.

"Name?"

"Levers, Gerald, Wallace, Sir," replied Gerry.

The sergeant looked up. "If you are planning on being a soldier, let's get one thing straight. I am not a Sir. Do I look like an officer? I am a non-commissioned officer of the Fort Garry Horse. You will not call me *Sir*. I am a sergeant, and you will address me as such. Understood?"

Gerry did know better. He'd known the rank structure of the army since he was a kid.

Without waiting for an answer, the sergeant barked out his next request.

"Present Address."

Gerry quickly recited his answer and added a crisp "sergeant."

"Date of Birth."

At that moment, Gerry feared his age would be considered too old for combat. He answered with only the slightest hesitation, knowing the sergeant was watching him closely due to the mistake he already made by calling the man Sir. "August 25, 1916, sergeant."[12]

The Canadian Army now considered Gerry Levers a little past his twenty-third birthday. He was definitely old enough, and it didn't appear a birth certificate was necessary to prove it. He was now exactly five years younger than his correct year of birth.

At this point, it wasn't just his date of birth he needed to change. His deception continued as he told the sergeant when he graduated and when he began working. Gerry quickly adjusted those dates by adding five years to each.

He answered the rest of the questions the sergeant barked out to him right, quick, and proper — questions such as name of religion, occupation, next of kin, and previous military service. With a sense of pride, Gerry told him he spent five years with the Queen's Own Cameron Highlanders cadets.

One of the questions included whether there would be a job waiting for him when he returned. He assured the recruiter he'd been promised employment when he returned from the war. When the interrogation was complete, the sergeant pulled the triplicate form from the typewriter and handed two carbon copies to Gerry. "Take these to the second floor. They'll do your medical up there. For a strong-looking chap like you, there shouldn't be any problems. Good luck, Levers."

"Thank you, sergeant," said Gerry. He made an army regulation right face and marched to the staircase, where he bounded up the stairs two at a time. Once again, there was a long line ahead of him. It would result in a long wait.

In the interim, nurses weighed him, checked his height, and took his temperature. The nurse even asked him embarrassing questions about any sexual diseases he might have and entered each answer onto his medical form.

Next, it was in to see the recruiting station's medical officer. *Just a formality*, he figured. He stripped to his undershorts and sat on an examination table. When the doctor entered the room, he did the usual assessments. The doctor listened to the rhythm of Gerry's heart, made him take deep breaths as he held the stethoscope over his lungs, and looked for signs of wheezing.

"How's everything sound, doc?" Gerry inquired.

"Jump off the table and pull your shorts down," came the reply.

"Wow, this guy certainly has personality," Gerry muttered to himself.

Using a tongue depressor, the doctor became a pecker checker. Gerry's genitalia were swished back and forth, lifted and inspected. Still not an *hmm* or an *ahh*. The next thing he knew, he was bent over the examination table. The doctor told him he was checking for hemorrhoids.

Gerry found the whole situation humiliating. He was sure that thousands of others were going through the same process and felt the same way.

"Okay, you can pull up your shorts and lay back on the table."

Gerry did as instructed. The doctor used his hands to prod here and there. The last thing he did was take a look at his feet. That's when Gerry heard the first "Hmmm."

"Get up. Stand with your feet flat on the floor," ordered the doctor.

Gerry did as the doctor told him. The doctor stood back, leaned over, and inspected Gerry's feet from the side.

"That will be all. You can get dressed now."

"What's the verdict, doc? Am I a good candidate to serve our country?"

"You seem to be in fairly good shape. Lungs are clear, and your heart's strong and steady. No indications of a sexual disease on your form and no hemorrhoids. There's just one problem. You have flat feet. This will disqualify you from active service." Having issued his diagnosis, he stepped to the side table.

Gerry was devastated. He wanted to serve. His feet never bothered him his entire life, whether playing sports or spending hours marching on a parade square as a cadet.

As he put his shirt on, he heard a loud thump followed by a second. The doctor turned and handed Gerry a copy of his enlistment paper with a stamp indicating his rejection for medical reasons. "Take these forms downstairs and give them to one of the men at the front desk," was the last thing the doctor said to him as he headed off to examine another potential recruit.

There was nothing he could do but go back to work at the grain exchange. He did his job, but with each news story printed in the *Winnipeg Free Press* or the *Winnipeg Tribune*, he became more determined to find a way to join the fight.

Part Three

If Day, Winnipeg

On the cold winter's day of February 19, 1942, Winnipeg experienced what it might be like "if" the Germans invaded Canada as they had many European countries. The day, including a simulated battle between German and Canadian Forces, was called "IF DAY."

There were mock bombings of bridges leading out of the city core. Anti-aircraft batteries fired hundreds of blank rounds to simulate their attempt to shoot down enemy aircraft painted with German insignia. Armoured track vehicles carrying German troops paraded down Portage Avenue, with the troops' arms held high in a Nazi salute.

Nazi troops parade down Portage Avenue during a mock invasion.

There was a staged battle between 3500 Canadian soldiers in the Winnipeg area. Many volunteers posing as the overwhelming invading forces were World War One veterans or young members of the board of trade. They were dressed in uniforms that had been rented from a Hollywood studio. The Canadian troops surrendered by 9:30 in the morning. Shortly after the end of the battle, radio stations began broadcasting orders from the German command.

The men posing as German troops lowered the British Ensign in Lower Fort Garry. Then, they replaced the Union Jack with a red, white, and black swastika.

**The Germans haul down the Union Jack and get
ready to hoist the swastika flag in its place.**

The occupying force arrested and imprisoned members of the Manitoba Legislature, the Mayor of Winnipeg, and other prominent citizens.

"If Day." Nazis arrest politicians at City Hall.

A special edition of the *Winnipeg Tribune* had its name changed by the German occupation.

Front Page, *Winnipeg Tribune*, **February 19, 1942, Special Edition.**

Its new name was *Das Winnipegger Lugenblatt*, and the entire edition was written in German.

Phoney Reichsmarks were handed out in place of change in some shops.

Fake Reichsmark, given out by merchants on If Day.

Outside the Carnegie Library, the occupying forces burned old books scheduled to be discarded.

Men portraying German soldiers burn books outside Carnegie Library.

The occupying forces disbanded Boy Scouts and Girl Guides groups, and Jewish organizations were persecuted. The exercise even included German troops taking personal items right out of people's homes.

Nazis escort Rev. John Anderson from All Saints Church.

Decrees posted around the city proclaimed what would happen to anyone who challenged the Greater Reich Forces' authority.

German Proclamation, posted around Winnipeg on If Day.

The tenth item on the decree included offences resulting in
death without trial:

1. Attempting to organize resistance against the Army of
   Occupation.
2. Entering or leaving the province without permission.
3. Failure to report all goods possessed when ordered to do
   so.
4. Possession of firearms.

At the end of the day's activities, a march took place to com-
memorate the day's event. Some members of the spectacle carried
banners proclaiming, "It Must Not Happen Here." "Buy War Bonds"
and "Buy the new Victory Bonds."

Victory Bond Poster sponsored by the Canadian Bank of Commerce.

Following the parade, a banquet was held at the Hudson's Bay Company for many of those involved.

The entire scenario, conducted to raise funds for War Bonds, was a successful campaign. Within six days of "If Day," Winnipeg alone raised over $23,000,000. Within twelve days, the province of Manitoba reached its goal, which would equal over $300,000,000 today. In total, Manitobans purchased over $45,000,000 worth of bonds.[13] [14]

There was hope that the simulation would increase the number of recruits from the Winnipeg area. Voluntary enlistment had tapered off since the first days of the war when Gerry first attempted to join.

On June 5, 1942, Gerry finally joined the 18th (R) Recce Battalion of the 2nd Armoured Car Regiment Reserve Unit. It seemed they didn't care about his flat feet. On his enlistment paper, titled

Certificate of Medical Examination, a line referring to descriptive marks featured a small written notation: *Slight degree Flat Feet*.

Now a proud member of the reserve unit, Gerry was excited about his new role and immediately headed to Shilo, Manitoba's annual training camp. He would not be with the reserve unit for long.

Part Four

The ill-fated Dieppe raid on August 19 claimed the lives of 907 Canadians, with 2,460 Canadians wounded and 1,946 men taken prisoner.[15] Perhaps the loss of so many Canadians at Dieppe meant flat feet were no longer an issue for enrollment. Gerry fulfilled his dream on September 5, 1942. He was transferred from the Reserve unit to Active Duty with The Royal Winnipeg Rifles, a battalion whose roots went back to 1883. The RWRs were one of the regiments that had come into existence during Canada's Northwest Rebellion.[16] Following a battle in 1885, the enemy began referring to the regiment as the "Little Black Devils".

Gerry Levers after Enlistment, 1942.

After eight months of training in Debert, Nova Scotia, and the small arms training centre in Long Branch, Ontario, Gerry received 30 days of embarkation leave. He returned to Winnipeg and spent time with friends and family.

On May 12, 1943, he boarded a ship leaving Halifax with thousands of other troops. Ten days later, he disembarked in England as a reinforcement with The Royal Winnipeg Rifles of the 7th Canadian Infantry Brigade, 3rd Canadian Infantry Division.

Gerry was unsure of his role in the war. The regiment trained for combat over the next twelve months. Little did any of them know it would be as part of the most significant invasion force the world would ever see: D-Day, June 6, 1944.

The following pages tell my father's story about D-Day and the days that followed. It tells about his "What If" moments, inspired by letters he wrote home, the diary he kept while in the hospital, and a radio interview conducted with CBC upon returning to England. It also uses historical accounts of battles 75 years ago and the official war diaries of Lieutenant-Colonel John Meldram, Gerry's regimental commanding officer. His diary helped pinpoint where he and the men of The Royal Winnipeg Rifles were as they proceeded from Normandy to Germany and the day-to-day activities they experienced.

Thursday, June 1, 1944

As a rifleman, Gerry was not privy to what took place before the invasion but felt they were getting ready for the big one. There was so much activity, more than any other scheme or exercise, since arriving in England in May of 1943. "There's no way this is another drill. Or if it is, it's the biggest we've ever been on," he thought to himself.

His battalion split into two groups, where they would wait for the anticipated invasion of Europe. B and D, the two first assault companies, bivouacked in a camp designated number 7. The rest of

A and C, the reserve companies, would be part of the second wave of assault landings and were assigned to Camp 8.[17]

Both groups were bivouacked in Cranbury Park in Hiltingbury, England, approximately eight miles from Southampton. There were over eleven thousand men in this marshalling area, along with two thousand vehicles, all waiting to head to the ships at the dockyard. They were kept busy with PT and rifle drills. Many camps were enclosed within barbed wire fences. The men were isolated from the outside world to ensure the secrecy of the planned invasion. Sentries posted to guard the perimeters had orders to shoot anyone who came too close to the wire.[18]

Gerry was more toned and fit than he had ever been, even fitter than in Canada, where he was a Physical Training instructor in the training camps. Still, like all the other men, Gerry was getting tired of the constant PT. He just wanted to get into the show.

Friday, June 2, 1944

Many of the Winnipeg Rifles were originals. They came over to England in August of 1941. They weren't battle-hardened soldiers, but from the officers, NCOs, and riflemen, each man felt they were one of the best-trained regiments in the Canadian Army.

There are various personalities in any large group, from those who are quiet to those who are more outgoing. Some can make friends with anyone. Others are like the class clown — trying to get a laugh from people no matter the circumstances.

The men knew it was only a matter of time until they were thrown into the fray. Each dealt with his fears and trepidations in different ways.

Gerry's company was issued two 24-hour ration packs, intended to make the troops self-sufficient for the first 24 to 48 hours. Soldiers ate these rations throughout their training many times while on field exercises, also known as schemes. They also received vomit bags meant for use while in the assault crafts as they headed for shore.

The platoon sergeant stepped forward. "Gather round, men," he ordered. When he had their attention, the sergeant held up a 24-hour emergency ration tin. Then, using the metal key attached to the bottom of the can, he removed the lid. "Inside, you will find two packages of crackers wrapped in cellophane and two bars of Cadbury chocolate. These *won't* be opened unless there is no alternative. Then, and only then, will you open them only on orders from your NCOs or officers. Is that clear?"

"Yes, sergeant," came the unified response.

Next, he held up the regular ration box, made to fit inside the soldier's mess kit. "I have been ordered to remind you about your rations, just in case you have forgotten. This one is expected to last you 24 hours," he called out, as he held the now-familiar package in the air. "As you can see, it is tagged 'B' for the type of meat inside. There are seven different main courses for your nutrition." The sergeant continued, "I know you've probably had your fill of these while on schemes, but orders are orders. I will tell you about these rations, and you will enjoy it."

"Don't know how we could forget all those lovely meals we've enjoyed the last couple of years," came one of the comments.

"Since you men are so well versed in our culinary delights, perhaps one of you would care to tell the rest of the men about our ration packs?" No one volunteered to demonstrate the meal kit. "I didn't think so," said the sergeant as he held up the package and removed each of the contents. "Now, as you all seem to be aware, you have one package with ten biscuits. Secondly, there are two packets of oatmeal. Item number three, two blocks of tea with milk and sugar. These blocks are wrapped together so you can enjoy two hot drinks."

One of the jokers in the platoon piped up, "I'm sure we'll be able to have a spot of tea and invite the Germans to join us. Right, boys."

"That's enough out of you, Combs. Next, we have one can of some kind of meat; this one's bully beef. Two bars of chocolate with raisins; one bar of vitamin-enriched chocolate."

"My mom will be pleased I'm getting my vitamins, sergeant," quipped Combs again.

This time, the rest of the platoon laughed and mumbled their agreement about how their moms would be happy that the army was so concerned about their health.

"All right. Enough. Next, we have some sweets, two packs of chewing gum, and two meat broth cubes. As you know, these you can mix with water. One bag of salt, four lumps of sugar, and four sheets of toilet paper and one set of instructions for use."[19]

Once again, Combs piped up. "Hey, sergeant, we won't need those instructions. My mother taught me how to wipe my arse before I turned three."

The uproar from the platoon was welcome. Even the sergeant was unsuccessful in keeping a stern-looking face.

"For your information, Private Combs, the instructions are for how you should prepare the contents and includes meal suggestions."

"Those two little boxes are supposed to sustain us for forty-eight hours?" grumped Whitely.

"Get them in your packs. You might think it's a four-course meal at the Fort Garry Hotel before we're done," joked Gerry.

The sergeant then handed out water purification tablets. "Place two or three of these tablets in your water bottles, then shake it around," he said as he demonstrated a procedure they'd done numerous times during training exercises. "It may be a few days before you see water tank trailers. Make sure you keep your water purified."

After completing the demonstration, the sergeant left the platoon to add the rations to their packs.

"Hey Gerry, want to get a haircut? King told me some of the guys are getting a trim before we head out," said McQueen.

"Sure, why not. A bit of a trim is about all I can expect. I think I've shed a lot more hair off the top since I've been wearing this damned helmet. Might be totally bald before we get home. I do want to look presentable when we meet some of those pretty

French ladies I've heard about," said Gerry. "Let me pack my rations. I'll be right with you."

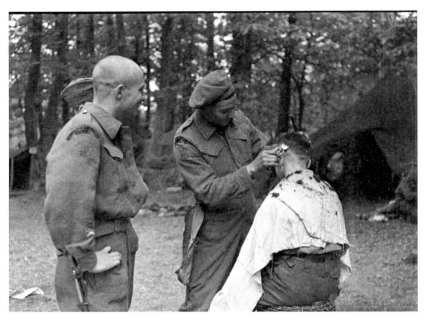

Infantrymen of The Royal Winnipeg Rifles, getting haircuts June 1944.

"This looks promising," he heard someone in the section moan.

"What's that?"

"The vomit bags. Guess the navy boys are afraid we're going to mess up the decks of their little boats."

Those who were still packing up agreed how ridiculous the idea was.

As they walked to get their hair cut, a group of men held a large tarp with one man sitting on it. Together they would pull it taut, then toss the man high in the air. The faces of those gathered were laughing and smiling. They didn't look as though they had a care in the world. They certainly didn't look like men who were concerned about the prospects of heading into battle in the days to come.

Men of the RWRs relaxing in camp before boarding ships to France.

The entire regiment wore their new helmets issued in the middle of February. Unlike the Mark II Brody style used by British and Canadian troops during World War I, the earlier design did little to protect the side of a soldier's head. The new one improved protection by over one-third.

Gerry wasn't sure where it came from, but the helmet was soon referred to by another name. It wasn't the Mark III, as officers called it as they proudly handed the helmets out to the troops. Someone with the new model commented that it looked as though the soldiers were wearing a turtle shell on their heads. Just like that, it became endearingly known as the "Turtle Helmet" because the overall shape looked like an empty turtle shell. [20]

At one o'clock, the order came to form up and prepare for transport. The men loaded onto the trucks for the nine-mile trip to the docks at Southampton.

Upon arrival, A Company would be loaded onto their LSI (Landing Ship Infantry) to take them to their final destination. Rumours were plentiful as to where they were heading. Nobody confirmed or denied the scuttlebutt.

The columns of trucks stretched for miles as they headed to Southampton. Gerry sat at the back end of an open-sided transport. "Will you look at that," he blurted as they began to roll through the city, then pointed toward a walled yard. "There are ladies out there doing their laundry. Hanging up their knickers," he laughed. "There's even an old guy out tending his bloody garden."

Residents hanging laundry and attending gardens as troops head to the docks.

Gerry couldn't help but notice the evidence of the destruction the city had undergone during the German blitzes earlier in the war. Although the roads were clear, piles of bricks were stacked where the remnants of shops, churches, and factories once stood.

"Sure glad the German Air Force seems to be out of planes," Gerry announced.

"You know, the buggers bombed the P.M.'s residence during the blitz. They say old man Churchill was not happy," uttered the soldier beside him.

The company could have forced-marched the nine-mile journey in less than three hours. However, it took over four hours to drive because of the thousands of vehicles moving toward the piers.

When they finally disembarked, the men were stiff and sore from sitting on hard wooden benches. A number were heard complaining about having sore butts.

"Shut your traps, you lot," came the booming voice of the platoon sergeant. "You'll be wishing for a sore ass and the comforts of a nice wooden bench a few days from now."

Canadian troops heading toward the docks.

At 1700 hours, they were queued up at berth thirty-nine, ready to walk up the LSI (L) Landing Ship Infantry (Large) gangplank to the 'Llangibby Castle,' a 507-foot former passenger ship. Since her refit, she could carry close to 1600 troops. Gerry could see nine of the Llangibby's eighteen LSAs (Landing Ship Assault) hanging from the davits. These were small cranes that hung over the s ship's side to raise or lower the smaller boats. There were five on the lower row and four above, each capable of carrying a crew of four and thirty-six troops. [There is a discrepancy, between the number of Landing Craft Assault boats (LCAs), between the official landing tables (14) and information found on the website about the Llangibby Castle. (18)]

The British-built LCAs hanging off the sides were six feet longer than the American Higgins Boat landing craft. Both had the same capacity, but the British design allowed the soldiers to sit on benches.

For troops making a run-in from a flotilla of ships as much as ten miles offshore, the seats were considered a luxury compared to the American design. Theirs required soldiers to stand the entire time or sit on the floor that was soon covered with water and vomit. The Canadian and British soldiers agreed the Yanks would be tired and wobbly or soaking wet before they made the run to the beaches.

The Higgins Company built the landing craft used by US soldiers. It was inspired by a small flat-bottom boat used in Louisiana's swamps. Like those of the Higgins boats, the bottoms of the British landing crafts were also flat. The British LCAs were constructed from mahogany planking with a layer of light protective armour plating. Besides their extra length, their boats were designed with two other features for the men's comfort and safety. The side benches were protected from the elements by an upper deck, helping to keep some troops dryer in heavy seas. In addition, the craft had armoured doors. They were six feet back from the landing ramp, affording troops extra protection between the time the ramp was lowered and the platoon headed for shore.[21]

Both crafts had landing ramps. The British design used a combination of wires and pulleys to drop theirs, allowing soldiers to jump from the boats onto dry land. It was a good concept if the LCAs could beach themselves high enough for a dry landing. The invasion plan was to hit the beaches a few hours after low tide. It was a compromise between the landing craft striking hidden obstacles, detonating mines, or having men cross a vast expanse of beach too close to the German guns located along the Normandy coast. Failure to reach shore would require soldiers to jump into frigid fifty-degree water, which could be over their heads.

The Canadians began practicing for beach landings in August of 1943, which included smoke and live ammunition. In other exercises, men were forced to swim in full gear as part of their physical training. A well-trained platoon could charge off the boats in less than three minutes. Gerry's platoon's unloading time was down to just over two-and-a-half minutes during rehearsals.

The Captain broke the spell Gerry was under as he gazed at the hundreds of ships in the harbour. He stood at the side of the gangway, shouting encouragement to the men: "Come on, boys! The sooner you're on board, the sooner they'll get us fed. I heard from the Colonel it just might be the best meal you've experienced since we left Canada."

As promised, the boys were well fed, and at eight o'clock, the engines were fired up. The Llangibby Castle began steaming south to meet with other Naval Force J ships. Their destination was the Solent Sea, a narrow strait between Southampton and the Isle of Wight, which leads directly into the English Channel.

Saturday, June 3, 1944

Gerry and his platoon were among 1530 troops on board their LSI. They were more comfortable than those on smaller LSIs, which were filled to the bulkheads with men. The meal the captain promised when they boarded the ship exceeded everyone's expectations.

In all, the flotilla of over five thousand ships was the most massive armada ever assembled. Many smaller vessels were open to the elements, carrying up to two-hundred-fifty troops crammed in shoulder to shoulder. The men in these ships would not be taking part in the initial assaults. Providing the original attacks were successful, the larger LSIs would land directly on the beaches. Ramps and gangplanks would be lowered, allowing men and equipment to come ashore without the fear of being shot.

Onboard the Llangibby, the men lazed around. The day began with a good breakfast. Following that, platoons took turns with various forms of PT, followed by yet another weapons inspection. The routines helped relieve boredom and keep their minds off the days ahead.

In the afternoon, the troops were assigned muster stations in the event of emergencies and became familiar with the ship. Afterwards, they were free to do as they wished within the crowded confines of the boat.

Each man dealt with the tension in his own way. Being in such close quarters with fifteen hundred men on a ship designed to carry four hundred passengers meant there were few places to be alone. A game of cards offered a good way for the men to relieve the stress many were feeling.

"Hey Adams," said Gerry, "how about a game of cribbage?"

"No bloody way, Levers; you took me for the last of my smokes last time we played."

Gerry tried to get a game with a couple of other chaps but didn't get any takers. Several poker and dice games were taking place. Neither of these interested him, so he settled for a few rummy games. He still managed to win a couple of smokes he would save for later.

"Attention on board. Attention on board. There will be a moving picture shown tonight at 1900 hours courtesy of your hosts of the Llangibby Castle. We hope you enjoy it, compliments of the crew and Captain McAllen."

The men went below, enjoying the show, if for no other reason than to quell the jitters many felt. Afterwards, they returned to the decks until lights out. They huddled together against the railings, re-telling stories of life at home and tales of women they knew. They wondered aloud what they might be doing if they weren't in the army. They had shared such anecdotes with each other dozens of times over the past year. Most wondered where they were heading.

Many wanted a cigarette, but smoking was strictly forbidden. "At night, a glowing cigarette can be seen from a great distance away," they were told. Some of those on board refused to take heed of the order. If caught smoking, soldiers found themselves in the brig for not taking the matter seriously, causing quite a stir for all those on board.[22]

Sunday, June 4, 1944

The weather was unpleasant, cold, and cloudy, with showers and a northwest wind. There was a church parade officiated by Captain E.W. Horton. The ship's entire contingent, including the Marine Flotilla Party, participated, along with the Regina Rifles and the Canadian Scottish Regiment from Victoria.

**Church service aboard Llangibby Castle
(Captain E.W. Horton on the right).**

Gerry attended several church parades while in England. Today he joined hundreds of soldiers on board as Padre Horton stood above the men and led them in prayers. He then recited the twenty-third psalm to those gathered on deck. At the end of the service, even men who never attended church regularly joined the Chaplain as they all recited the Lord's Prayer.

At noon, Lieutenant-Colonel Meldram received discouraging news from the Supreme Headquarters Allied Expeditionary Forces (SHAEF). The orders postponed the invasion due to the inclement weather. It didn't take long for rumours about the delay to make their way around the ship. Men were grumbling, and Gerry was elected by his section's men to find out about the delay. He approached his sergeant to ask about it. "Let's go ask the lieutenant," he offered.

The lieutenant didn't have the answer they were looking for either. Even the lowly rifleman knew full moons and high tides went together. A full moon under a clear sky would make their crossing easier. It also meant the ships' silhouettes would make clear targets for enemy submarines or attack boats. After leaving the lieutenant, the sergeant said, "If we don't get on with it before Tuesday or Wednesday, we might have to wait. It'll be another fourteen days before we get favourable tides."

"Where the hell will they put all these guys if the delay goes any longer?" Gerry asked as he looked at the sea of faces standing on the deck.

"Damned if I know, Levers. I'm just a sergeant, remember."

"Like I mentioned to the boys when we were in the convoy coming through Southampton. "It's lucky for us the Luftwaffe don't have much of an air force left. We'd be sitting ducks."

The men were disappointed by the delay. The sea was still rough as the men headed to bed, and even the five-hundred-foot Llangibby Castle was rising and falling with each wave. Gerry was glad he wasn't on one of the small transports. Infantry troops weren't used to the constant motion, preferring to have both feet planted on solid ground. Whether it was the ship's motion or nervous jitters about the days to come, none of the soldiers enjoyed a restful night.

Monday, June 5, 1944

When Gerry came on deck that morning, he was greeted with the promise of another dismal overcast day. He felt positive there would be another delay and began the day expecting little action. He and the men of his section discussed where they would be if the landings had taken place as planned. Their rifle section consisted of ten men, including a corporal, six riflemen, a lance corporal and his two-man Bren gun crew. "By now, I'd say we'd be halfway to our objectives. Who knows, maybe we'll be in Paris in a couple of weeks," beamed MacDonald.

Not all were quite as cock-sure. "Let's not forget what happened to the boys from the Calgary Highlanders at Dieppe," chided Davis.

There was another round of weapons inspections. "Don't know how they thought my Enfield was going to get dirty sitting on the bloody ship," said one of the riflemen.

"Well, with all the oil you're putting on the damn thing, it sure as hell will never get rusty," snarled Gordy McQueen. "Make sure you keep it dry as we land and keep it out of the sand. That won't be any good for it, either."

At 2100 hours, the engines, which had idled since arriving off the Isle of Wight, began churning harder. Finally, the Llangibby Castle weighed anchor and slowly headed to the English Channel to join the other ships heading to Juno Beach.

Once in the open, they met their destroyer escorts: the HMS Stevenstone, HMS Venus, and a Free French Navy destroyer, La Combattante. Their job included keeping the troop transports out of harm's way from German U-Boats or the fast-attacking E-Boats with their torpedoes. The men were happy to hear that two-hundred-fifty mine-sweepers had left hours earlier to clear a path for them.

The speaker system crackled to life:

Attention Ships Company. The show is on, and I assure you it will be the greatest show ever. With tremendous air cover, I repeat tremendous air power, which cannot be too much emphasized. I require you all to be on your toes and to carry out your duties to the best of your abilities. Remember, it is our privilege to take part in this the greatest operation in history. We have waited long for this opportunity. By your determination and resource, we shall again prove to the world the great spirit of Britain, which will inspire the world.
May God Almighty speed us in this great enterprise. Good luck to all of you.[23]

"Wow, those Limeys really know how to make you want to do their duty for God, King, and Country, don't they," quipped McQueen.

They were now steaming past the massive Nab tower, built as part of a defence system during World War I. The men on board began to point out a fantastic sight. On the tower's top platform was a brightly lit V that seemed to be pointing its way toward France.[24]

"Hopefully, that's a good sign," said Gerry. He could still see the brilliant V miles after leaving the English coastline as they headed to wherever their final destination would be.

Envelopes marked *Top Secret* were now being opened. Regimental commanders and senior officers had already been informed of their exact destination. Until this moment, the platoon's officers and all other ranks were practicing with bogus maps marked with code names. It was now time to let the rest of the men in on the destination. As the Captain of the ship announced moments earlier, "The show was on."

Gerry's lieutenant returned to the platoon with his orders, and the men gathered in front of him. He pointed out where they would be landing with the rest of A Company, twenty minutes after B and D Companies' initial assault. They would be loaded into their LSAs from the SS Canterbury and the SS Laird's Isle.

Over the next hour, he went over detailed maps of a beach, code-named 'Juno.' The plans showed a sector referred to as Mike Green. "This section of beach is where A Company will land. From there, we begin the long road to liberate Europe," said the lieutenant.

The detailed reports included the positions of gun emplacements and pillboxes. Comprehensive maps were given out, right down to the section leaders, each with directional arrows on them, indicating the route of advance to their first three objectives. These points were code-named Yew and Elm, and finally, the Oak line. This was an overly optimistic target of fifteen kilometres from the coast.

"Who comes up with all these bloody code names anyway?" McQueen whispered to Gerry.

"Damned if I know. Maybe the powers that be want us to think it's going to be a walk in the park."

The next thing the lieutenant read were letters from Generals Eisenhower and Montgomery.

SUPREME HEADQUARTERS
ALLIED EXPEDITIONARY FORCE

Soldiers, Sailors and Airmen of the Allied Expeditionary Force!

You are about to embark upon the Great Crusade, toward which we have striven these many months. The eyes of the world are upon you. The hopes and prayers of liberty-loving people everywhere march with you. In company with our brave Allies and brothers-in-arms on other Fronts, you will bring about the destruction of the German war machine, the elimination of Nazi tyranny over the oppressed peoples of Europe, and security for ourselves in a free world.

Your task will not be an easy one. Your enemy is well trained, well equipped and battle-hardened. He will fight savagely.

But this is the year 1944 ! Much has happened since the Nazi triumphs of 1940-41. The United Nations have inflicted upon the Germans great defeats, in open battle, man-to-man. Our air offensive has seriously reduced their strength in the air and their capacity to wage war on the ground. Our Home Fronts have given us an overwhelming superiority in weapons and munitions of war, and placed at our disposal great reserves of trained fighting men. The tide has turned ! The free men of the world are marching together to Victory !

I have full confidence in your courage, devotion to duty and skill in battle. We will accept nothing less than full Victory !

Good Luck ! And let us all beseech the blessing of Almighty God upon this great and noble undertaking.

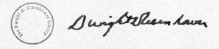

**Letter from General Eisenhower given to troops
on the eve of D-Day.**

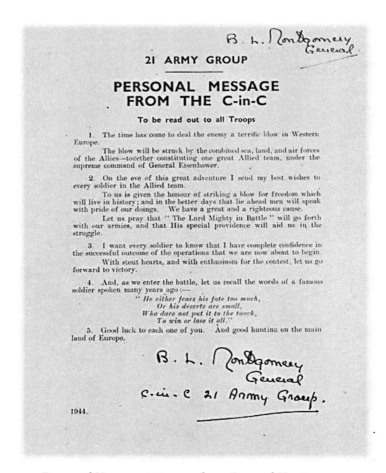

Personal Message to troops from General Montgomery.

After reading the letters, the lieutenant added his comments. "We've been training for what will take place in the morning for a long time. I know you will do yourselves, the regiment, and our country proud, and each of you will do their best and then some. Good luck, and, like our ship's captain so eloquently stated, Godspeed to all of you.

"Now I'll get the sergeants to pass out seasick pills. I hear it's going to be a tad rough going across the channel."

Nobody would be sleeping again this night. The ship's crew kept busy serving hot meals to all the men, and there were hot drinks available to all aboard throughout the night.

Those sitting on the open deck could hear the constant drone of hundreds of bombers as they passed overhead. It was a comforting sound and confirmed the ship's captain's statement about the tremendous air power. In the distance, the bombings could be heard as the air force dropped thousands of tons of bombs on the shore batteries in the landing zone. The bombing would continue throughout the night, ending just after 0500 on June 6. The bomber command flew over 1100 sorties and dropped more than 5200 tonnes of bombs.[25]

Part Five

Tuesday, June 6, 1944, D-Day

It was indeed a rough night on the open channel, making most of the men violently sea-sick. At four a.m., the navy boys offered everyone hot tea and a cold snack.

"It'll help to settle your stomach," claimed more than one of the sailors.

"Hey, Gerry. You scared?" asked one of the younger men as they began priming their grenades.

"Not sure. I'm not sea-sick, but my guts are sure churning."

At 0500 hours, orders were given to line up and prepare to board their respective LCAs. Although the sunrise was not due for another hour, the sky had been getting brighter since just after four in the morning, despite the cloud cover.

There was a northwest wind blowing; the sea was rising and falling and didn't look the least bit inviting. The wind seemed to die down slightly as the men waited to board their landing craft. Since coming on deck, the men on the Llangibby Castle listened as hundreds of bombers flew above them and dropped their bomb loads over the beach area. At 0515 hours, the sounds of the bombing campaign by the air force on the beachhead stopped, leaving a disturbing silence in its wake. The men were left with the distant drone of planes heading home. Reality soon set in that the ensuing battle was being placed squarely on their shoulders.

Men of the 3ʳᵈ Canadian Division Preparing to Load onto LCAs.

The order was given for LBDs to form up at the davits, holding the landing craft. Waiting to load on the LCAs were 386 men, including A and C Companies, men from the battalion headquarters, medical personnel, beach reconnaissance parties, and beach signallers. One of the six landing craft assigned to A company also carried the 7ᵗʰ Canadian Infantry Brigade – Padre, attached to Royal Winnipeg Rifles, Captain H. E. Horton.[26]

In awe, Gerry gazed at the panoramic view of Invasion Force J as he stood on the ramp leading to the LCAs. Looking over the heaving seas, he whispered to himself, "This isn't going to be like a day out on West Hawk Lake."

"Take a look," the soldier standing next to him announced. "There must be thousands of ships out there."

"Look at all those barrage balloons. There are hundreds of them too."

Convoy and barrage balloons en route to D-Day.

The loading went as practiced. At 0530, Gerry heard the ship's anchor release, then splash into the water. Captain McAllen gave the order to lower the boats from the davits. Three-and-a-half minutes later, the Llangibby Castle had offloaded hundreds of men. The engines were rumbling, and the men who would land at H-hour plus twenty minutes were on their way.

Some of the landing craft began having issues moments after they were untethered from the mothership. They were bobbing up and down on the choppy seas like corks. Though the waters were somewhat calmer, Gerry's boat, like the rest of them, was lifting, then dropping into troughs with each wave.

"Bloody Hell," shrieked the rifleman sitting next to Gerry. "If this is supposed to be better than yesterday, I'm sure as hell glad we weren't out here then."

Gerry looked at him. The man's face was pale and as green as his tunic. He watched as the man turned away, leaned over, and vomited all over the floor of the landing craft. *So much for the cold tea and snack they were given at 0400*, he thought.

The men who were sea-sick earlier were in worse shape in the tiny boats. At 0530 hours, their LCA eased away from their ship, and the naval bombardment began. The HMS Warspite, a Royal Navy Battleship, was credited as one of the first to fire.

HMS Warspite lobbing Shells during the Battle of Normandy.

The racket of nine destroyers and two cruisers of the Juno naval task force as they began pounding shoreline defences was mind-numbing. The thundering boom and report from the guns created a racket like no other the men on the landing craft had ever heard.

Also firing off the coast was the HMS Belfast, which could send ninety, six-inch shells per minute toward the heavily fortified enemy positions. On other beachheads, battleships were firing guns as big as sixteen inches.

Inside their little boat, even with the engines of their landing craft running full speed, the sound of the guns was deafening. As they progressed toward the beaches, the sky lit up with streaks of flame from the Landing Craft Tank with rocket launchers (LCTRs). Each of them contained hundreds of rockets tipped with explosive charges. They fired salvo after salvo of missiles toward the shore.

Gerry was a guy from the prairies, a landlubber, not a seaman by any stretch. The regiment had practiced amphibious landings in the past but never encountered seas as rough as this. He could hear the sounds of other men retching and throwing up. Gerry couldn't figure out why he wasn't doing the same as the other platoon members, as the boat continually rose and fell in the swells. Some of the men were now dry heaving because there was nothing left to throw up.

Canadians inside a British-made LCA, wearing their invasion helmets.

Men sitting close to him laughed nervously. Many weren't sure they would have the strength left to jump onto the beach once they landed. Even with seawater breaking over the bow, the air inside the landing craft smelled rancid, and the deck was slick with vomit.

Gerry couldn't believe his ears. As they continued to circle before making their run for the beach, one of the men began singing, "Pack up your troubles." Others soon joined in. When the boat finally made its turn for shore, the singing died off. The mood became sombre as each man dealt with the growing tension. Some mumbled prayers, while others appeared lost in thought.

Gerry looked at the men near him. Their faces showed a range of emotions between panic and quiet inner resolve. He was sure most of them were wondering if they would live to see another day.

**Infantrymen of The Royal Winnipeg Rifles
in Landing Craft Assault (LCA).**

The men of A Company were scheduled to land behind D Company on sector Mike Green twenty minutes after the first assault wave hit the beach. Some of the men were now standing, attempting to catch a glimpse of what lay ahead.

As they made their run to the beach, the boat's pilot was one of the few with a good view. He was too busy lining up his route to shore to say anything. Perhaps he'd been silenced by what he was witnessing.

One of the men nearby yelled nervously, "All the shelling from the ships and bombers should have beat the hell out of the defensive positions on the beaches. Surely our boys have made it off the beach by now."

Following the landings, The RWRs War Diary reported:

> The bombardment having failed to kill a single German or silence one weapon, these coys (companies) had to storm their positions "cold" — and did so without hesitation.[27]

When they were within half a mile from shore, the engines sped up. Gerry joined the others who were standing and was able to see the backside of the beach. As the bow rose, he spotted one of the pillboxes built into the side of the terrain. He could see spots where shells had burst around the bunker. There appeared to be little or no damage. Gerry could see tracer rounds from the German MG 42 machine guns as they continued to spit out deadly fire. As the boat dipped, he saw men lying on the beach, many of them not moving.

By the time they were ready to land, Gerry and the others had been bobbing up and down in the channel for over two hours.

Some men felt that death might have been a welcome relief for how sick they felt. For the second assault wave of The Royal Winnipeg Rifles, their baptism of battle was only moments away. This morning would be the first time most would be facing live fire from an enemy trying to kill them.

The intensity of the landing is reflected in Gerry's own words:

Machine-gun bullets are starting to whine around our craft. Even though they are standing, the boys are keeping their heads down. Here we go, the doors are open, and the ramp is down, and our officer is off, followed by the rest of us.

It didn't go as smoothly as practiced. The landing craft had failed to land directly on the dry beach requiring men to jump into waist-high cold water.

We are in the waters off the beach up to our waists and sometimes up to our chests. We wade ashore, and it's pretty slow work. As my feet stepped out of the English Channel onto the damp sand, there was no time to celebrate that I hadn't drowned. Machine guns are making us play hop scotch as we cross it at the walk.

On many occasions, my dad told me that he was sure if they had landed farther from the beach, he would have drowned. While wading to shore, he was also concerned about keeping his rifle dry. He later found it humorous that the flat feet the doctor had concerns about were sloshing around in his new high-top invasion boots.

There is only one man hit in all this time. I couldn't tell who it was. I just know he was hit pretty bad.

According to my father, this man was beside him as they jumped off the ramp, only feet away to his right as they stepped onto the beach. He saw him hit by machine-gun fire, then fall to the ground. Their orders were clear: "Do not stop to assist the wounded."

Constant enemy fire made him zig and zag. Gerry tried to move faster, knowing that stopping to help the injured soldier was not an option, knowing that slowing down might make him the next target. The man was face down in the sand. Every casualty lying on the beach looked the same. He didn't know who it was because initials and service numbers were marked on the packs' underside. He knew one thing for sure. The man was hurt pretty badly.

Whether by luck or good fortune, Gerry continued onward without being struck by bullets and reached safety behind the dunes. This protection meant he and the others were no longer in the direct line of sight from the hail of bullets. He took a moment to relish being alive, knowing the pull of a trigger or having a mortar shell tear him to shreds could change that in an instant.

Other than the man shot as they stepped ashore, he hadn't noticed others lying on the beach until he reached the dunes. Men had been cut down as they came ashore. Some were dead; others appeared severely wounded. Lying on the beach, many of them were writhing and screaming. Looking toward the shoreline, he saw bodies floating in the surf. Gerry had no idea that by the end of the day, thousands of men would be killed or wounded before stepping even two or three feet onto the shores of France

"There but for the grace of God," he whispered, as sounds of battle raged around him.

Unlike other locations along the Normandy coast, this stretch of Juno Beach had no sea wall. Though they were lying safely behind the dunes, the constant machine-gun fire made it evident that other parts of the company were still being shot at on the left flank. The machine gun was set in a Tobruk, a turret, deep enough to provide shelter from gunfire while giving the machine-gun operator a 360-degree vantage point.

An explosion silenced the gun to their left, and a cheer erupted from the RWRs when the firing stopped.

The beach was by no means quiet; mortar fire and 88-mm shells were landing all around. The explosions sent plumes of coarse sand into the air, leaving shell craters in their wake. There was the constant unmistakable sound of other German MG 42 machine guns from the not-yet-silenced pillboxes in different Juno Beach sections. The men later described the long bursts of the MG 42s as a buzzing sound. Others remarked that it sounded like a piece of fabric being torn; others said it sounded like a zipper going up and down.[28]

Burning its way into Gerry's memory was the smell of gunpowder and explosives mixed with blood and the rancid smell of death and seawater. He didn't know it then, but there would be times throughout the rest of his life when certain smells would remind him of this exact moment.

They rested behind the dunes for three or four minutes until the commanding officer of A Company, Major Hodge, ordered the company to move forward. At that instant, Gerry understood what thousands of Canadians during World War I did when the whistle would blow. It was the signal for wave upon wave of brave soldiers to rise from their slit trenches and run head-on toward the murderous enemy fire in the hopes of winning a few feet of ground.

Each company was assigned a specific exit point to get off the beaches. As Gerry's company moved forward, the lead men cut the barbed wire strung for miles along the coast. Soaked to the skin, sand caking his uniform, they began moving to the predetermined exit point. What felt like an eternity was less than half an hour since landing on Juno beach.

The company reformed on the backside of the dunes. Major Hodge pointed his men in the direction of Ste. Croix-sur-Mer. Moving inland, they came upon rows of tank ditches, six to eight feet across. They were four to five feet deep, filled to the brim with water. The Germans put these in place to prevent the forward movement of armoured equipment through the fields between the beaches and Graye-sur-Mer. In his journal, Gerry wrote:

> *Heavy machine-gun fire churned the ground in front of us. We headed off to the left flank to try and round them up. Bullets came close but did not hit anyone. Our group flanking the machine-gun position eliminated the threat with a combination of direct fire and grenades.*

Farther ahead, D Company took a different exit point off the beach. They were now clearing the town of Graye-sur-Mer.

Along the roadway, they came across the village washhouse. Several Germans and Canadians lay dead around the old structure. A section of the rear wall had collapsed, apparently blown away by the blast of a grenade. Gerry's platoon continued toward town without resistance from the Germans.

As he looked toward the town, Gerry saw the local church. The top part of the steeple was smoking, with a massive hole in the upper section.

Al Miller, one of six riflemen in his section, pointed to the smoking, gaping hole. "I wonder if it was the navy that almost destroyed the church. The steeple would have been an ideal position for a sniper. If there was someone up there, I don't imagine there would be much of him left, eh Gerry?"

"Probably not. Sure as hell made a mess."

As they gazed at the steeple, they observed a Canadian soldier waving from the bell tower, letting them know there was no threat from the elevated position.

The steeple of the Graye-sur-Mer church, destroyed in the aftermath of D-Day

Plaque at Graye-sur-Mer showing the bombed-out steeple.

The following statement was taken directly from the plaque:

The steeple of the church in Saint-Martin had been destroyed by lightning on June 4th, 1873. Father Raphael Blin, the parish priest in Graye-sur-Mer, who officiated in this church, succeeded in raising funds for the reconstruction of his steeple between 1940 and 1943. It was inaugurated on September 5th 1943. On 6th June 1944, it was once again destroyed by gunfire, as were most of the bell towers along the coast, which it was supposed the Germans were using as look-out posts. Undaunted, Father Blin had his steeple repaired, and

it was unveiled on September 9ᵗʰ 1945. As Father Blin had thus twice overseen the reconstruction of his steeple, and in accordance with his expressed wish, he was granted a special dispensation to be buried beneath the steeple, inside the church, on his death in November 2001.

Less than half a kilometre from the washhouse, they reached their first objective: a large farmhouse across the road from the town church. After making a cautious approach, they found no sign of the enemy. Gerry's platoon was ordered to surround and search the farmhouse while the rest of the company moved toward the next objective. They would catch up as soon as they cleared the house. The Major did not want to leave any Germans behind them as they made their way forward. If they discovered the enemy had occupied the place, they were to look for any papers the Germans might have left behind.

There were craters throughout the area; evidence of the bombing runs in the early morning hours. The air force was instructed to keep their airstrikes to the beach areas, but cloud cover caused entire bomb loads to stray off-target. Some landed in the area surrounding the farmhouse. The barn across the courtyard displayed extensive cracks in the walls caused by the concussive force of the explosions. The fence built from the same rock was crumbling in places, but none of the wayward bombs seemed to have struck the house. The men could hear the sporadic sounds of gunfire coming from the town, the farmyard itself eerily quiet.

During training, some men learned several key German phrases. The sergeant called out, "Lass deine waffen fallen und komm mit erhobenen händen heraus" (Drop your weapons and come out with your hands held high). If the enemy did occupy the home, it appeared they were no longer there. The platoon surrounded the house, keeping their weapons trained on all the doors and windows, as two men entered and called out again.

Inside, they heard voices coming from the cellar and called out again. A French mother and her two children emerged from their hiding place in the basement.

When the woman came outside, she began shouting, "Merci, Merci, you have finally come. Bienvenue, Welcome, Welcome," she said. "Americain?"

Several men in the regiment were from Quebec, including three Choquette family members who could speak French. "Non, mademoiselle. Nous sommes Canadiens."

"Choquette. Ask her if she's seen the Germans," ordered the Lieutenant.

"Excuse moi madame, avez-vous vu les allemands?"

"Je ne sais pas, Monsieur. Nous étons dans la cave toute la nuit," she stammered, then pointed to the house, then down to the ground. "Quand le bombardement a commencé."

"She doesn't know, Lieutenant. She and her kids were in the basement all night once the bombing started."

"All right. Leave the family here. We'll work our way to the Elm line position and rendezvous with the Major there. There's supposed to be a minefield along the way." Clearing mines was one of the jobs of the pioneer company, known as sappers. "Let's hope the sappers did their job and marked a path for us. Before we get to Elm, we have to get through Sainte-Croix-Sur-Mer, then it's on to Creully."

Gerry had met his first French civilians. The mother seemed grateful, but there was no time to dawdle. The platoon immediately set off up the lane leading away from the farmhouse. The young boy and girl ran beside them for a moment or two, saying thankyous and goodbyes. The lieutenant gave the children small pieces of chocolate and sent them back to their mother as the platoon carried on.

When they reached the suspected minefield area, they were relieved that the sappers had been through and done their job. There were areas marked by signs in German warning of *Minen*. There were no mines where indicated; instead, the Germans set them in unmarked areas, making it tricky for company sappers to work their way through these minefields. The platoon spread out into the fields and began advancing to their next rendezvous point.

As they moved forward, they saw giant stacks of straw. These haystacks provided camouflage for the pillboxes inside from aerial reconnaissance. Believing they were empty because other LDBs would have already passed through the area, the lieutenant said, "Leave those for engineers coming up behind."

With those words hardly out of his mouth, the men began taking fire. Rifleman Tony Hubert noticed movement under one of the haystacks and began firing into it. Each ten-round magazine for the Canadians' rifles held a minimum of two tracer rounds (bullets with small pyrotechnic charges). When fired, the chemical composition burned brightly, making the shell easily visible to the naked eye in the dark. One of the tracers set the straw ablaze. Moments later, a group of Germans came out from the haystack with their arms held high.[29] These prisoners, members of the 716th German Infantry Division, were gathered up, searched, and escorted back toward the beaches by two riflemen.

The LBDs fanned out into an arrowhead formation. They began walking through a field of waist-high barley that would soon be ready for harvest. Rifleman Dawson of Gerry's section was on point. He stopped suddenly and held up his arm with a clenched fist as he crouched down on one knee. The rest of the men did likewise. As he looked ahead, Gerry saw two Boches walking towards them with their hands in the air.

"Looks like more prisoners, lieutenant," pointed out the sergeant.

"Pay close attention. There's bound to be more Germans hidden out there. If you haven't done so already, fix bayonets and tread carefully. If these Nazis are hiding in the fields, you may not get a chance to shoot," suggested the lieutenant.

One of the sections moved forward to meet the surrendering Germans. Like the other soldiers who fled the burning straw stacks, these men were quickly patted down and searched for weapons and documents. Finding neither, the lieutenant ordered two more soldiers to return the prisoners back to the beach. As the Germans were escorted away, the remaining men headed off again.

As they advanced, Gerry heard a rustling sound from his left. The lieutenant was right. There were more. Using his bayonet, he carefully spread the stocks of grain, knowing there was likely an enemy soldier lying in wait. Gerry was still surprised when he found the man lying directly in front of him. The man rolled from his prone position onto his back. Gerry was about to ram his bayonet into the man lying before him. With a look of terror on his face, the man screamed, "Rusky!" Gerry managed to stop the deadly momentum within two inches of his enemy's chest.

The look of relief on the Russian's face was unmistakable. Gerry called out for the lieutenant: "This guy says he's a Rusky, Lieutenant." After bringing the man to his feet, he patted him down. Gerry was busy with his Russian and didn't see the men capture another soldier, who turned out to be Polish.

The new prisoners also needed to be sent back toward the beach. "Johnston, see if you can catch up with the others. Turn these guys over to them, then get back here on the double. All right, the rest of you spread out and stay sharp."

According to the map, the platoon was approximately three kilometres inland and closing in on Sainte-Croix-Sur-Mer when they caught up to Major Hodge. He was trying to find a way around a defensive position located on the high ground outside of town. The Germans were dug in and prepared for a fight.

The maps indicated a potential defensive position ahead. Various enemy positions had been pinpointed with the assistance of aerial photographs over the previous months. Now he needed to know exactly what lay ahead.

Gerry's platoon was given the task of scouting the extent of the enemy position. As they advanced, the point man again motioned for everyone to halt. After working their way forward, the men gathered in a semi-circle. The lieutenant pointed out movement near a small bluff, approximately eight hundred yards ahead. He lifted his field glasses to survey the situation. "Got a couple of machine guns up there. They have to be eliminated."

The following is how Gerry described the situation:

As we get close, we come under a crossfire of machine guns. By this time, I am pretty cocky and have all the confidence in the world. (I expected to be frightened a little but can truthfully say that I was not. It was just like one of our exercises, but this time they were playing for keeps.)

"I was ahead of my section, which was in the lead and was on the right flank. We were in grass about a foot high which gave us cover from the machine-gun fire. I crawled up to a barbed-wire fence which was about a hundred yards from the enemy slit trench. The slit trench seemed to be about a hundred and fifty feet in length with a blockhouse on the left flank.

Turning to the rear, he realized he was on his own. The rest of his section was lying low under cover of the high barley field they had come through. Without backtracking, there was no way to warn the rest of the men about what he was seeing. Peering forward, he could see the German position.

I saw a Boche, well exposed and like a sucker, raised myself to take aim. I drew a nice bead and was just squeezing the trigger when I saw a small puff of smoke to my left and a light machine-gun bullet smacked me down. It hit me in the right leg and went right through the thigh from left to right.

As he lay there, he could hear the cracking, pinging, and popping all around as men on both sides began shooting and throwing grenades. The smoke and dust from grenades rose in the air, then settled toward the ground for a few moments before being whisked away by breezes coming inland off the channel.

Gerry was out of the battle, figuring he was going into shock. "Jesus Christ," he cried, then muttered to himself, "That'll teach ya for getting so cocky."

As the fighting continued, Gerry lay quietly. He could hear the enemy calling out. He figured they might be getting a better fix on his position. Several German stick grenades, potato mashers, were thrown his way. With a hundred yards between him and the slit trench, he knew there was no way for them to throw their grenades far enough to reach him.

After forty-five minutes, when the worst of the shock wore off, Gerry figured he should move back and find the rest of his section. His leg hurt like hell, but there were still Germans yelling, and he was afraid they knew his precise location; he didn't want to be lying there, waiting for them to come out and check on him. He feared being captured or killed.

Crawling back to where he left the rest of the section, he found his corporal and another man pinned down, and together they withdrew. With slightly better cover, Gerry made good time despite his wound. He finally made it back to the rest of the platoon.

Since a frontal assault on the German position would be a suicide mission, the platoon prepared to head to the left flank, hoping to make an end-run on the enemy. Before leaving, the medic bandaged Gerry's wound with a field dressing and gave him a shot of morphine for the pain.

"You're one lucky guy. It looks like a clean shot straight through. You're going to have two nice scars," suggested the medic. "How long were you lying out there?"

Not sure. At least forty-five minutes. I could hear the Boche calling to each other once in a while, so I decided to start crawling back. Thought they might come out and have a look at me and didn't want any part of that.

"Jesus, Gerry, you're damned lucky you didn't bleed out."

"Don't I know it? Thanks for fixing me up."

Sergeant Donaldson came over to check on Gerry, telling him to head back toward the beach. "You should come across more of our boys coming up from the beaches."

While getting my wounds dressed, there had been constant fire from snipers to bother us. They sure make life very uncertain.

Searching for a medical officer as he headed toward the beach, Gerry saw two sappers join the platoon. He was confident they would help eliminate the threat from the slit trenches.

At the same time, Major Hodge met with the company officers to discuss their options. Afraid of being pushed back by a counter-attack, the Major put in a request for reinforcements. He also asked for tanks to help eliminate the enemy from the fortified position near Sainte-Croix-Sur-Mer.

Gerry began working his way back to meet up with others moving in from the beachhead, hoping to find a medical officer. The mortar sections were firing their two-inch mortars toward the slit trenches, but they didn't seem to have any effect. Since they were already a few kilometres inland, he figured more troops would now be streaming uncontested across the beach where so many men had already died. "What the hell. I made it up here without firing a shot, and I still haven't," he said to himself.

After leaving the company, he heard loud explosions. Then the gunfire from the area where he was wounded stopped abruptly. "Never heard any tanks." He wondered if some of the Shermans from the 1st Hussars Armoured Regiment or the 6th Armoured had come to lend a hand. Gerry hoped sappers, mortars or tanks had cleared the Germans out of their positions.

Colonel Meldram reported in his War Diary:

> Portions of A and C Sqns, 6 Cdn Armd. Regt. Went to the help of A Coy, with cool disregard for mines and A Tk guns, beat down the mg positions and permitted A Coy to mop up and advance to the South.[30]

Gerry limped and hobbled with his bad leg. The morphine the medic gave him helped dull the pain. Figuring it was time for a rest, he leaned against a bank on the side of the road. He was afraid if he sat, he might have trouble getting up. "I guess I could take time for a smoke," he thought. "Haven't had one all day." Pulling out his pack of smokes, he found they were soaking wet. "Damn it. What the hell did you expect? You almost drowned in the Channel. Is it any wonder your smokes are wet," he mumbled.

While leaning back, wishing for a dry smoke, he couldn't help but think of the letter he'd written home in November of '43, six months after arriving in England. He'd addressed the letter home to his dog Topper because when a parcel arrived from Winnipeg, it seemed good old Topper, his Cocker Spaniel was the sender. The package contained a couple of cartons of Canadian cigarettes. In his letter, he told Topper:

I received your parcel of cigarettes yesterday and certainly was glad to get them. I only had two packets left out of Bertie's parcel, so was just about out, as you can plainly see.

The rest of the letter spoke to his family:

Guess that sounds kind of silly, but after all, Tops sent the cigarettes, and I had to thank her. As I said in my letter to her, they arrived at an opportune moment. Am smoking pretty heavy these days, and the Limey cigs are terrible.

In another portion of his letter to Topper, he wrote:

The dogs I've seen over here are a pretty mangy-looking bunch. I don't think you would enjoy meeting them, also don't think that you would care very much for the country. The weather has turned quite cool the last couple of days, and it has rained some.

While recovering in the hospital in England, Gerry wrote:

While resting at the side of the road, I was still cussing myself about my wet smokes. I saw a bunch of Boche coming down the road about a hundred yards away. They were marching in threes, so figured that some of our boys must be around. I pushed myself off the bank and angled over to them. There were four RWRs and one Can Scot soldier guarding the prisoners. Some were Poles, and some were Russians. I fell in with our boys and helped to guard them. They were quite docile and never attempted to give us any trouble."

The prisoners included a German battalion commander, his second-in-command, two officers, and forty-six other ranks. When Gerry took a close look at them, he figured they were a pretty sorry-looking lot.

Gerry didn't know the Canadian Scottish soldier but recognized the other four men. He waved to Sinclair, Hubert, Chartrand, and McLeod. They'd all been friends since Gerry arrived from Canada.

McLeod snorted, "We've got ourselves a big lot here, Gerry. The funny thing is, there's a bunch of Poles and Russians mixed in with the Germans."

"I know. I almost stuck my bayonet into a guy a little while ago. Just before I rammed it through him, he starts screaming, 'Rusky.' What the hell; I thought we were here to fight Germans," Gerry announced.

"I've got no idea. The Captain told us to take this batch back to the beach and get back to the company double-quick," grumbled McLeod.

Gerry hadn't seen stretcher-bearers or any members of the Canadian Field Ambulance sections. They were supposed to be following directly behind the advance, so he helped escort the prisoners toward the beach.

They marched their prisoners back to the coastal town of Graye-sur-Mer. Upon arrival, they paraded the POWs through the narrow streets, searching for a cage to put them in. The French citizens were excited to see the Germans on the opposite end of a rifle. Dozens of them were hooting, hollering, and catcalling. The townspeople screamed at their prisoners. Gerry figured they wanted the German officers beaten or worse.

An older-looking Frenchman ran over to Gerry and passed him an open bottle of wine. He took a drink and was almost sickened by the taste. It was terrible. In an effort not to insult the man, he managed to choke it down. He thought anything would have tasted good at this point, but he was wrong. He later found out that it was probably Calvados, a local liqueur or brandy-like drink made from apples. After he'd passed the bottle around, he noticed that the other men guarding the prisoners didn't seem to enjoy it any more than he had.

A lot of the enemy soldiers were young, some not looking much older than fifteen or sixteen. They appeared terrified and concerned the Canadians would shoot them right on the spot since they were unable to find a suitable cage to keep them. After four years of occupation, the prisoners appeared concerned about the civilians beating them to death as revenge.

Canadian Provost Corps (C.P.C.) guarding the first German prisoners.

Gerry and the other five Canadians escorted the prisoners safely back to the beach near Courseulles-sur-Mer. It was one of the first big batches brought to the beach. It wasn't far from the spot Gerry left only hours earlier.

"That's quite the lot you boys have there," called out one of the officers from the Provost Corp as they marched them onto the beach.

"What's going to happen with these guys?" Gerry asked.

"For now, sit them down over there, right on the beach. Then, when we get a chance, they'll be loaded onto one of the LSTs and taken back to England. A lot of them will end up in Canada long before you get home, I'm afraid," announced the officer.

The four men from A Company and the Can Scott told Gerry they needed to get back to the fighting. "Hey, Levers. Get your leg fixed up real quick and get back here. I think we're going to need all the help we can get," hollered McLeod.

After shaking hands, his pals took off at a slow trot to rejoin the men on the front lines.

Gerry sat down on the sand against the wall below one of the German gun emplacements, not far from where the prisoners were being guarded. As he looked out into the channel, he marvelled at the scene before him. Large Landing Craft Tanks (LCTs) landed directly on the beach, disgorging Red Cross Units, Jeeps, tanks, transport trucks, and thousands of troops onto the shore in a steady stream.

While resting on the beach, he learned that the walls and ceilings of the gun emplacements were so thick they could withstand almost anything the air and naval bombardment threw at them.

As he finally relaxed, he decided it was time for a drink. There hadn't been a chance to even take a sip of water since being wounded. While resting at the roadside, he'd been thinking more about having a smoke than a drink.

He removed his water bottle from its pouch, surprised to find it empty. Looking closer, he discovered a hole on one side of it. He shook the canister and heard something rattling around inside. After pulling the cork, he poured out the bullet and realized it must have gone right through his leg and ended up in his water bottle. He undid the button on his tunic pocket and dropped the copper-jacketed projectile inside.

He could see dozens of wounded men on the beaches. Many were worse off than he was, some with missing limbs or bad blistering burns. There were a number with bandages on their heads; in some cases, those bandages covered their eyes.

Wounded Canadian soldiers, awaiting evacuation.

He took note of the white tarps covering those killed in action. Training with his company over the past year, the men had learned a great deal about each other. He wondered how many of the dead might be from Winnipeg.

He also saw young girls, who must have been from the village above the sea wall, assisting the wounded. Captured German soldiers were helping to bandage the injured Canadians

Medics prepped the worst casualties for return to the ships sitting offshore. Since Gerry could limp, he didn't need a stretcher. It was late afternoon before he was on a DUKW, an amphibious landing craft called a 'duck boat,' and driven off the beach into the water. These six-wheeled truck boats could run right onto or off the beaches loaded with troops or gear.

The sea was calmer compared to the trip in hours earlier. Gerry realized he hadn't swallowed anything but seawater since the hot tea he'd had at 0400. Even if it was rough, there wouldn't have been anything to throw up anyway.

The ride back to the ship was quicker than the run to shore hours earlier because the ships were repositioned closer to shore and now sat anchored only a mile from the beaches.

They pulled alongside the vessel that would return Gerry to England. He saw other boats discharging trucks onto smaller ones being used to ferry equipment to shore. The men securing the gear belonged to the RWRs. He didn't know them by name, but their distinctive shoulder patches indicated they were with the Little Black Devils.

On board the ship, he was placed on a cot. Others were on beds spread around the decks. When he and the latest bunch were lying down, the navy medics began to treat the wounded with great care. The first-aid man gave Gerry a shot of a new drug called penicillin. "It'll help ward off infection," the medic said before giving him another dose of morphine. Even with the screams and constant sound of men moaning, he finally managed to fall asleep, something he hadn't done in over twenty-four hours.

Part Six

June 7 – 16, 1944

Gerry was one of the thousands heading back to England in convoy on June 7. Finally, somewhere after 2100 hours, they disembarked in England. That's when he came to the realization he'd left his equipment on Juno Beach. "What the hell? My smokes were all wet anyway."

When the ship pulled into Portsmouth, they were taken off on stretchers and loaded into waiting ambulances. The piers were teeming with hundreds of people, including civilians, all lending a hand with the task of helping the wounded soldiers.

There were no shortages of smokes here. On the contrary, as they came off the ship, the soldiers were cheered by army medical personnel and civilians alike and were handed cigarettes by the dozens. Gerry drank so much tea he figured he might float to the nearest hospital.

Upon arrival at the Haslar Royal Hospital, he and the rest of the wounded received truly royal treatment and care. The doctors were exceptional, speedy, and efficient, making short work of stitching both sides of Gerry's leg. He showed his doctor the bullet he poured out from his canteen while waiting on the beach.

The following morning, the doctor who sewed up his leg handed him back the bullet while doing his rounds. There was a hole drilled in it. "Get something to wear around your neck and hang this bullet on it. You're a lucky man. Think of the bullet as your good luck charm. Might keep you safe 'til you get home."

While at the hospital, Gerry met three other men who arrived at the same time. All four were considered walking cases, giving them more freedom to move around than the more gravely wounded soldiers.

While the doctors were good, the nurses were prettier. He and his newfound friends convinced the ladies to give them their addresses. Margaret and Gloria told them they would come and visit them at the convalescent hospital where the Canadians would be sent to recover.

On June 9, Gerry and a contingent of other Canadians were transferred by ambulance to Canadian Hospital #9 in Horsham. The previous day, the hospital had received seventy-six patients. By the time Gerry and his pals arrived, the place with a capacity for six hundred wounded soldiers was mostly empty. The building was a combination of one and two stories, complete with a substantial inner courtyard where those in recovery could walk and exercise.

Gerry and other walking cases were getting impatient to get back into the fight. They complained when told they would be convalescing for quite some time. The medical staff wanted to make sure everyone was in fighting shape before being sent back to France.

"Ain't that just like the army? Make sure we're good as new, then send us back so somebody can start shooting at us again," grumbled one of the patients.

Late that evening, Generals Crerar and Stuart visited the hospital. General Crerar was in charge of the entire Canadian Army. He walked through the hospital, stopping to talk to the men. Gerry was surprised when they stopped at his bedside and spoke with him.

"How are they treating you, soldier?" asked Crerar.

"Just fine, sir. Thanks for asking."

"Where were you hit?"

"Upper thigh, sir." Gerry wasn't about to tell him about being shot just below his manhood.

"You men have done a real good job. Some of our units have advanced further inland than any of the others, British or American," boasted Crerar.

**Lieutenant General Henry Crerar,
commander of the 1ˢᵗ Canadian Army.**

"That's good to hear, sir. The boys and I are just waiting to get back to the fight, sir. After a couple of days lying around here, there's a bunch of us getting pretty restless. Guess you can't keep us Canadians down."

"Glad to hear that. Good luck with the leg."

The day after the generals left, Gerry and his three friends were approached by the CBC and invited to London to make a radio broadcast for the people back in Canada.

Over the following days, he and hundreds of other soldiers fell into the routine of ordinary hospital life.

As more wounded soldiers arrived, they brought word from the Normandy area about some German Regiments, including Colonel Kurt Meyer's 12th SS Panzer Division and the Hitler-Jugend. They learned that many of the men taken prisoner by Meyer's men had been murdered, including fourteen men from Gerry's company.

On the evening of the 12th, Gerry wrote home to tell his family about his exploits since June 1. His letter was on a sheet of Armed Forces Air Letter paper, so thin it would tear if he sneezed on it. Hoping his letter would not be censored, he wrote:

I happened to come across him first and am just going to sink the bayonet home when he shouts, "Rusky." I pulled up my rifle when the bayonet was about two inches from his chest and turned him over to our officer. Kind of wish I hadn't listened to him now that I've seen some of our chaps.

Gerry wrote about being cocky when he attempted to shoot the German soldier, only to be wounded with a bullet through the right thigh:

Two inches higher, and I would have stopped being a man.

He finished off his letter:

It's 10:00 PM. Four of us are going up to London to make a broadcast. How do you like your famous son? They will notify you by cable when the broadcast is to take place. So long, for now, everybody, and write soon. Love Gerry.

Along with his new friends, George Russell, Al Trotter, and Ralph Spencer, Gerry made the eighty-mile trip to London on

June 16. When they arrived at the BBC studio, they met with Lieutenant Jack Scott. He would do the interviews with the men, and the broadcast would air across Canada.

At the start of the broadcast, Scott told his listeners how the four were probably the first wounded to reach London since the invasion. Then, he introduced the men, talked about how they were injured, and finally referred to Gerry, the only man to make it off the beach.

"And finally, we have rifleman Gerry Levers of Winnipeg. His wound was a machine-gun slug through the right thigh."

"I got further in. It was about three miles inland. We were just going into a small town called Sainte-Croix-Sur-Mer. That was our second objective."

"What were the things you remember most about the whole show, Gerry?"

"The way the Canadians went in. They were like a bunch of veterans who'd been under fire for four years. It wasn't running so much as walking. We were all pretty waterlogged from going through the water."

"How does it feel to be back in London?" asked Scott.

"We trained for this for two years. It's just plain tough luck to last for less than a day. We figure we'll be getting back as soon as these scratches get okay. I've been hurt worse than this playing hockey."[31]

While still in London, Gerry and his new mates visited many local pubs and were treated like conquering heroes. The locals were excited to hear their accounts of the landings. Of course, it didn't go unnoticed that each of the men had been wounded. Gerry, still limping badly, took pride in showing off his souvenir slug that went through his leg.

As hard as they tried, nobody would let them buy a drink. Spencer even offered to buy a round of drinks for the locals with a 100-franc note. No one took him up on the offer.

Londoners Fete Canadian Wounded

LONDON, June 14—(CP-Reuter)—Londoners Tuesday opened their hearts to the first casualties from France they had seen —four Canadians who called themselves "the unluckiest" because they couldn't follow their colleagues in.

They were Cpl. George Russell, Kinistino, Sask.; Tr. Alex Trotter, Stratford, Ont.; Spr. Ralph Spencer, Londonderry, N.S., and Rfmn. Gerry Levers, Winnipeg.

In pubs they visited nobody would let them buy a drink. People gathered around to hear their stories and buy a round. Spencer volunteered to pay with a 100-France note. But no one would allow it.

It wasn't hard to tell they were casualties. Spencer had shrapnel in his left leg. Levers, who displayed a machine-gun slug taken from his leg, limped badly.

Russell, who had shrapnel wound in his right wrist which he got three minutes after he hit the beach, and Trotter, who was hit in the shoulder by shrapnel when his tank was knocked out by direct hits on the turret, killing his crew commander, had their hands slung inside their tunics.

Winnipeg Tribune story from London, June 14, 1944.

Gerry and other wounded soldiers ended up spending more time in the hospital than they would have liked. He still felt like one of "the unluckiest." In hindsight, however, it may have been the luckiest thing that could have happened.

Part Seven

On September 5, 1944, Gerry again found himself on the English Channel heading to France. At this point, the transports were still unloading in the Normandy region. He finally made it back to his regiment and was taken on strength (TOS) on September 17.

Gerry was back with his company; it was good to see some of the men. He was well-rested and ready to get into the fight. He arrived just in time to help with the second day of operations as the LBDs attacked the gun batteries on Cape Gris-Nez.

The initial attack by The Royal Winnipeg Rifles at the Cape Griz-Nez batteries was unsuccessful. It was decided to turn the final assault on these bunkers to the Canadian 9th brigade. The 7th brigade, including the RWRs, Regina Rifles, and Canadian Scottish, would now assist in the assault on Calais.[32]

Before the regiment could move on to the city of Calais, they needed to go through Vieux Coquelles, some eighteen kilometres from Cape Gris-Nez. On September 25, the regiment would meet stiff resistance from pockets of Germans. They were in defensive positions on the outskirts of Calais. Fields of cereal crops and hay for the dairy farms covered the landscape around the city. Only ten metres above sea level and less than three miles from the Straits of Dover, the lay of the land was as flat as a prairie grain field. The topography and lack of cover made the advance toward Vieux Coquelles dangerous. The Germans made their advance more difficult by flooding the fields between the town and Calais.

This phase of the battle plan called for the RWRs to take Vieux Coquelles. Then they would head across to Fort Nieulay to avoid the flooded region between where they were and the city of Calais. Gerry's company was in the lead as they approached the town, advancing in a line abreast formation. This required heading towards their objective in a straight line, with a few feet of spacing between each soldier.

There were dozens of small farms on the town's outskirts; the area appeared calm and tranquil as they moved forward. It felt like the perfect day for an autumn walk, not much different than the day he headed off to enlist back in 1939. As they approached one of the farmyards, all seemed quiet. There was no definitive sign of the enemy. They anticipated German resistance but hadn't come under any sniper fire or mortar bombardment.

When they were within two hundred metres of the farmhouse, the enemy opened fire on the men of A Company. Jimmy Branch, an American who joined the regiment before America entered the war, was on Gerry's right. After arriving in England, the two men had become close friends. Jimmy's family lived in Goliad, Texas; thus, someone decided his nickname should be Tex. On Gerry's left was another rifleman by the name of Landry; he came from the Maritimes.

When the shots rang out, Gerry dove to the ground in the field of tall grass, which would soon be ready for the second cutting of the season, hiding him from the sightlines of the farm ahead.

Gerry heard Landry call out, "I'm hit."

"How bad?"

"Took one in the shoulder; I think I'll be okay," came the reply. "How about you?"

"Bastard's missed me this time," scoffed Gerry, "Hey, Jimmy, you okay?" he called to his right.

There was no answer. Gerry crawled in his direction.

He saw Jimmy lying flat on his back. As he moved closer, he called to his friend, "Tex. Tex. You okay?"

There was still no response. The evidence was clear from the hole in the helmet where the bullet passed through and hit Tex in the forehead. His friend was likely dead before he hit the ground.

Gerry gently removed Tex's helmet. Very little blood came from the wound, but his eyes were wide open. Gerry looked at his friend as he put his fingers over his eyelids and closed them for him one last time.

While attending to his friend, the rest of the regiment managed to flank the farmhouse. After a short battle, the guns went silent. Gerry took his friend's rifle. After attaching the bayonet, he stuck it in the ground. This would mark the position of Tex's body, making it easier for the men following to find him.

With the danger of snipers eliminated, Gerry checked on Landry and arranged for a medic to take care of him, then joined the rest of the regiment as they made their way through the town.

Vieux Coquelles was usually a sleepy little town, but the Germans had built considerable fortifications, including bombproof concrete shelters in strategic locations. The Canadians received stiff resistance. Fighting went from house to house; in some cases, it was hand-to-hand combat.

Once the company cleared Vieux Coquelles, they moved toward the village of Coquelles. Along the way, they encountered more sniper attacks, and came across several minefields. As they neared their next objective, the enemy began to find their range and started dropping artillery rounds on the regiment.

When they arrived in town, fighting took place from house to house on almost every street. By late afternoon the LBDs were getting the support of Allied artillery, which helped drive the Germans out of town. Since it was late September, darkness was coming earlier than when Gerry landed on Juno Beach. By seven-thirty, the sun was setting, and the town was finally quiet.

The battalion again sustained heavy casualties. Once again, A Company took the worst of it. There were eleven wounded and five men, including Tex, were dead. The total losses for the RWRs in the engagements during the afternoon were the equivalent of an entire platoon.

When Gerry returned to France, Tex was the first to welcome him back. In his deep Texas drawl, he asked what Gerry was doing while the rest of the regiment slugged it out from the beaches. He told him how he survived the mess they found themselves in around

Putot-en-Bessin. This is where many of their pals were captured, then murdered at the Chateau d'Audrieu, including Major Hodge, the company commander. Gerry learned his friend had a close call during the attack of the Carpiquet airport. It was a grim reminder to Gerry of how many friends he lost while recovering in England.

Since D-Day, Gerry's company had lost a total of seventy-five men who were killed in action, murdered or died later from their wounds. This included replacement troops, many of whom Gerry had become acquainted with. Eighty-eight men, including Gerry, were wounded, and twenty-four men had been taken as prisoners of war.[33]

"I think I've managed to kill one or two Germans myself along the way, but not enough to make up for what they did to Major Hodge and the others," said Tex.

After Jimmy had gotten everything off his chest, Gerry told him about his time in England, the hospitals, the pretty nurses, his meeting with General Crerar, and his time in London following his CBC interview.

Tex lowered his head and began speaking softly. "Now that you're back, Gerry, I want to give you this." He handed Gerry a piece of paper.

"What's this?"

"It's the address for my parents. If anything happens to me, I would like you to let them know what happened. I want them to have more than the impersonal telegram that the families are receiving. Will you do that for me?"

"I'm sure it won't be necessary, but if something does happen, I'll make sure to let them know."

While still fresh in his mind, Gerry took out his paper and pen and wrote a letter to Tex's parents. He would save them the details other than saying they had been good friends and how it was a pleasure to have known him and explain how he was with Jimmy when he died. Somehow he would make sure they knew Jimmy didn't suffer.

As he wrote the letter to Jimmy's folks, he wondered if Jimmy somehow knew his number was coming up soon. He could have given the address to any of the guys before or after they landed on the beaches. For some reason, he waited to give it to him after his return.

"Jesus Christ. He died within a week of giving me his folks' address," swore Gerry.

 "What if I hadn't taken it?" he asked himself. "I should have known not to take the damn thing."

The Cape Gris-Nez Batteries were finally put out of action by the 9th Infantry Brigade, including the Highland Light Infantry and the North Nova Scotia Highlanders, with the assistance of the 14th Field Regiment of the Royal Canadian Artillery and several British Armoured Regiments. Late in the morning of the 29th, sappers' hand-placed charges. They finally silenced the massive guns, including the Todt Battery that fired fifteen-inch shells that could hit the Dover coast.[34]

Gerry avoided being wounded again throughout the rest of the war but experienced another close call in November of 1944. One story he told over the years involved the loss of the "Good Luck Charm Bullet" that he found in his water bottle. He never mentioned the date or the town. I do know, however, that it was after The Royal Winnipeg Rifles crossed into the Netherlands. Using the war diaries, I followed his regiment's route after the battle at the Leopold Canal. I didn't walk in his footsteps from that period, though I did trace his movements on a map.

After a costly but successful battle at the canal, the 7th Canadian brigade spent the next month on a circuitous route of more than 325 kilometres through the Netherlands and Belgium. The war diary does not indicate that RWRs were involved in any battles on November 11, 1944, the anniversary of the end of the First World War. This is contradicted by the nominal rolls that indicated six men were killed in action and another was wounded.

At 2230 hours on the 11th, their convoy came to a halt less than twenty kilometres west of the German border in Grave,

Holland. The RWRs would be relieving the US 325th Glider Infantry Regiment, part of the 82nd Airborne Regiment. They took part in the famous airborne operation known as Market Garden. The 325th had landed in the middle of the area on September 23, six days after the assault began.[35] It was during this same time that Jimmy Branch was killed.

When the Canadians arrived at their destination, the Americans left an excellent picture of the enemy dispositions. They went to no end of trouble to assist them every way.

Over the following two weeks, the weather was mostly cool and cloudy, combined with either light showers or heavy rain. The battalion was sporadically shelled by mortars and 88s and also subjected to intermittent bombing by enemy aircraft.

During this relatively quiet time with no major battles, A Company still had eight men killed, three taken prisoner, and twenty wounded. The casualties resulted from small encounters with enemy patrols or the sporadic shelling landing in the area.

He never told me the circumstances, but based on the information I have pieced together, this is where Gerry lost his lucky bullet.

At 2200 hours on November 27, a fighting patrol was sent out from A Company to attack a house. According to intelligence reports, this location had been occupied by the enemy on the previous night. My father always referred to the place as a farmhouse.

The patrol's size is not mentioned in the war diary. When the patrol arrived at their destination, the house appeared empty. It would not have been a good house-clearing tactic to leave the main floor unguarded. Still, at some point during their investigation, the whole patrol ended up in the basement.

While clearing the downstairs area, the men heard footsteps on the floor above. With no idea who was entering, they realized too late that they were trapped in the cellar. The only exit was up the stairs, where they all heard the boots tramping across the floor. Gerry was no longer the cocky man wounded during his first day of the war. He knew if it was the Germans, their patrol was in a dire situation.

According to my father, men crouched behind some boxes and laid out several ammunition clips in hopes of reloading if they lived long enough. They knew one grenade tossed down the stairs could mean the death of the lot of them.

I was old enough to have seen Fess Parker portraying Davy Crockett at the battle of the Alamo. My dad told me that's how he felt, and he was afraid that this would be his last stand, just like Davy Crockett.

Gerry reached for his good luck charm. To his dismay, the shoelace around his neck no longer held his lucky charm. Having worn through the string, the bullet was no longer attached. Knowing the Germans had occupied the house, a sense of dread came over him as he thought his luck might have run out.

Clomping boots were approaching the cellar stairs. My dad said the sense of relief he felt when the voices he heard were speaking English rather than German was indescribable. He did say the men were Americans but never mentioned what unit they were with.

As he related the story to me over the years, I could tell he was relieved that his last moments weren't spent in a basement in the Netherlands.

Would this qualify as a "What If" moment, or was it fate that it wasn't the Germans returning to the place they were the night before?

Just before Christmas of 1944, Gerry received a letter back from Jimmy's mom. He was glad he sent his note to them, if only to assuage the helpless feelings his family was going through.

Isabel N. Branch
EPISCOPAL RECTORY
Goliad, Texas

December 6, 1944.

Dear Gerry,

Words cannot express my appreciation or gratitude
to you for your kindness in writing to tell me just what
I wanted to know about my darling son. He was very
precious to us. When the first telegram came from the
Canadian Minister of Defence it told us that he was
missing in action on September 25th. Six days later it
was followed by another saying that Jimmy was officially
reported killed in action on September 25th. The first
news only raised our hopes but when the second came well-
we felt as if our world had stopped.

I am so glad that you were with him when he met
his end and I know God will bless you for what you did.
Let me assure you that you have the prayers of a grateful mother and father and sister. We do hope you will
be spared to go home to your loved ones.

In Jimmy's last letter to us some time in the
early part of September, he said he had received a
package we sent on August ninth. On September fourth,
we sent him another which I want you to have when it
arrives at the Company Headquarters. We are having a
shortage of cigarettes here but as soon as I can manage
to get some I shall send you a box. It will not be long,
I hope, before I am able to do so.

You must be well, on into winter by now. In Texas
we never have very severe weather- that is in the part
where we live. We have not seen snow since we left
Wyoming.

God grant that the New Year may see an end to
this hellish behaviour of man, and that we may live
in brotherly love with each other for all time.

God bless and keep you, dear boy.

My husband and Barbara (Jimmy's sister) join in
this wish.

Again thanking you for your lovely letter,

Very sincerely yours,

Isabel B. ...

Thank you Letter from Isabel Branch to Gerry Levers.

After Germany's unconditional surrender in May, Gerry volunteered to take part in the battles that would soon take place in the
Pacific Theatre. On June 22, 1945, he left Europe with a short stop
in the UK and was back in Canada by the middle of July. He was

given a month's repatriation leave before having to report back for training for the upcoming battles in Japan.

Gerry Levers in Victoria, BC, August 1945.

Though he volunteered to stay in the army to fight against the Japanese, Gerry was still on leave in Victoria, BC, on August 6, when the atomic bomb was dropped on Hiroshima. This was the day that essentially ended the war against the last remaining member of the Axis powers. It came as quite a relief to the hundreds of thousands of allied troops who were scheduled to participate in the invasion of Japan. The official Japanese surrender came nine days later, on August 15. Then on September 2, 1945, the official surrender documents were signed aboard the USS Missouri in Tokyo Bay.

Upon completion of his leave, Gerry returned to Winnipeg. Japan officially surrendered on September 2, 1945. On the 25th, he was assigned to the 2nd Battalion PPCLI and granted six months of industrial leave without pay.

On December 18, 1945, Gerry received his official discharge from the Canadian Army (Active). His release certificate indicated his current age was now 29 years, four months old. The army never did find out that he skimmed five years off his age when he attempted to volunteer in 1939.[36]

"What If"

Winning D-Day, the battle of Normandy, and, eventually, World War II would come at a terrible cost. The nominal rolls from The Royal Winnipeg Rifles indicate there were over 100 casualties on June 6 alone. Two days later, the number climbed to over 320 brave men who were no longer in the fight for which they trained so hard. The casualty numbers included men killed in action, wounded, or taken prisoner, including 58 men murdered by the 12th SS Panzer Division and Hitler-Jugend.

Local newspaper accounts reported 400 Canadians killed in action on the first day alone.

I'm only here today because my father was one of the lucky ones. Was it fate or luck he was assigned to A Company? This story may not have been written if he had been assigned to B Company. They took some of the highest casualties of any Canadian company on D-Day.

B Company landed on the beaches as part of the first assault wave on Juno Beach at H Hour, with an oversized Company of 164 men. After fierce fighting, Captain Gower, the company commander, left the beach with 28 men and four stretcher-bearers.

I don't know if my father wondered about his "What If" moments during his recuperation after D-Day. He may not have known the extent of the casualties the Little Black Devils suffered at that point. Did he think about the man next to him who was shot in those first few moments as they set foot on the beaches of Normandy? "What If" they had disembarked in a different order? Would the machine-gun fire that cut him down have hit my dad instead? Did he continue to dwell on what might have happened if he jumped from the landing craft farther from the beach, or whether the weight of his pack might have drowned him if the water was only a few feet higher?

Did it haunt him when he thought about "What If" the bullet that struck him followed a different trajectory? Would he have been one of those buried in the Canadian cemetery above the beaches of Normandy near Beny-sur-Mer? "What If" he had been hit a little higher? Did he think any more about the fact he would never have children? Or "What if" it hit the femoral artery?

He mentioned the four men he helped with escorting prisoners back to the beachhead in his letter home. At the time he wrote the letter, did he know the fate of those men? Chartrand was taken prisoner on the 8th. Along with over 57 other men from his company, he was murdered at Le Chateau d'Audrieu by members of the 12th Waffen SS under the command of Colonel Kurt Meyer.

There were eight men by the name of Chartrand listed on the Winnipeg Rifles' nominal rolls, two of whom were in A Company. The 12th SS murdered both after they were captured.

Tony Hubert, the man who set the haystack ablaze with the tracer rounds, was also captured on June 8. His fate was better than the prisoners the SS murdered. He ended up on a train for transport to a POW camp in Germany. While on a second deportation train from Rennes, France, on July 5. Hubert managed to escape from the train near Tours, France and began to fight with the resistance.

There were three men by the name of McLeod in my dad's unit. The first one killed in action was J. McLeod. He died on June 16. Another J. McLeod, as well as N.A. McLeod were both severely wounded on July 4, when their company came under heavy fire from German positions while advancing toward the airport near the town of Carpiquet, on the outskirts of Caen. The second J. McLeod later died of his wounds.

Memorial Plaque for Murdered Soldiers in Putot, France.

A.C. Sinclair was the fourth man my dad helped with the escort of prisoners. The regimental records don't give the exact date he was captured. After being taken prisoner, he was sent to POW camp 4D, only 140 kilometres south of Berlin.

There have been varying accounts of Canadian soldiers' actions when they fought against the 12th SS and Hitler-Jugend, following D-Day. Various reports say there was no evidence of Canadians executing German POWs. On the other hand, I believe there were never many of those enemy combatants taken prisoner. Perhaps because these troops were so fanatical that they chose to fight to the death rather than surrender.

If he did know about what happened to those men on the 8th, would he have realized that getting wounded probably saved his life? Did he know when he was signing the letter home how many men were wounded, captured, or killed in action on the first day, or how many would die from the wounds they suffered?

Did he know when he did his radio broadcast how many men The Royal Winnipeg Rifles lost at Putot-en-Bessin? Was he aware that the Canadians who landed on Juno Beach experienced so many casualties: a total of over 950, including 369 who were killed during the initial assaults? In comparison, the Americans who landed on Omaha's beaches suffered close to 2400 total casualties.

Many "What Ifs" took place after he first joined the regiment in September 1942. My dad never really talked about his friend Jimmy Branch (Tex). He only said he was beside Tex when they approached the farmhouse: "He was there one moment, and the next thing I knew, there was a bullet in the middle of his forehead." Did he wonder how lucky he was? What were the odds of him surviving when men on both sides of him were shot?

He used to tell my brother and me about volunteering to take part in the invasion of Japan. The few times he spoke of it, he said, "If we needed to invade Japan, I don't think many of us would have made it out of there alive." "What If" the war with Japan didn't end on September 2, 1945, a full six years after the beginning of World War II?

While I was growing up, we had a copy of Dad's radio broadcast transcript from London. The original document seems to have disappeared during one of several moves. I always believed his interview was with the BBC and attempted to find a copy of it in their archives. Then, a few years ago, I heard old World War II broadcasts on the CBC. It was then I realized I'd been searching not only for the wrong broadcasting company; I wasn't even looking in the correct country.

I sent an email to the CBC, hoping to get a copy of the transcript from them. Within weeks, they contacted me. They found the complete interview that I had grown up knowing about but never heard. It is now posted on their archives site for all to hear. It was surreal to listen to my father's voice from 1944. At times, it was difficult to believe it was him speaking because he didn't sound at all like the man who would become my dad.

Throughout our lives, we can all look back and reflect on "What Ifs." For most people, our daily "What Ifs" don't mean life or death. There is no time for soldiers in war during a heated battle to think about "What Ifs."

It's easy to analyze a football or a hockey game twenty-four hours after the final whistle. It's easy to ask "What If" your team tried for a field goal instead of attempting the third and long, or "What If" your hockey team scored in the third-period breakaway. It's hard to comprehend how even a moment's hesitation might have made a difference with the "What Ifs" of those days over 75 years ago.

How many men who landed on those beaches spent the rest of their lives with survivor's guilt? Did they think about how those who died would never be fathers? Who knows what the unborn children of those fallen soldiers might have contributed to the world? Would they have been doctors, inventors, statesmen, or just good fathers and citizens? Men or women whose children might have made incredible discoveries, inventions or medical break-throughs for our country and the world? How many children made contributions that would have remained unaccomplished if their fathers hadn't survived? I'm sure these are questions after the conclusion of any war throughout history.

"What If" Adolf Hitler was killed instead of only suffering a shrapnel wound in his leg while fighting near Bapaume, France, in World War I? Would there even have been a World War II?

"What If" famous Canadians who survived injuries during the First World War had died instead? These included men like Frederick Banting, one half of the duo of Banting and Best, who discovered insulin. If Banting had died of his wounds during the Cambrai offensive, would people with diabetes have the insulin they need today to carry on healthy lives?[37] "What If" Lester B. Pearson, 14th Prime Minister of Canada, had died when his plane crashed. Later, during the blackout in London, he was hit by a bus. Would the Red and White Canadian Maple Leaf flag, known worldwide, have been different if he was not the Prime Minister in 1965?[38] George Vanier was the Governor-General of Canada between 1959 and 1967. "What If" he had died from his battle wounds when shot in the chest? "What if" he didn't survive the surgery after losing his right leg? Who would have taken his place? During World War II, he was a Major General. Now, Canadian University football teams compete each year for the Vanier Cup. In 1988, he was named one of the most significant Canadians in history.[39] "What If?"

There are famous Canadians who survived the Second World War. Not all saw combat or landed with the troops at Normandy. Just the same, "What If," they didn't make it back. Would the fabric of Canadian life have been different? Among the notable surviving veterans is James (Stocky) Edwards, fighter ace with the RCAF. In 2009, he was named one of Canada's 100 most influential Canadians in aviation.[40] Howie Meeker, was a hockey player and legendary broadcaster, survived a blast from a hand grenade.[41]

Another notable Canadian survivor of D-Day was James Doohan, better known as Scotty from the original *Star Trek* series. He served as a lieutenant with the 14th Field Artillery Regiment. His unit landed east of my dad's regiment. Someone said fate was with him that day. After arriving on the beach under heavy enemy fire, he managed to kill two German snipers. However, all did not go well for the future actor. On the evening of June 6, he was shot six times by friendly fire. He was hit four times in the left knee and once in the chest, and the sixth bullet took off the middle finger on his right hand. The shot to the chest would likely have killed him if not for the cigarette case he had just put back in his pocket.[42] "What If" he had died of his wounds? Who would have helped Captain Kirk (William Shatner, another Canadian) propel the Starship Enterprise through the Galaxy?

We hear people talking about their lives and how they wouldn't change a thing. I'm not sure I believe them. Take a moment to consider your own "What Ifs?" If you changed just one thing, would your entire life have taken a different path?

As I prepared to attend the 75th Anniversary of D-Day, I looked forward to walking in my father's footsteps across Juno beach toward Sainte-Croix-Sur-Mer. I was apprehensive about visiting the site where my father's friends died at the SS's hands. I began wondering, "What If" he wasn't just wounded 75 years ago?

My dad didn't go on to be a great statesman or hockey player or do anything famous. When discharged in December of 1945, he returned to his job at the Grain Exchange. During Winnipeg's "Big Flood" in 1950, he once again volunteered for service, assisting with dyke construction and helping at evacuation centres. Following the floods, my dad left the Grain Exchange, and he, my mom, and my brother headed west to British Columbia.

He began working for Queen Charlotte Airlines as an accountant. QCA would later become Pacific Western Airlines, and my dad would continue to work for them until he retired.

In 1954, the year I was born, our family moved into the Fraserview area of Vancouver. This was a new subdivision filled with veterans of World War II and their families. The vets could rent their homes from the Central Mortgage and Housing Authority for around $75 a month or even purchase them for a mere six or seven thousand. Dozens of schools in the area were filled to the seams with baby boomers. I had the privilege to be one of the boomers.

My dad maintained his passion for cars, and during the 1960s, he purchased his pride and joy, a 1967 fast-backed Barracuda. Each time the car returned to the garage, it needed to be dusted or wiped down with a damp chamois. I learned how to drive in the

Barracuda. When he died in 1986, there were only 67,000 original miles on it. To this day, I wish I still had his classic.

After World War I, many veterans returned without physical injuries. Still, they suffered from what later became known as shell shock or battle fatigue. Many of those returning from World War II suffered the same afflictions. Today, we call this Post-Traumatic Stress Disorder. It can affect anyone who constantly works in high-stress situations. There can be nothing more stressful than putting your life on the line day after day or watching friends die beside you when a difference of inches could mean you were the one in harm's way.

I'm happy to say my dad didn't show outward signs of suffering long-term effects from the war. I do know the war was one of the reasons he never wanted to go camping. He told us he'd slept enough on the ground in the mud to last a lifetime.

While looking through the Official War Diaries of The Royal Winnipeg Rifles, his aversion to camping became evident. Conditions in the Leopold Canal area during the second week of October 1944 were miserable.

According to the War Diary:

Prolonged exposure to wet and cold still had to be endured in flooded slit trenches or smashed buildings as unusually bold enemy snipers and machine-gunners were continuously on the lookout for any Canadians they could shoot.[43]

In 1983, I suggested we go to the 40th anniversary of the Normandy invasion being celebrated in 1984. Despite watching many fictional and fact-based war movies, my dad had no desire to return. After seeing how many friends he lost and discovering what happened to some of these men, it is only now that I truly understand the reasons. Perhaps it was the possibility of bringing back painful memories. As a result, I never had the opportunity to walk beside him as I traced where he was all those years ago. Fortunately, I did get the chance to take a walk in his footsteps in June of 2019, 75 years after him.

Many recollections of my father stand out. For example, he always took the time to watch our baseball or football games. In addition, he attended any function in which we participated. These included talent shows, stage plays, or annual inspections when my brother and I were members of the army cadet corps.

The other is how he was there for a simple game of catch in the yard. How many children born before their fathers headed to war, whose fathers failed to return, didn't have the opportunity to throw a football or baseball with their dad? He was never too busy, and it taught me a valuable lesson. I tried to carry on the tradition with my two daughters. I coached their soccer teams and made sure I attended each dance or music recital and all their Christmas concerts and sports days.

Lastly, he taught my brother and me the meaning of respect, hard work and being a good Canadian. It has served both of us well throughout our lives, and my brother and I like to think we have passed his legacy down to our children.

I have always been proud of the small role he played on the beaches of Normandy 75 years ago. After learning the fate of the four men escorting prisoners back to the beach, I'm thankful my dad was wounded when he was.

"What if," he wasn't? Would I be here today? I often joke about how I consider June 6 kind of like an unofficial second birthday. The fact is the next two generations would not be here if his close calls had ended differently.

My dad suffered his own other "What If" moments throughout his life, including surviving three heart attacks and open-heart surgery.

Another one of the hobbies he took up was photography. He became a decent amateur photographer and enjoyed the simple pleasures of taking imaginative pictures.

He continued to play golf for the rest of his life until he died in 1986 at age 75. Some of my fondest memories are when he, my brother, and I would play golf together. Mom would make us a hearty breakfast before we headed off to the links.

In his final year, there was nothing he enjoyed more than heading to the site of EXPO 86 in Vancouver. Three or four times a week, he and my mom would walk the grounds to get exercise and take in the sights and sounds of that great exposition.

His final act was to continue to volunteer after he died. He finally got his opportunity to go to university when he donated his body to the UBC medical program. He hoped this might help with the education of new doctors, especially those in heart research.

Looking at my daughters and granddaughter, I wonder: was it luck, destiny, or something predetermined, that allowed all of us to be here today because he survived his "What If" moment?

John (Johnny) Grant Nearingburg
HIGHLAND LIGHT INFANTRY OF CANADA
Inspired by stories from Johnny's daughter, Patt Nearingburg

Part One

John Grant Nearingburg was born in Galt, Ontario, in 1919. He was one of nine first-generation Canadian children born to Henry ("Harry") Nearingburg, an English immigrant to Canada whose roots were in Scotland. His mother, Alice, was also born in England.

During World War I, Harry volunteered for the Canadian Expeditionary Force. He headed off for training, leaving his wife and five young children at home. Perhaps Harry's son Johnny's first "What If" moment occurred when his father was in Halifax. After completing basic infantry training and being prepared to go overseas, they discovered a medical condition associated with his eyes, making him ineligible for service. Harry was discharged at age 33 for medical reasons on July 4, 1916.

If Harry hadn't returned home, he might have been involved in the campaigns where so many Canadians were killed or wounded, places such as Vimy Ridge or Passchendaele. There were over eleven thousand casualties during the Canadians' battle for Vimy Ridge between April 9 and April 12, 1917. In the second battle of Passchendaele, from October 26 to November 11, 1917, the Canadians suffered another staggering toll of over 12,000 men killed, wounded, or missing in action.

After returning from training, Johnny's dad, Harry, remained in Galt and worked at Hilborn Hockey Stick Company, then as a gardener for Mr. Hancock at Hancock Textiles and later at Narrow Fabrics until retirement. The textile plant was close to home and was a situation that worked out for the family. Johnny's mum was affected by advancing rheumatoid arthritis, meaning that Alice spent most of her day in the confines of a wheelchair. Being close to home allowed Harry to return during the noon hour to prepare lunch for her. By the time World War II arrived, Harry was working in the shipping department of Narrow Fabrics. He was a good worker and respected by all accounts by management, staff, and co-workers.

In 1919, Johnny was born, the eighth of nine children. Like thousands of others, his parents were considered working poor, but they were a closely-knit family. There was enough money to keep them all fed and to occasionally splurge for a few simple extras. Occasional music lessons were Johnny's indulgence when he was young. In addition to music class at school, he joined the Galt Kiltie Marching Band. He learned to play the trumpet, becoming proficient enough to participate in several competitions, including an esteemed music competition at the Canadian National Exhibition when he was nine. For this occasion, his mother, Alice, made him a new pair of trousers from a set of curtains. Johnny won the competition for his age group and continued to play the trumpet for years to come.

Gold medal certificate from the Canadian National Exhibition.

During high school and in the community, he excelled in sports and became one of his high school's star players. Johnny was 5'11" in his senior year, which helped him lead his Galt high school basketball team to many wins. Local papers praised him for his contributions on the court.

Johnny's mum and siblings clipped out and kept articles from the newspaper. Many citations and stories written about Johnny through the years were about the various sporting teams he played on — especially basketball.

At fifteen, while still in high school, Johnny joined the Highland Light Infantry Cadet Corps, where he used his trumpet skills as a band member. He continued to train with them while taking courses at the Galt Community Institute (GCI). Upon completion of his GCI program in 1938, he went to work with the B.F. Sturtevant Company in Galt, Ontario as an office clerk. The Sturtevant Company was renowned for ventilation and cooling fans and was on the air conditioning business's cutting edge. By this time, Johnny left the Cadet Corps and joined the HLI's militia.

After working for Sturtevant for a year, Johnny moved to the Gore Insurance Company as an underwriter. He earned the princely sum of $20 a week, the equivalent of $350 a week in 2019, or around $8.75 an hour in today's dollars, an amount less than the current minimum wage anywhere in Canada.

He consistently improved himself in his new profession, taking numerous courses while building his career as an insurance un-derwriter. At home, he proudly tucked away one of the first certifi-cates he earned in business: a "Certificate showing Proficiency in Filing."

At the end of 1939, his high school friends began enlisting with the regular army to fight the Nazis. When the war started, Johnny was already training with the reserve regiment of the HLI, and although still living at home at this point, he felt he was doing his part. Johnny also felt his meagre paycheck helped his family to make ends meet. They were getting by, but it was a struggle.

In June 1941, an envelope addressed to Mr. J.G. Nearingburg arrived at the family home. The brown envelope had no date on the postmark from London, Ontario. The green postage stamp cost the sender one cent. There was no return address on the letter, just the initials O.H.M.S. centred along the top.

Just the sight of the envelope made Johnny's mum shiver. When he arrived home from work, Johnny and the rest of the family gathered around the table while he carefully opened it.

Inside was a letter from the Department of National Defence:

DEPARTMENT OF NATIONAL DEFENCE

HQ, M.D. No. 1
London, Ontario, 17 June, 1941

Dear Sir:

You are aware of the present Recruiting Campaign and the urgent need for men at this time of crisis when the very life and liberty of the Nation is at stake.

The Prime Minister of Canada, The Right Honourable W.L. Mackenzie King, stated in Ottawa on June 12th:

"I call on young men to enlist in this great cause. I make this appeal to young men who will live here after the war is ended. I appeal to them to enter the armed forces as a recognition of the sacrifices made by others on their behalf."

Every physically fit and worthy man, if he has not already offered his services, must be considering his responsibility and duty at the present time.

To assist and guide you in your decision the enclosed article is forwarded for your perusal. This article written by Elmore Philpott, who served with distinction in the last war, appeared recently in the Victoria Times.

When you decide to enlist you should apply to your nearest Recruiting Office or Armoury.

Should you wish further information, please write the undersigned.

Yours truly,

(T.G. Tilley) Major
District Recruiting Officer
M. D. No. 1

Letter sent to Canadian men encouraging enlistment.

His mother feared the worst when he first opened the letter. She knew the country hadn't incorporated the draft but felt the tone of this letter was worse than being drafted.

The request did what it intended. It made Johnny and thousands like him feel a sense of guilt about not doing their part.

"Well. What are you going to do, son?" his father asked.

"Not sure, dad. I kind of thought I was doing my part. Maybe it's not enough to carry on with what I'm doing here. I'm exactly what the letter says they're looking for. Mum, there are relatives of ours who have been under attack with nightly bombings since last September. Let's not forget about all the men who barely made it out of Dunkirk."

"But you have responsibilities here, Johnny," cried his mum.

"I know, but the regiment is going to be needing more full-time men to train. The first nine hundred are due to leave for England in July. They're heading off with a total of 39 officers, and only 26 of them are Lieutenants. My colonel figures I have a good chance of becoming an officer."

During the first week of July in 1941, the Highland Light Infantry boarded a train, and Johnny was at the station to see the troops off.

"Hey Nearingburg," yelled Lieutenant Doug Kennedy from one of the windows, "If you don't hurry up and join, we're going to win this war before you even get over there."

"I know. I'll catch up real soon. Save some of the action for me," called Johnny as he watched his friends pull out of the station.

The train would take his friends to Halifax, where they would board the S.S. Strathmore on the 21st for their trip across the Atlantic.

Over the next two months, each time he reported to the armouries, Johnny felt uneasy. Finally, at the beginning of October, he approached the commanding officer of the reserve unit. He told him he was ready to apply for Officer Training Camp.

The Colonel respected Johnny and was pleased he finally agreed to join the regular forces. On October 21, his colonel signed the papers regarding Johnny's OTC application. Included in the section of general remarks, the colonel added, "In civilian life, he has shown himself to be a reliable and conscientious worker."

Finally, on October 31, Johnny, now 22 years old, was Taken on Strength (TOS). This meant his permanent military records would show him as a soldier in the regular army as a member of the Highland Light Infantry. The HLI's roots went back to the 1880s, and its history included battle honours during the First World War at The Somme, Ypres, and the Hindenburg Line, to name a few.

Highland Light Infantry Hat Badge.

Johnny told the Gore Insurance Company he needed to do his service and join the regulars with his friends. Like all good employers across the country, the company assured him his job would be waiting when he returned.

It wasn't as though he was getting wealthy working for the insurance company at $20 a week, but it was a steady job. His mum was now very much suffering from her Rheumatoid Arthritis, and his dad still worked for the textile mill. His sister Kathleen was the only other sibling living at home. The rest were married and beginning their adult lives in the rural area around Galt. This opportunity seemed to be the answer to the day-to-day struggles of an average Canadian family. The absence of the voracious appetite of a tall, healthy male at the table each night might make the food bill stretch a little farther.

Johnny's mum was dreading the day he would join the regular army, ever since the night the letter arrived from the District Recruiting Officer. She knew, from the moment he opened the appeal for volunteers, that this day would come. It became more evident after the first group of men headed off by train to Halifax. She wasn't happy with his decision to enlist but knew Johnny needed to do his duty.

Johnny Nearingburg with his Mum.

From the day he transferred to the regular force, the smile she attempted to show to the family, despite her arthritis, seemed to disappear. It hurt Johnny immensely to see his mum so upset and concerned with his decision.

Johnny was posted to Brockville, Ontario, a week after enlisting. Upon arriving in Brockville, Johnny had mixed emotions about leaving the family. After settling into his barracks, the first thing he did was sit down and write a letter home. In his impeccably neat, cursive handwriting, flowing straight across the page without the aid of lines, he wrote:

Dear Mother and Dad.
I got your little note, Mum, and you know how I feel. My heart is every bit as full as yours. I tried my hardest to keep from showing it, Mum, and I know just how brave you and Dad and the rest were.

Johnny went on to say:

We had another Medical this afternoon, and I was in perfect condition. My eyes are perfect, the medical officer said, so I'll be able to see all of your England.

At the end of the first letter, he needed to ask for some of the money he left at home:

I need this because I won't be getting paid for a while." Ending the letter to his mom, he said, *"any time my money comes home, Mum, take it for anything you or Dad need and, please send me another picture of you and Dad & everybody.*
Goodbye – just for a little while.
All my love, Johnny.

While in Brockville, he completed his training successfully and, in February 1942, was promoted to the rank of second lieutenant. A month later, he was promoted to full lieutenant.

Courses and training were Johnny's way of life in Canada, preparing him to become a proper officer and leader of men. He worked and studied hard for each of the courses trained, often getting the highest marks in his class. Taking these courses meant travelling to various bases around Ontario, including Brockville, Hamilton, and Borden.

During his time at the Officer Training Centre (OTC), Johnny went on leave several times, taking the train home from Brockville for a 260-mile trip to Galt. Despite her concerns, his mother was incredibly proud of her son. "You look so handsome in your uniform," she would tell him.

Johnny Nearingburg's military picture, dressed in his tailored uniform.

He would give her a loving hug each time he packed his bag and returned to camp. He dreaded the day he would tell his mum and dad goodbye when the army shipped him to Europe.

In May, while at Camp Borden in the Army Training School, Johnny learned he would be heading overseas. He took a furlough after his travelling orders came through. On June 5, he headed home to spend time with his family.

There was no big going-away party with the family as Johnny prepared to go. He did enjoy spending time with each of his brothers, sisters, nieces, nephews, and of course, with his mum and dad.

Each family member insisted he keep up with his letter writing.

"I'll do my best," promised Johnny. "I'm sure they will be keeping me swamped once I get there, but I will try really hard."

When he left for Halifax, the entire family knew there was a possibility of never seeing him again. It was a sad departure for all, especially his mum.

On June 14, 1942, Johnny boarded a ship bound for Great Britain. Upon arrival, he would be joining up with the other members of the regiment. They preceded his crossing eleven months earlier. Johnny travelled the high seas aboard a ship for eleven days and disembarked in Scotland on June 25. He had no idea it would be over two years until he set foot on Canadian soil again.

As soon as Johnny arrived, he made sure to send his mum a telegram, knowing she would worry until she heard from him. This telegram would be his first from overseas:

MRS H NEARINGBURG
44 ELLIOTT ST GALT ONT=
SEVEN DAYS LEAVE WITH JOE KING, MET DICK STAUFFER
JOE MANION LONDON LAST NIGHT GOING TORQUAY
TOMMORW=
        JOHN NEARINGBURG

The training in England and Scotland was hard. For security reasons, in his letters home, Johnny never wrote about the specifics of the *schemes* (training exercises) he was frequently on.

In August 1942, shortly after arriving in Britain, the disastrous Dieppe Raid took place. The HLI was not involved in the battle, but everyone heard how many casualties the Canadians suffered. Of the 6000 men who landed ashore, over 3600 were killed, wounded, or captured.

The public was led to believe that Operation Jubilee was supposed to be a test to find out if an amphibious landing was possible. The other objective was to temporarily hold Dieppe's port, gather intelligence, and destroy enemy defensive positions. However, the raid's primary goals failed.

Even though it was a disaster, it provided valuable lessons. Over the following 22 months, the Allies would use what they experienced from the high cost of failure at Dieppe to assist in preparing Operation Overlord. They learned the need for better intelligence of enemy defences, the requirement for absolute secrecy regarding any planned invasion and the realization it could not take place near a fortified port. Planners for D-Day realized they needed better naval and air bombardments of the landing sites. A final requirement was a better option for re-embarkation if necessary.[44]

According to author and historian David O'Keefe, this was more than a trial run for the eventual invasion of Europe. In his book, *One Day in August*, the culmination of 15 years of research of the intelligence archives of 5 countries, O'Keefe outlines his discovery that the raid on Dieppe was actually a "pinch raid" organized by British Naval Intelligence. The Dieppe mission, under cover of a raid, was to secretly steal the German codebooks that would unlock the Enigma cipher machine that held the key to the German High Command's plans. If the operation had successfully captured the codebooks, it might have saved countless lives and shortened the war by several years.[45]

In late August and September 1942, the tone of Johnny's letters home never changed. There was no indication when writing home about the South Saskatchewan Regiment or the Queen's Own Cameron Highlanders experiencing huge losses at Dieppe.

When his platoon found Johnny had never been on one of their infamous route marches, they were all interested in finding out how he would hold up. His men did appreciate how generous Johnny was with his cigarettes. He said so to his family in the summer of 1943:

Tell Dad, thanks for the cigarettes. I still don't smoke, but often when we are out on schemes, the fellows run out, and they sort of look to me to have them, why, I don't know?

In a letter sent out before Christmas 1942, he wrote:

We had another scheme. We were marching with full packs for days at a time. I think they want to know how long we can go without sleep.

He finished this letter with a request:

By the way, do you think you could send me the mouthpiece? I might get a chance to play a little while I'm here.

On January 31, 1943, Johnny sent off another of his almost weekly letters:

Have just returned for the office where we have been making out all of our returns for the month. Sunday makes no difference – the forms have to go in. I received your parcel with my mouthpiece in it on Thursday. Now, if I can just manage to pick up a trumpet, I should be all set. One of the Captains from the Home Guard sent me an invitation to their dance next Friday. Maybe I'll get a chance to play then.

After his mouthpiece arrived, Johnny took any and all opportunities to play on one of the trumpets he would borrow.

In many of his letters, Johnny would talk about sports like playing left field for the baseball team or spending an afternoon on the tennis court. Each time he spoke about those activities, knowing how much his mum loved her gardens, he also remarked about all the flowers.

His letter of April 2, 1943, was typical of what he wrote:

Dear Mother, Dad & Everyone.
It has been lovely today. All the daffodils are out all around the houses, and the bushes are bursting into bloom. We played tennis nearly all afternoon after having a church parade this morning. Then we tried to get a tan. Last night we had our Regimental Dance.

It didn't matter how many letters Johnny received from home telling what was going on back in the colonies; it was business as usual for him and his pals.

Another of his weekly letters again finished off with more talk about flowers:

The roses are all in bloom here now, and they are very lovely.
They climb all over the houses, and some of them are the
grandest colours. Rhododendrons grow wild over here, too, and
they are all in bloom now. I hope everyone is keeping fine and
keep writing. — lots of love, Johnny.

One day Johnny showed up for one of their schemes on a motorcycle. "You lucky bugger," grumbled one of his fellow officers as they formed up. "How the hell did you manage to get yourself a motorcycle?"

"Just another perk of taking the courses I've been on – especially the transport assignment. I even have my licence now. The thing is, I not only had to learn how to ride but to pass, but I needed to know about every blasted part of the bike. Don't know why? We have mechanics to look after that."

"Just count your lucky stars. You get to ride and not walk."

Johnny took other courses to prepare him for the battles he knew were coming, including one on specialized weapons. Then he completed a demolition course. All his extra training resulted in his assignment to the Headquarters Company. During his time in England, he held positions as the billeting officer and transport officer. Johnny was now in charge of a headquarters platoon consisting of both sappers and riflemen.

In a letter in July of 1943, he wrote:

I am playing left field on the ball team too. The roses are out
now and are really beautiful. I will write again on Monday. Bye
for now. Lots of love, Johnny.

In Great Britain, the HLI spent time in both England and Scotland. "You know, it seems almost every time I write home, we're about to head to a dance or have just returned from one," Johnny commented to Dick Stauffer, one of his best pals from home.

"It's okay, Johnny, we all have to make a sacrifice for King and Country," laughed Joe.

"The folks back home are going to think all we do is have parties, play ball or tennis, take long marches, and go on leave. I can't tell them any more about what we do to earn our pay, other than to say we were out on another scheme. I tell Mum all is fine and how I want more letters from the folks in Galt. If I tell them anything else, I'm sure this will be the time the guy who censors our mail will open mine. The next thing you know, I'll be busted down to a bloody private."

"Don't worry about it, Johnny. The Regiment has too much time and money invested to bust you now."

At the end of April, Johnny took a sniper course. When he returned, one of his close friends, Joe King, asked, "Why the heck did you take that?"

"I didn't have anything better to do this week. If I make a career of the army, I figured it would be good to know the basics. You never know when being a crack shot might come in handy. Besides that, Joe, somebody has to watch your back. I might just save your life."

Part Two

Thursday, June 1, 1944

Johnny and the rest of the Regiment were in Southampton's marshalling areas, waiting at the docks to board their landing craft. He had no idea where they were heading. He didn't have to be on the planning staff to know they were waiting to be loaded onto ships for transport somewhere. The place where the regiment was sequestered was sealed off from the rest of the world. It was army life as he knew it for the past 31 months: hurry up and wait — until now.

An ENSA concert party entertaining troops.

There were no official inspections or parades on this day. Still, one of the companies did marching drills around the marshalling area. The weather was reminiscent of a pre-summer day in Galt. Other than a weapons inspection, Johnny and the rest of his platoon relaxed. They enjoyed watching some entertainment put on by the Navy, Army, and Airforce Institute (N.A.A.F.I.). Many of the men were writing letters home, not sure when the next opportunity would arise.

Friday, June 2, 1944

It was another glorious day. During the afternoon, Johnny didn't do much in the way of training to earn his army pay. Many of the men were working on their tans. "Careful, Fletcher, you don't want to get yourself a sunburn. Putting your uniform back on will chafe like the devil," cautioned one of the officers. Then, Johnny and others headed out for a baseball game against the rival Stormont, Dundas, and Glengarry Highlanders Regiment (SD & G) from Cornwall, Ontario.

**Canada vs US Servicemen baseball game,
Wembley Stadium. August 1942.**

"It's not like I'm doing it in the buff, sir," replied Fletcher. "I'll make sure I don't get a burn, sir."

The two regiments played another exciting ballgame with the HLI up 16 to 3 at the beginning of the ninth inning. Unfortunately, the Highlanders blew the lead. If not for an incredible diving catch of a line drive by Johnny's best pal, Dick Stauffer, the game would have been lost. When completed, the score was 16-15.

Saturday, June 3, 1944

Someone told Johnny it was one of the hottest days in a decade for this time of year. "They say it reached over 100 degrees in the straits today, Johnny. Lucky it's not as humid as Ontario when it gets this hot," remarked Dick. There were a few showers overnight, but not enough to put a stop to another ball game, which the HLI won again.

The unit's scheduled move to the docks at 2230 hours was postponed. "You won't be getting a lot of rest tonight, I'm afraid. Our new schedule calls for us to be ready to go by 0400 in the bloody morning," Johnny told his men.

The regiment was issued Tommy cookers, portable heating stoves to cook their rations on. Even though they were notoriously inefficient, most men were pleased. As usual, there were still grumblings from some of them. "Just great," snapped one of the men. "By the time these little buggers heat our water, it'll be time to push off again."

In the morning, they were finally issued cots to sleep on, complete with blankets. In the afternoon, the items were returned to stores. Each of the soldiers thought they would be heading out that night. Hours later, the bedding was redrawn again due to another postponement. Like all the regiments getting ready to load onto the ships, Johnny and his men were issued seasick pills and vomit bags.

Sunday, June 4, 1944

Highland Light Infantry in Southampton on June 4, embarking aboard LCI 250, LCI 125, and LCI 306.

The regiment was awakened at 0200 hours to turn in their blankets again. At 0300, they were served a hearty breakfast, and by 0400, the HLI was on the way to the docks. Johnny discovered his Landing Craft Infantry (LCI) ended up with some of the worst accommodations in the regiment. "Not quite as nice as the quarters we enjoyed in Scotland, are they, Dick?"

"Not by a long shot. So much for rank having privileges. What I wouldn't give for some of those Scottish comforts. I might even put up with some of the mud we slogged through when it seemed it would never stop raining."

Other companies enjoyed the comfort of cots strung up in tiers of three. On Johnny's boat, there were no bunks and nothing but cocoa matting on which to sleep. It was very crowded, which meant the men would be taking shifts to sleep on the floor of their LCI.

It all ended up being a moot point. At 1600, the ships were held in port. The HLI War Diary indicates:

A south-westerly wind of half-gale force lashed
the Straits into great white-crested waves.[46]

"What the hell is a gale-force wind, sir?" asked one of the
privates in Johnny's platoon.

"Pretty brisk, I imagine. Why don't you ask one of those navy
types?"

A short while later, the private returned after being educated
by the sailor. "For your information, lieutenant, the navy guy over
there, says a gale-force wind can hit up anywhere between 40 and
55 miles an hour. You think that's why we've been stood down?

"I would say it's a pretty safe bet, private."

Disembarking the LCI, Johnny, his platoon, and the rest of the
HQ Company were escorted by a security detail to a recreation
complex near the docks. They were allowed to clean up with hot
water, have a real shave, and eat a good meal. The boys were each
provided 25 cigarettes, courtesy of the Canadian Government. At
this point, Johnny would have an occasional cigarette, although he
was not much of a smoker. He saved his to pass out later when an
occasion called for it.

Most men still didn't think this would be the real thing, despite
the elaborate preparations. They were disappointed it was called
off. In 24 hours, they would be begging to get off their landing
craft.

Monday, June 5, 1944

There was another round of sick pills handed out. Dick Stauffer
muttered, "Hey Johnny, I sure as hell don't like the sound of us
getting more seasick pills. Maybe it means it's going to be a go."

"Well, the weather doesn't look at all promising. We might be
thankful we have those pills if it's this windy in the Channel. The
sky looks pretty angry and grim."

At 1330 hours, Johnny's LCI slipped out of the harbour. There
were no crowds of cheering people, just a few dock workers sending

a hesitant wave their way. Men in the brigade's boats waved and hailed to each other as the regiment's Piper played "The Road to the Isles."

The men were given another round of seasick pills as the wind in the open channel picked up. At 1600 hours, they knew this was the real thing when maps were handed out. There was no shortage of them. Each unit's maps showed specific objectives, right to the section level, so the entire group would know precisely where they were going. The plans showed the destination of their first day's objective. Johnny also received his own set of maps to assist him in briefing his men. There was also a detailed list showing the order in which the various regiments' landing crafts would be hitting the beaches.

When he opened his packet, Johnny and the other officers realized that the locations used during training, indicating Poland's invasion, were bogus. Operation Overlord was truly underway. They were excited to see the landing would be taking place on the beaches of Normandy, France. One of the regiment's first day's objectives listed the city of Caen.

**Briefing infantrymen of the Highland Light
Infantry of Canada aboard LCI (L).**

The rest of the day and early evening involved going over all the locations where they were heading. The details were meticulous. As a platoon commander, Johnny went over the plans with his soldiers until they were familiar with their job.

After the briefings, letters from Eisenhower and Montgomery were read to all the troops. It was lucky they rehearsed for this day so often. As the channel grew more turbulent, many men were much too sick to pay attention and didn't give a damn what the generals said. "Those buggers are probably sitting around having a nice hot rum while we're out here puking our guts out," complained one of the men who was deathly ill with seasickness.

The final note of the HLI War Diary on June 5 states:

> So the day ended, and the HLI of C, many thousands of miles away from Galt, where they started, many of them four years previously, were on their way to France to "fight our countries battles, til the day of victory.[47]

The Highland Light Infantry of Canada aboard LCI (L) 306 of the 2nd Canadian (262nd RN).

The weather heading to France was far worse than any exercise they experienced during their years of training. The men were heaving what little food remained in their stomachs over the side of the boat and lost faith in the seasick pills' ability to do their job. Some men were trying to rest, but nobody was getting any sleep. Others were curled up in the fetal position on the floor of the ship. Many men of both B and HQ companies were wondering if fighting the Germans might be better than the battle their stomachs were waging against the frothing sea.

With the briefings complete, Johnny wondered how he would write about this to his mum and dad. How could he adequately describe just how rough it was in this little boat, the relentless bobbing up and down like a tiny rowboat on Lake Huron when the winds picked up? In between the swells, he could see hundreds of ships just like theirs doing the same.

Johnny wondered if his folks had received his most recent letters by now. They must have the one he wrote about attending a party for a young lady's 21st birthday. She was a lovely girl who was studying singing. Also, she was serving with the Women's Royal Naval Service (WREN). She had the voice of an angel to go along with her good looks.

He thought about the $350 war bond he purchased in April, knowing it would get better interest than the money he sent home for his mum to put in the bank. Johnny was proud about selling more war bonds than anyone in the platoon, close to $3000. Now, he hoped to survive his time on the boat long enough to cash them in.

He remembered writing in a letter:

By the time this war ends, I'll have so much money we'll have two cars instead of just one.

Then thinking more practically, he suggested that his mum and dad buy the extra ten feet of land next to the neighbour's and maybe the forty feet into the bush behind the house. *"Then, you could really have a lawn."*

"Could that have only been eleven days ago," he wondered? It seemed more like a year. Johnny recalled rambling on about another baseball game and poker games. He told them how the regiment's adjutant was in one of his 'better' moods and how all the men laughed their heads off. That night the medical officer even gave up writing his letter home because he was laughing so hard.

"Sure wish somebody could lighten the mood for the men who are so sick right now or that the MO could give the boys something stronger to make them feel better," he thought.

He knew his folks wouldn't have the letter he wrote just three days ago while sitting in camp. In that one, he talked about what now seemed to be silly and trivial subjects, like more baseball and poker games with even bigger pots, or about the Charlie McCarthy show on the radio. Johnny finally came to terms with the English weather; maybe not at that exact moment out there on the channel, but when he wrote his last letter, it had been grand:

The weather here has been lovely of late, and if it keeps up, I may begin to think this country is better than my opinion of it was before.

He thought about all the letters he received since joining the army. Johnny was more than pleased with the support from all his family and friends back home. He'd even had a message from the pastor of the Presbyterian Church his family attended.

Many men were lucky to get an occasional letter from home. It felt as though a week hadn't gone by since joining the army that there wasn't a letter for Johnny. Many times there were packages from home, often including baked goods and food. Getting letters from home were responsible for keeping many a man's spirits up.

There wasn't a special girl back home in Johnny's case, but the letters from family and friends were always the high point of his week. He hadn't counted them, but he must have sent a minimum of one letter each week, which would add up to over 130. "Sure hope they kept them. It might be fun to relive some of the better memories when I get back," he snickered to himself.

Part Three

Tuesday, June 6, 1944, D-Day

Like over 100,000 other men sitting on the ships off the Normandy coast, many could not sleep. Johnny never did go below decks during the night. He preferred the open air as compared to the close confined quarters below. The putrid smell rising from the sleeping area was enough to make even the heartiest of men gag.

There was no marked improvement in the weather overnight. There were light showers, and the wind and seas were still tossing their LCI up and down. The bows were smashing clumsily into the swells. Some men who spent the night below began arriving on deck at 0400 hours, many still wrapped in blankets. They were eager to watch the start of the show. There were flashes in the distance on the left flank. They knew from their briefing that the 6th airborne and commandos were attacking the fortified coastal batteries and bridges.

Throughout the early morning hours, the men on Johnny's ship could hear the pounding the coastline was getting from aerial bombardments. At 0515, it turned eerily quiet along the coast. The bombers were finished their missions. Now the rest of the softening of the defences would be up to a naval bombardment. Ultimately the men landing on the beaches in the next several hours would determine if Operation Overlord was a success or failure.

At 0530, the silence was broken when the destroyers, battleships, and cruisers began pounding the coast with their naval guns. Lieutenant Nearingburg couldn't figure out how any man still below decks could sleep through the barrage now taking place. Those men obviously preferred the opportunity to try and sleep in hopes their stomachs might calm down a little. Like Johnny, those coming from below were in awe of the spectacle before them. There were thousands of ships as far as the eyes could see. The men on deck looked longingly toward the shore in hopes they would soon be back on solid ground. The beaches of France is where their war would now begin.

As 0700 came and went, Johnny could see the LCAs carrying the initial assault waves getting ready to make their way to shore. From his vantage point, it looked like he was watching newsreel footage like the ones played in the London theatres before the feature film. Johnny was getting his bearings about where his boat was in relation to the war being played out before his eyes. At 0730, he watched the LCAs speed up to make their final run to the beaches. From where he stood, Johnny could see shells sending up plumes of water all around the smaller craft, each filled with 36 members of an assault platoon.

The men on deck then witnessed a fireworks show like never before. Salvos were let loose from the LCTRs. The 192-foot modified tank carrying ship held an average of 1000 rocket tubes welded on a platform mounted to their deck. Each fired a five-inch diameter projectile loaded with seven pounds of high explosives.[48] These ships began firing as the assault boats came alongside them while still a mile from shore.

Johnny could see fires burning in many of the homes and buildings along the coast. Echoes from the rockets took several moments to reach them after witnessing the flare trailing from the projectile.

By 0830, many LCAs were passing by, returning to get more troops from the larger ships anchored beyond where the HLI waited for their turn. There were not nearly as many as they saw heading in during the initial waves. The men aboard Johnny's LCI could see countless boats damaged or destroyed along the shore. Dick Stauffer leaned over the side and yelled at the pilot of one of the LCAs. "Hey, how's it going in there?" Dick asked as he pointed toward the beaches.

It was hard to hear the man, but Johnny understood the gist of it. From the look on the man's face, it didn't look as though it was going well at all.

After getting word from the company commander, the call came at 0900. "All right, you men, start getting your gear together," ordered the Company Sergeant Major (CSM).

Johnny gathered his platoon around. Though many were still feeling the effects of upset stomachs, the adrenaline started to flow through their bodies. Most were looking forward to getting their feet onto the beach. "We are about to put all your training to the test. I have faith that each of you will do your job once we land. Remember, if anyone is wounded, do not stop to help them. Keep moving forward and leave his care to the medical team."

"What about you, Lieutenant? You want us to leave you too?" asked a lance corporal.

"I can still run circles around all you boys, and I don't plan on staying still long enough to let the Germans get a bead on me. Still, if they do happen to knock me down, you are under orders to leave me too."

From his vantage point on the LCI, Johnny could see dozens of the smaller LCAs drifting around the beach. When he checked his map, he realized he was looking at the towns of Courseulles-sur-Mer on the right flank, with St. Aubin-sur-Mer on the left.

Captain Stark called for an officers' meeting just after 0930. "We have a delay," he reported. It will be after 1100 before we make our run-in. So tell your men we'll be going around in circles a little longer. Keep their spirits up. I'm sure they don't want to be stooging around out here any more than the rest of us."

Johnny returned to his platoon and told them the news. "Bloody Hell, the fight will be over before we even get a taste of it," remarked one of his men. There were nods and grumbles of agreement amongst the entire platoon.

Platoon commanders were called to another meeting as 1100 hours approached.

"Okay, boys. Here's the latest news. We won't be landing at our original point of Red Beach near St. Aubin. We've heard the North Shore Regiment is having a tough time with it. Initial reports indicated the tanks were running behind, and those boys paid a hell of a price. I'm happy to report the tide is turning in our favour. We'll be following the Queen's Own Rifles. They've moved off the beach into the town of Bernieres-sur-Mer, so we're going to be heading there. We should be landing high and dry on the beach."

Close to four hours after the first troops landed, the LCIs carrying the men from Galt stopped circling and began their run to "White Beach."

The HLI war diary described the landing as follows:

All the LCIs bearing the rifle coys touched down almost together. The Navy did an excellent job getting us ashore as it was one of the driest landings we managed in some time, being only knee-deep. As soon as the ramps were lowered, men began to stream off carry bicycles. The only mishap was in the beaching of the B Coy boat, which carried the CO and his command group.

It came in fast, but the bow swung to the right and stove in the ramp on the neigh-bouring craft. It tried again and this time hit an underwater mine, blowing a hole about three feet in diameter in the bow. No one was injured.[49]

The Highland Light Infantry aboard LCI (L) 306 of the 9ᵗʰ Brigade landing at Bernières-sur-Mer, France, June 6, 1944.

The sound was deafening. It took Johnny a moment to shake it off. The men were shouting to find out if everyone was all right.

"Sounds like there weren't any casualties, sir," offered the platoon sergeant.

There was evidence strewn along the shore of the carnage that the initial assaults suffered. Bodies floated in the shallow water. Several LCA hulls were underwater after striking mines similar to the one Johnny's boat hit.

Thousands of defensive structures were built along the entire Normandy Coast. Over 3600 of them were on Juno Beach.

The War diary reported:

> The approaches to the beach were sown with obstacles, such as hedgehogs, element C and poles. Teller mines were placed on top of many of these as underwater obstacles to craft. Several LCAs from the assault wave were lying underwater where they had hit these mines.[50]

Hedgehogs were made of steel angles or rails between five and six feet long. Two rails were crossed to make an X, and a third piece was set crossways on the rails. Some were anchored into the sand with concrete. They were placed in shallow water to tear the bottoms out of the landing craft or to make it difficult for tanks to cross the beach

Hedgehog.

Belgium gates, also called Elements C's, were made of steel plate, angle iron and rebar. It stood roughly six to ten feet high, weighed more than 2000 pounds and had a rough resemblance to a barn gate.[51]

Belgium Gate – Element C, or Cointet-element. On display in France.

The men of Johnny's platoon were streaming ashore, carrying their bicycles. Johnny looked around and found his pal, Lieutenant Dick Stauffer. The beach was in utter confusion. Only twenty-five yards of beach now separated the shoreline and the promenade of Bernières-sur-Mer.

'Nan White' Beach on D-Day.

It appeared Johnny's statement about not stopping to assist the wounded was unnecessary because they were not taking direct fire. The first assault brigades had done their job but had done so at a terrible cost in casualties.

"This place is a shambles, Dick. It seems a vehicle no sooner gets started than the one in front gets stuck. Even the tanks are getting bogged down. So far, the beach group has only opened up five exits."

"Looks like it's going to be a while getting off the beach. This is nothing like those organized rehearsals. If the Germans get a couple of 88s ranged in on us while we're sitting here, a couple of well-placed shells will take out half the regiment. I'll check with the Captain and see if there's any revision of the plan," offered Johnny

"Just be glad there's a good air umbrella keeping the Luftwaffe out of the skies," said Dick as he pointed upward.

While they waited, Johnny checked with his captain to see if anyone had come up with a better plan to get off the beach.

"According to the colonel, we just have to wait our turn," was the response to Johnny's question.

The medics were trying to set up and function, which seemed to be an impossible task. The solution was to "nest" all the casualties together until the 9th Brigade made it off the beach.

Finally, Johnny's platoon began to work their way inland. It didn't take long for the HLI to catch up with the back end of the 8th Brigade. The roads were a mess of rubble from collapsed buildings. Once again, the congestion brought the entire regiment to a complete standstill. Up ahead, the Queen's Own Rifles were coming under pesky sniper fire, and German 88s were making forward progress difficult.

Word came from the colonel; the regiment would be getting off the road: "Even though the air force has done a fine job, there's still a chance of German planes getting through. If they hit us from the air, the regiment will get cut to pieces by strafing fire. We're getting off the road. We'll settle in behind the church on the grounds of a large estate."

At 1330 hours, orders were given to Lieutenant Nearingburg to get his platoon dug in, settled, and ensure they ate something. For most of the men, it had been 36 hours since they last tried to eat — those who were sick while aboard had little left in their stomachs. The prospect of eating hardtack, bully beef, and a mug of self-heating soup or cocoa was a little demoralizing.

While preparing his meal on his tommy cooker, Johnny thought of some of the fantastic meals he had enjoyed while on leave at various places in Great Britain: fresh vegetables, linen table cloths, fine china and silverware, and being waited on by servants while dining at a castle in Scotland.

The sun poked its head out from the clouds for the first time since they played ball against the SD & G's, and it slowly began to warm up. At the same time, it was getting humid due to the rain of the past several days. "Hey Dick, it looks like the sun's finally visiting us. It feels grand, doesn't it?"

"Sure does."

Johnny was called away to an officers' meeting and told they would be moving out shortly. Their transport vehicles arrived, meaning the HLIs could get the regiment organized to move farther inland. Seven hours after the shelling began, no one had fired a shot.

They were soon on their way toward a place called Beny-sur-Mer. As they left the coastal town of Bernieres-sur-Mer for the five-kilometre trip, the townspeople were treated to quite a sight. Over three hundred men departed the confines of the estate on their bicycles. The HLIs travelled through the streets of the town as though they were out for a tour. The lucky ones were the boys from D Company, who rode in the back of the regimental trucks. There were hoots and hollers from the men in the vehicles as they shouted to those riding their bikes. The catcalling was returned in kind. "You're all a bunch of lazy sods," they cried, getting the opportunity to use one of the terms the English soldiers were so fond of using.

It took hours for the regiment to reach their destination, which was only five and a half kilometres from the estate grounds. It was 1845 hours before the advance party arrived in town and after 1915 when the whole battalion was in place at what would be the start line for their next objective.

With sunset hours away, the battalion still anticipated moving forward. Unfortunately, the road ahead was jammed with vehicles of Le Regiment de la Chaudière from Quebec.

At Beny-sur-Mer, the HLI encountered its first contact with the enemy when the regiment came under constant mortar fire. There were no casualties, but several bombs landed uncomfortably close, giving the men a small taste of what the other Canadians had experienced and what to expect in the future.

Though the Germans had retreated from the village of Beny-sur-Mer, the men knew they would be down the road somewhere. They were probably setting up defensive positions to delay the troops coming off the beach.

Once again, the HLI sat and waited. Johnny approached the company commander. "This is getting pretty old, Captain. The men want to get into the thick of the action. They haven't spent two-plus years training for this, just to sit around. Look at them," he suggested as he pointed toward the troops. Some of the men were propping themselves up on one elbow while reading a French phrasebook. With the evacuation of the enemy troops from their barracks, the local citizens soon began looting the homes where the Germans had stayed over the past four years of occupation.

Johnny watched the systematic looting of the village taking place by town residents. People were carrying away wheelbarrows full of army boots. Others had chairs and clothes, and another lugged a box full of black rye bread. Men struggled with flour bags; one carried a hind leg of beef, and women came by with chickens, butter, curtains, and eating utensils. One of the funniest sights he saw was the parish priest carrying a pile of dishes down the street. "Perhaps he's simply gathering up what was previously his," Johnny speculated to himself.

The people of the town were excited to see their liberators. They were talking and gesturing their thanks to the men. There were a few HLIs who could speak Canadian French. Though not the same as the local dialects, they could translate the townspeople's appreciation. The villagers did not seem to be bothered by the sporadic mortar fire. They scurried around to various groups of soldiers, offering them milk or wine. The wine ended up being more popular, though none of the men drank too much after stern warnings from the officers.

"Feels nice to be appreciated, doesn't it, sir," remarked Nearingburg's sergeant.

"It feels wonderful, sergeant, really great."

The colonel gathered the officers together to discuss the next objective; when his radio operator received word that the HLI would be standing down for the night. It was now 2145 hours, and darkness was creeping in faster by the minute.

"Well, I guess we're calling it a day. Spread your platoons around the perimeter of the village and dig in for the night. It looks like we won't be heading off till early in the morning," instructed the colonel.

This was how the HLI's first day of helping to liberate France and the rest of Europe from the German Third Reich ended. While the men were happy to have survived the day, they were disappointed they had not had the opportunity to do more to help their comrades. They knew there were a lot of dead and wounded Canadians back on the beaches. While landing, their boat bumped bodies floating along the shore. For most, it was the first time they'd seen a dead body. The knowledge that the dead were fellow Canadians and that there was nothing they could do for them began to sink in amongst all the men of the HLI.

After checking the men manning defensive perimeters in their slit trenches, Johnny and Dick found an opportunity to sit and have a rest.

"You know, Dick, I'm feeling a bit guilty. I sure hope those boys we left back on the beach don't think we've let them down by not doing our part today."

"Don't you go worrying about it, Johnny. I'm sure we'll soon be seeing plenty of action. When we find ourselves staring down the barrel of a Tiger tank, we'll all be wishing we were still sitting in this little town."

Part Four

Wednesday, June 7, 1944

At 0545 hours, the brigade held an officers' meeting. All platoon commanders reported that it was a quiet night. Major Anderson of D Company announced having sent out patrols just before dawn, hoping to capture some prisoners.

The Colonel addressed the officers: "Have your men ready to pull out at 0730. We'll be picking up where we left off yesterday. HQ wants us to be at the objectives they set for us last night, and we're already ten to twelve hours behind schedule."

Lieutenant Nearingburg gathered his platoon together. They were part of the headquarters company but were not stationed directly outside the Colonel's door. Johnny went over their assigned objectives with his men once more.

At 0620, he heard a commotion coming from the area of D Company. He stopped the briefing as a soldier came through his part of town. "What's going on, corporal? Where you off to in such a hurry?"

The corporal slowed momentarily. "Sorry, sir. I have to get up to HQ. The boys on patrol just brought in our first prisoner," he managed to spit out with evident pride as he once again took off in the direction of regimental headquarters.

"Tell your men they did well." Lieutenant Stauffer shouted to the corporal as he disappeared.

"Hey, Dick. Check with the Captain. See if you can head over to D company and find out more about their prisoner," suggested Johnny.

A short while later, Dick returned. "Guy was a sniper. Believe it or not, they caught him wandering close to the edge of town. The boys also confirmed reports of the enemy dropping paratroopers during the night. They'll probably try to reinforce the guys who hightailed it out before we arrived."

Delays, once again, halted the HLIs. While they waited, they heard several planes overhead. High above, they could see an aerial dog fight taking place.

The men stood and watched the drama above them play out. Standing beside Johnny was his sergeant. "Look at those guys go at it lieutenant. I think the two-engine job is a Junkers 88; the other one's ours, and it's a Spitfire. He should have no problem. Ours is faster and more maneuverable. It also has a bigger profile for the Spitfires to shoot at. Can't turn as tight as our boy can either. It has a pretty big turning circle compared to the Spit. They suffered heavy losses from the RAF Spitfires and Hurricanes back in 1940."[52]

"You know your planes, sergeant. I'll give you that."

"Yes, sir. My cousin is with the RCAF. He got here in '43. I've been down to see him a few times. Told me he wishes he'd been around for the real dog fights back in '40."

Private Henwood, one of the other men watching, cleared his throat, then began to mimic Winston Churchill: *"Never in the field of human conflict was so much owed by so many to so few."*[53]

Johnny was bothered by Henwood's sense of bravado and let the men know he was displeased. "Those guys lost over a thousand planes back in 1940.[54] Let's not be so glib. If they didn't have air superiority, we might not have made it out of Southampton. The outcome could have been a lot different if some of those ME 109s came around, strafing the beach while we were landing. They don't call it a dog fight for nothing. Our guy up there is fighting for his life," scolded Johnny.

"Sorry about that, lieutenant. I didn't mean any disrespect. I think we all know those pilots kept the Germans off our back," conceded Henwood.

They continued watching the battle in the skies above and cheered as the Spitfire won the day against its two-engine foe. When they lost sight of the Junkers, it was trailing smoke and headed off in a north-easterly direction.

By 1100 hours, the regiment had travelled a mere three-and-a-half kilometres to Colomby-sur-Thaon. Along the way, they were often forced to stop and wait again due to the overcrowded roads. The regiments ahead were clearing out pockets of resistance. Bringing up the rear, as they were, meant that the HLI was still untested in battle.

"Sir, these delays are sure affecting morale. Even the privates are complaining," Johnny said to the commanding officer of his company.

"They're not the only ones exasperated, lieutenant. Once we get into the fight, they might have different thoughts. The North Novas and Chaudiers have been taking the brunt to this point. Tell your boys not to worry. They'll get their chance to take it to the enemy," the captain said.

According to the HLI War Diary:

> Another trick used effectively by the Germans during the day was the use of our code signs on the wireless. At vital points of the battle, they would come on the air, use our call signs and give orders that, if followed, could have wrought havoc. For example, in the midst of a shelling, they would say, "Don't stand down in the trenches. Get up and face it." Reports that whole Coys of the NNS had been wiped out originated in the same way.[55]

By the end of D-Day plus one, June 7, the HLIs came under sniper and mortar fire a few times. The North Novas and the Stormont Dundas and Glengarry boys both had tough goes of it, having been bloodied in battle, but held their positions. At one point, the HLIs were targeted by the Fort Garry Horse armoured regiment when tank commanders mistook them for a group of enemy paratroopers.

After the near miss, the CSM could be heard bellowing at the top of his lungs in a voice capable of bringing a raw recruit to tears or silencing an entire parade square. He began cursing about how colour blind the tank crew must be: "Stupid buggers. We're all dressed in Khaki. The bloody enemy's uniforms are grey. How tough can it be? How about we go back to wearing Red Coats. Would that bloody well help?"

Shortly after the near miss from their tanks, a German Messerschmitt strafed the area. Fortunately, no one was killed, but a few men were wounded.

One event helped to raise the men's morale. Two of the officers travelling around in the C.O.'s carrier were investigating buildings believed to have housed German soldiers and officers. They hit pay dirt in one of the houses after discovering a strongbox belonging to the 12th SS Panzer Grenadier Regiment. The box was such an important find that it was immediately dispatched back to the coast. Confirmation came through in the days to come. The chest's contents included a treasure trove of secret codes, organizational structures, and orders, which would prove to be valuable intelligence in the months ahead. It was a real feather in the HLI regimental cap, making all the fruitless searching of houses and farm buildings a worthwhile endeavour.

At the end of D + 1, almost all the other regiments had their baptism by fire. The stress of not doing their part was probably higher than if the HLI had been immersed in battle. On a positive note, the men were fresh and anxious to push on the following morning.

Thursday, June 8 – Sunday, June 11

The regiment moved another seven kilometres and set up a perimeter around Villons-les-Buissons. There were continuing reports of enemy armour concentrating in the area.

The next 72 hours seemed to run together. Other than the men who were wounded by the strafing incident, the regiment didn't have many casualties. C Company suffered their first injuries during an exchange of grenades being tossed back and forth between German soldiers who infiltrated the company lines. Sergeant Coburn died from the wounds he suffered, and one of the German soldiers was killed.

The men of Sergeant Coburn's company liked and respected him and were upset by his loss. It didn't take long for word to get around about Coburn. His death reinforced to everyone the harsh truth: war is real.

Orders varied between being told to be ready to move or advised to stand down, dig in, and wait. Evening patrols were sent out to ensure there were no more infiltrations by the enemy. Reports were circulating about German armoured divisions moving to the area. Undoubtedly, their orders were to push the invasion force back to Normandy's beaches.

Constant shelling throughout the day kept the whole unit pinned down. At noon, a private from C Company made it to head-quarters with a report for Colonel Griffiths: "Sir. The captain says to tell you it's barely possible for the men to lift their heads from the slit trenches without bringing more shells down on us."

Johnny's headquarters platoon engaged in a few skirmishes with the enemy. They would head out of their defensive position and advance through the knee-high grass and cereal crops that were almost ready for harvest. When they spotted enemy troop movements, his company would drop mortars on those positions and lay down fire into the grassy areas. The enemy would slip away without engaging. The Germans seemed to be merely testing the regiment's defences. They were starting to think the enemy was living underground.

On the 9th, plans had been drawn up for Johnny's platoon to join up with B Company to be ready to break through the lines now being held by the SD & G's. Their unit would head towards Buron, approximately four-and-a-half to five kilometres from the objective. This was the goal set by the planners for the 9th Canadian Brigade by nightfall on D-Day. They were supposed to have reached the airfield at Carpiquet, which was only nineteen kilometres from the Normandy Beaches. Still, when the time came, the attack was once again called off.

While they waited, they stayed dug into their positions. "Our men are starting to look like the earth they've burrowed into," was a comment made during one of the officers' meetings.

Every man, from the company clerk to Lt.-Colonel Griffiths, felt the strain. The enemy had been embedded in the area since the Germans overran France in May of 1940. They were familiar with the territory, knew the terrain, and had maps indicating predetermined points to concentrate their artillery barrages. These coordinates meant the regiment's positions were constantly subjected to shelling.

The only time the regiment's mortar unit could fire toward the enemy was during an artillery barrage. If they tried at any other time, the Germans would immediately shell the area with accurate counter-battery shelling of their own.

Johnny was again called up to HQ and thought they might get the order to move out. He arrived at the officers' meeting just as a screaming shell from a German 88 cut the signal wire at headquarters.

"I'd say that was a bit of a close shave, Colonel," said the company adjutant.

While stationed in England, Johnny often wrote to his mum and dad expressing his hope of becoming the company adjutant. Unfortunately, at least ten other officers were vying for the position. In the end, Johnny didn't get it, but at least he was with the headquarters company.

Around the same time, two privates were sitting in their slit trench when an 88-millimetre shell passed between them. Neither spoke for several minutes. Then one of them rose out of this trench and announced to his pal, "I think I'll go write a letter."

The HLIs were beginning to capture prisoners, including a number taken from the 12th SS Panzer division and the 736 Infantry Regiment. However, the enemy's delay tactics began to slow down the allied advance. This became a concern for everyone right up to the brigade command and beyond.

If the delays the Canadians were experiencing meant the Germans had enough reinforcements, there was fear a significant counter-attack could push the allies back to the beaches. The HLI's observed and recorded a continuous stream of German Paratroopers dropping into the area to bolster their defences.

On the morning of June 10, C Company was scheduled to head to Buron to determine the enemy's strength. Before leaving for the town, they met a civilian, who was able to communicate that he came through town earlier and hadn't seen any enemy troops. Next, they spoke with a Royal Canadian Engineer who had done a reconnaissance (recce) of Buron and Vieux Carron the previous day. He'd been looking for water and indicated he hadn't seen any enemy troops in either location. To prepare for an incursion the following day, C Company stood down. The NNSs were given the job of watching for activity around the town.

On June 11, Major Hodgins of C Company arranged for Johnny to accompany him and a one-hundred man fighting patrol. When Hodgins left Canada for England, he was one of twenty-six lieutenants with the first group of HLIs that departed on July 30, 1941. Both Lieutenant Colonels, who commanded the HLIs since arriving in England, were confident in his abilities. His excellent leadership skills resulted in Hodgins being promoted twice and becoming the commander of C Company.

When Johnny reported to Major Hodgins, the senior officer explained, "We're going to scout out the town, check for enemy positions and engage them as required. If we find them, our job will be to destroy them along with any equipment we find, so we'll take twelve sappers with us. Your sniper skills might come in handy."

Johnny was sure he would be getting his first taste of action and was keen to join the major, and they headed off to Buron at 1030 hours. As they worked their way into the town centre, they found it was occupied only by dead Germans. Proceeding farther down the narrow streets, Johnny looked for a spot to place C Company's snipers. At the same time, he kept an eye out for where he might set up if he was an enemy sniper. As they neared the centre of town, the Germans began dropping mortar shells on the advancing troops, and machine guns began firing from the far edge of town. The men of Major Hodgins' unit returned fire and managed to kill approximately fifteen enemy soldiers. The major realized a patrol of this size was too unwieldy and decided to withdraw the troops.

In the middle of the exchange with the enemy, Johnny was wounded by machine-gun fire. He was hit in the leg, and the bullet broke his femur. One moment he was returning fire toward the enemy; the next, he was lying on the cobblestones bleeding and writhing in agony.

Two men grabbed him by the shoulders and pulled him to safety around the corner of a building. A couple of men immediately bandaged his leg with one of his field dressings and called for stretcher-bearers, who moved him to the edge of town. Never in his life had Johnny been in this much pain.

During the short exchange of gunfire, the only other casualty was R.L. Harvey, one of the lieutenants from C Company. Both men were transported by jeep back to the regimental aid post (RAP). By the time they arrived, word had spread about incoming casualties.

The first thing Johnny thought while being transported back to the regimental aid post was how upset his mum would be when she heard the news of what happened to him.

When the jeep carrying the wounded arrived, his pal, Dick Stauffer, heard Johnny might be one of the casualties and came over to check on him. He was both surprised and upset to see his friend lying on the stretcher. Blood was already leaking through his bandage and his leg throbbed from the shattered femur. The pain was intensifying, despite the small dose of morphine he was given before being transported. The medics at the RAP cut off the field dressing and slit his trousers open to inspect and bandage his wounds properly.

"I thought you were more agile than this, Johnny. Hate to tell you, but your days of setting up a cross-country run for the company are behind you for a bit," he laughed.

Johnny would have liked to laugh. Instead, he gritted his teeth; his facial features became scrunched up, and then, taking short breaths, he glanced up at Dick and let out a deep sigh. "I know, I know. Guess I'll have to tell my folks I'm laid up. Mum is not going to be happy with me. Sorry to let you guys down, but don't worry about me. I'm sure they'll get this thing patched up and have me back with the regiment real soon."

The medics loaded both Johnny and Lieutenant Harvey into the back of an ambulance for transport to a field hospital. Dick shook hands with Johnny and said, "You behave yourself around all those nurses. I'd hate to tell your mum you've been misbehaving,"

As the doors were closing, Johnny heard Dick say, "You know I'll do it too."

"I bet you would. I bet you would." Despite his pain, he laughed as he said it.

The second shot of morphine he received at the regimental aid post kicked in as they headed back to the coast. The following day, Lieutenant Nearingburg was on a hospital ship, heading to England.

Part Five

Sunday, June 11, 1944

At the aid station, Johnny completed a pre-printed Field Service Postcard to send to his mum. It required regular postage and clearly stated that the postcard would be destroyed if anything else was added. The other side was reserved for the address.

NOTHING is to be written on this side except the date and signature of the sender. Sentences not required may be erased. If anything else is added the post card will be destroyed.

[Postage must be prepaid on any letter or post card addressed to the sender of this card.]

I am quite well.

I have been admitted into hospital

{ sick } and am going on well.

{ wounded } and hope to be discharged soon.

I am being sent down to the base.

I have received { letter dated ....

telegram ,, ...

your { parcel ,, ...

Letter follows at first opportunity.

I have received no letter from you

{ lately

{ for a long time.

Signature only }   *J. Nearingburg*

Date ....11....June....44....

Forms/A2042/7.
Wt. 18709/314 45,000M. 7/41. W. & S. Ld. 51-726. 192326F.

The Field Service Card Johnny sent home.

He knew it wouldn't be long before his family received official notification. Johnny felt it best to downplay his injuries and crossed out the references regarding his injuries. At the time, he thought it was the right thing to do and even crossed out the line referring to being wounded.

This postcard did not arrive at the Nearingburg home before the dreaded telegram from Ottawa on June 16. The telegram was made out to Johnny's mum. The good news for the Nearingburg family was that Johnny was still alive:

5256 MINISTER OF NATIONAL DEFENCE SINCERELY REGRETS TO INFORM YOU LIEUTENANT JOHN GRANT NEARINGBURG HAS BEEN OFFICIALLY REPORTED WOUNDED IN ACTION DATE AND NATURE OF WOUND NOT YET AVAILABLE STOP WHEN ADDRESSING MAIL ADD WORDS IN HOSPITAL IN BOLD LETTERS AFTER NAME OF UNIT FOR QUICK DELIVERY STOP IF ANY FURTHER INFORMATION BECOMES AVAILABLE IT WILL BE FORWARDED AS SOON AS RECEIVED.
    DIRECTOR OF RECORDS

During the Battle of Normandy, the men and women working with the Director of Records were responsible for the horrible and onerous job of sending telegrams to over eighteen thousand families. Their job was to inform the families about wounded, captured, killed or missing soldiers. In too many cases to count, the family would have received more than one of these notices. In the case of the Westlake family, three brothers were killed in June of 1944. Albert and Thomas were killed fighting side by side; their other brother George also died in June.

Three Kimel brothers from the Township of Langley, BC, all died serving in the army.

The Rivaits of Windsor, Ontario, also received devastating news about two of their sons dying. Two brothers, Leon and Alphonse, were killed at Dieppe. Their mother received a third notice from the Director of Records when her third son died in the Netherlands, and a fourth spent years in a prisoner of war camp.[56]

Personnel working on the index of battle casualties.

The same day that Johnny's family received the news, they sent a return telegram to him:

LIEUT JOHN NEARINGBURG
HIGHLAND LIGHT INF OF CDA IN HOSP CANRECORD LDN
RECEIVED THE TERRIBLE NEWS IF WE COULD BE WITH
YOU IT WOULD HELP DON'T FRET AND WORRY JUST
TRY AND GET WELL SON AND COME HOME WE ARE ALL
THINKING OF YOU LOTS OF LOVE
    MOTHER NEARINGBURG

It was three days before Johnny was back in England. His first destination was the Royal South Hants Hospital in Southampton. He didn't know when his folks would get the news about his injuries, and he wanted to send a note home but had lost all his personal effects in France. After he had lain in the hospital for a couple of days, he was finally given a pencil and paper.

In his letter, he told them he was sure by now they would have
heard the news from the War Office and knew the entire family
would be worrying:

*I'm feeling fine, and all I got out of the whole works is a hole in
the leg and a broken leg by the same bullet.*

 He went on to tell them about the hundreds of nurses flocking
around. Then, finishing off the letter, he wrote:

*Please don't worry, Mum & Dad, because the best doctors in
England are doing the work. I'm just a minor case. Bye for now.*
      Lots of love, Johnny

June 21, 1944

Johnny's mum received another letter, postmarked the 20th.
The return address was from the Officer in charge at the Adjutant-
General's branch.

Although the first few telegrams said Johnny was okay. Alice
Nearingburg feared her son might have taken a turn for the worse
when the Ottawa letter arrived. She gently opened the end of the
envelope, removing a folded sheet of legal size paper.

The correspondence contained a follow-up to the telegram the
family received on the 16th. Alice didn't realize she was holding her
breath the entire time she opened and read the first part.

The letter explained the procedures that might help the
family in the anxious moments they were going through. It was
only a form letter that told the recipient how injuries are reported
initially from Overseas:

Dangerously wounded or injured
Seriously wounded or injured
Severely wounded or injured
Wounded or injured

Slightly wounded or injured
Slightly wounded, remained on duty.

When the letter was written, there was no date or nature of the trauma, nor was there any indication of the injuries he received. The document explained only that Johnny had suffered his wounds in action. It said:

"As he has not been placed on either the Dangerous or Serious Lists, it may be reasonably assumed his condition is normal under the circumstances."

The last paragraph seemed to appreciate the anxiety the family would be feeling. However, they could rest assured that as soon as additional information became available regarding the nature and extent of Johnny's wounds, it would be forwarded to the family.

The following week Johnny's postcard from the Field Service arrived. Right behind it came the letter he wrote in pencil from the hospital.

With the arrival of her son's letter, Alice wept for joy. For the first time since receiving the telegram, she knew for sure he was alive. By the sounds of it, he was doing fine. She figured she might now be able to make it through the day without breaking down and quickly informed the rest of the family about the good news.

Alice Nearingburg received another letter from the Department of National Defence at the end of June telling her what she already knew. Canadian Military Headquarters, Overseas, advised her that a further report from the battle area established the confirmed date Johnny was wounded as June 11, 1944.

Various hospitals and rehabilitation centres would become Johnny's life for the next several months. He was told it wouldn't be long until he was transferred to one of the Canadian Hospitals.

Up to June 25, two weeks after Johnny was wounded, the regiment lost eleven men killed in action (KIA). A total of sixty men were evacuated, including Johnny and two other officers. This was considerably fewer than any of the other regiments who stormed the beach.

One piece of news Johnny heard while sitting around the hospital was about Colonel Griffiths. It was reported in the war diary as follows:

> While on a Recce, Col. Griffiths Lt. Campbell, Capt. Kennedy and Lt. Glanville ran over a 75 grenade used as a mine with the right wheel of their jeep. It blew up the whole front of the jeep. Col. Griffiths had his right eardrum burst by its blast and sustained minor scratches to his arms and legs. The rest of the passengers received a shock but were uninjured.[57]

Johnny always made friends wherever he went. His stay in the hospital was no different. One thing was sure: his appetite was voracious. He ate like a horse. The Red Cross made regular visits, and on one such visit, they gave him a pipe. Johnny rarely smoked cigarettes but had previously enjoyed a good pipe from time to time.

While being treated at the City General Hospital in Carlisle, England, Johnny met a nice chap from a British commando unit. Johnny never mentioned his full name in his letters home. Merely referring to the man as Billy.

He told Johnny he was with the 47th Royal Marine Commando Unit. "We took a hell of a beating coming in. Five of our LCAs were sunk as we came into Gold beach. We lost over seventy men during the landing."[58]

"My LCI also hit a mine as we got to shore. Fortunately, we didn't lose anyone," said Johnny.

Billy continued with his story. "A few days later, we were pinned down by snipers. Then a mortar round landed a few feet away. Two of my best mates died outright, I ended up with a whole lot of shrapnel in my backside, and one of them made a mess of my bloody knee. Don't expect I'll be playing a lot of football after the bloody war."

Their similar wounds helped them form an instant friendship. Johnny's new friend was a handsome fellow who knew how to charm the nurses. Johnny was more reserved and shy when it came to interacting with the young nurses treating him. During his stay at the Carlisle hospital, Billy's mom and dad came up from Sussex, staying in a hotel close to the hospital.

It seemed anytime Johnny was short of something, Billy lent him what he needed. It seemed a day didn't pass where he wasn't lending something to Johnny. "Hey Billy, I think I'm starting to look a little scruffy. Have to make sure I get Mum to send me a razor and a brush. People are going to start thinking I'm in the Navy if this beard grows longer."

Whenever his folks brought treats, Billy happily shared them and always gave Johnny some extra chocolate.

Near the end of June, the doctor in charge of Johnny's case came in to tell him he would soon be on his way to a Canadian Hospital. "Not sure when it will be, lad, but pretty soon, you'll be on your way."

While in the General Hospital in Cumberland, Johnny received the worst news of the war. On July 8, the Highland Light Infantry made a final assault on Buron, the same place he was wounded almost a month earlier. Like other men, by a twist of fate, or luck, he wasn't in the wrong place at the wrong time. Did being wounded after only five days in France save Johnny's life? Was that Johnny's "What If" moment.

On that day, the HLI battalion shrank by over 250 men, including sixty-two killed in action. The unit was now at approximately fifty percent of the original battalion's strength. Late in the evening, following the fighting, the command group was sheltered inside a building previously used by the Germans. While working on plans to consolidate what remained of the regiment, the building received a direct hit from an enemy shell.

The blast killed Lieutenant Sparks, a man Johnny had known since his arrival in England. He was another member of the original group that came across in 1941. The wounded included: Lt.-Colonel Griffiths, Major Durward of A Company and Major Hodgins of C Company. The blast also killed three of the regiment's signals men and injured four other ranks. Now, the only company commander to land with the battalion on D-Day was D-Company's, Major Anderson.

Late that evening, the adjutant wrote in the Regimental War Diary:

> Night fell on a quiet, smoking village which had witnessed one of the fiercest battles ever fought in the history of war. It was the HLI's first big fight, and the 8 July will go down in its memoirs as a day to be remembered.[59]

Others who survived the day merely referred to it as "Bloody Buron."

If Johnny was in Bloody Buron during the battle, would he have been amongst those killed, or would he have suffered worse injuries than he sustained on the 11th? The other possibility might have been a battlefield promotion.

Johnny's feelings were mixed, but he was happy his regiment had done their job. Hearing the extent of the casualties, including those who didn't survive, Johnny was saddened to the point of tears. When he received word of the battle, he still didn't know the fate of some of his best friends. He could only pray they were okay.

Like The Royal Winnipeg Rifles, the HLIs at Buron were fighting against battle-hardened SS troops. In this case, it was the 25th Panzer grenadier regiment, including fanatical Hitler youth members. At one point during the fighting, one of the companies was engaged by eight tiger tanks. Many of the SS soldiers refused to surrender. Instead, they fought to the death.[60]

On August 1, Johnny got a letter from his pal Joe King, telling him about the regiment and the grand job they had been doing. Joe finished off his letter by saying: *"Of course I can't tell you anything but just remember to ask me when I get back home."*

Following the Battle of Buron, Johnny was visited by other officers who were wounded there. He already knew how badly the regiment had been beaten up. However, getting first-hand accounts of what happened at Buron reinforced his feelings of guilt.

Visitors gave Johnny a detailed account of the battle. Hearing the names of the men who died brought the reality of the war to his hospital bed.

"Do you remember Corporal Weitzel?" he was asked.

"Yeah, I think so. Came over with the first batch back in forty-one, didn't he? I heard he was a good kid. Didn't his mom and dad die when he was young? "

"Yeah, that's the kid. Funny to think of him as a kid, though. He was only a couple of years younger than us."

"Anyway, there was a well-sighted machine gun causing holy hell on his company. Weitzel and two others headed off to take care of it. Firing a Bren-gun from his hip, he kept going, even after the last two guys with him fell. The trenches were filled with Boche. Weitzel killed or wounded an entire German platoon. They found his body the following morning riddled with holes."

"The boys in D Company figure he saved the whole lot of them. They want to put his name up for the V.C."[61]

Johnny was proud of the men he knew and how they proved themselves under fire. Once again, he was saddened by the terrible loss of lives, and their deaths weighed heavily on his conscience. The visitors saw the look of anguish on Johnny's face

"Johnny, I've got a little story to share. It might help to lighten your mood. Remember, nothing would have changed if you were there. So don't go beating yourself up about lying in here while the boys were out there."

"I understand, but it doesn't make me feel any better," sighed Johnny. "What were you going to tell me to lighten the mood?"

"You might recall the men were looking after the cows and chickens from the farms around Villons-les-Bussion. Well, some of the boys were even arguing about who owned what cow. The cow couldn't have cared less. It just stood there chewing its cud. The afternoon after you were wounded, there was quite a ruckus. I think it was Myer and Lovell. All I heard was, 'Where the hell are you going with my cow?' It's not your cow; it's my cow. I've been feeding it for two days. I think she was just happy somebody was milking her.

Private F.G. Lane of the HLI of C milking one of the cows.

The next thing you know, they decided to milk it right then and there and ended up sharing a helmet full of milk. A few of the others were gathering some potatoes, onions, and a couple of chickens. They ended up with a pretty nice stew out of the whole lot."

Johnny was getting a kick out of the good-humoured storytelling. "What was the final decision on who owned the cows?"

"Well, the Germans decided the dilemma for the boys. The day after you got your leg shot up, we thought we would be in for some well-deserved rest. The next thing you know, their 88s started up a pretty concentrated barrage. The boys weren't hit, but they sure killed a whole lot of cows. For the next couple of days, there were numerous explosions as the sappers blew big bloody holes in the ground to bury the dead cows.[62] The boys felt badly about not saying goodbye after you got nicked up that day. They told me to say hello if I ran into you. Anyway, a couple of patrols went out to try to capture some prisoners while the rest of us got our first chance to have a real scrub down and wash up some of our clothes. It was the first time most of the scruffy lot shaved since the night before we loaded up in Southampton."

**Private H.B. Willis of The Highland Light Infantry
of Canada using a truck mirror to shave.**

"Sounds like you boys were having a grand old time. Did you manage to get in a game of baseball too?" Johnny kidded.

"Not quite. There were too many trees in the orchard to set up a good diamond." laughed his visitor.

Johnny was enjoying hearing about the antics of the HLI boys. Billy listened to the stories as well and laughed along with the other two men. "You know Billy, a lot of the boys in our regiment, are from farms back home. They're a hard-working bunch. I think you'd like these kids."

"Well, if they're anything like you two, I'm sure I would, mate."

"I have one more for you guys before I have to go."

Both patients smiled as their visitor continued his story.

"By the way, your buddy, Dick, went out on a couple of late-night patrols. He managed to make it back in one piece, I'm happy to report. You remember Sergeant Pringle, don't you, Johnny?"

"Sergeant Al Pringle?" Johnny asked.

"The one and only. Anyway, Pringle ended up in a bit of a mess. One afternoon when the Germans started shelling us, he went running for cover and did a perfect swan dive into the nearest slit trench. Well, he was up and out of there lickety-split and running for the village pump. It seems it wasn't a slit trench. It was the bloody, open latrine. I must say he smelled like crap for days."

Both Johnny and Billy were now laughing so hard; tears were rolling down their cheeks.

"Oh my God, that's just too rich," laughed Billy.

"Just one more slit trench story before I finish off about the cows."

"As you know, jumping into slit trenches can be a dangerous business. Well, the same afternoon, Captain Kennedy and his batman Eldred ended up trying to get in the same one at the same time. Well, Eldred ended up with a broken and bloodied nose from Kennedy's hard head."

The laughter from the three of them was infectious; even men in nearby beds who couldn't clearly hear the stories began laughing.

"Okay, back to the cows, or maybe it should be back to the livestock. The brigade kept us moving around. We no sooner settled into Colomby-sur-Thaon than they were shifting us to Villons-les-Buissons. Anyway, here we are heading to Colomby and D Company decides they want to take their twelve cows. It looked like the bloody circus coming to town. Here's the regiment riding their bicycles down the road with the cows tethered to the back. They needed to ride slowly to ensure the cows didn't trot because they didn't want the milk spoiled. There were a couple of pushcarts as well. The carts carried some of the bikes and several chickens they had managed to adopt en route."

"I don't imagine the local farmers were overly impressed with us Canadians stealing all their livestock," scoffed Johnny.

"Well, I guess if the Germans counter-attacked, they would have done the same thing. It was better for us to look after our newfound pets than have the whole lot of them blown up in the fields. The boys were pretty upset about how many were lost during the earlier barrages."

"Word is the signals boys wanted to bring the horses too. They thought they could use the horses to get back and forth between the units. This idea was soon kiboshed by the brass to keep peace with the locals. As it was, they managed to stow away a little calf into the back of one of the trucks. It bawled non-stop until we got to our next camp. In their defence, the signallers claimed they took it so the little thing wouldn't starve to death. It's a good thing General Dempsey didn't decide to visit the front, or he would have received quite the shock. While all this was going on, Captain Sim lost track of Wilber."

"Who the hell is Wilber?" Johnny asked. "Name doesn't sound familiar."

"Wilber isn't a who. He's a what. Wilber was Sim's pet rabbit. It was only a wee little thing, and the last anyone saw of it, the little guy was running through a cabbage patch with Sim running around like a crazy man trying to catch it. He finally found it and brought it over to Villons. It seems to have disappeared sometime after that because no one ever saw it again."[63]

The attentive audience was again laughing heartily. Finally, a nurse came in and broke up the party and sent their rowdy visitor on his way. He promised to try and stop in again. On his way out, he gave both Johnny and Billy a firm handshake, telling them to get better soon. Walking past the other beds, he gave the other patients a wave and wished them speedy recoveries.

Johnny and Billy talked about some of the antics they had both experienced since joining the army. They regaled each other with pleasant memories of the friends they knew that were no longer with them.

Johnny never did get any more visits from men in his battalion while he was in the hospital. Within a few days, he and Billy would also be parting company.

Just like Johnny's entire military life, nothing happened as scheduled. On August 1, he wrote and told his family he was finally settled after being transferred to the Canadian Hospital number 19 at Marston Green. It had been a twenty-two-hour ordeal on a hospital train.

Arriving at his new location, the Colonel of the hospital examined his leg.

"I've looked at your x-rays. I think we can do a better job here. How does that sound to you, lieutenant?"

"Sounds terrific, sir."

Days later, Johnny tried to write a letter home. It proved to be an arduous task:

Well, I woke up and was really suspended in the air by all manner of gadgets. Colonel Spooner said I would be up like this for a month. He tells me my days in the army will soon be coming to an end and that he will be sending me home. Not sure when, but hope to be home in time for Christmas.

It was early September before Johnny was released from his rehabilitation contraption. During that time, the therapy nurses had many men working on projects to keep them busy and help them with dexterity recovery.

Johnny ended up making a leather wallet and a beautiful needlepoint picture of a floral bouquet:

You should see our ward right now. Everyone is doing needlepoint, if you can imagine, including the majors. I have a huge bunch of flowers to do, and it will take a least a couple of months to finish at the rate I'm going. I'll bring it home to prove I did it.

At the end of September, in one of his last letters home from overseas, he wrote:

I have almost finished my needlepoint. I do think I had better leave part of it to prove I can do it. Never again, though." His closing line was to tell his sister, Dot. Turn down the bed cause I'll soon be needing it. Lots of Love, Johnny.

On June 20, shortly after being wounded, the local paper published Johnny's picture and a small article about him being injured in action. The entire town now knew the 22-year-old former basketball star, John Nearingburg. He was now a statistic, another hometown boy wounded on or following D-Day. The article stated Johnny had served in the army for two years and eight months.

Since the day Johnny was wounded, the family received letters of condolence from the Regimental Guild and the Salvation Army. In addition, friends and neighbours were constantly inquiring about Johnny's health and any news regarding his return.

In the middle of September, Johnny's sister received a letter directly from Colonel Spooner. He informed her about Johnny's pending release and how he was fit enough to head back to Canada on the next hospital ship. The colonel told her that Johnny's general condition was excellent and went on to say:

"Despite the compound fracture of his leg, he will eventually have an excellent functioning femur, with the only skeletal issue being a half-inch shortening of the limb. The damaged tissue will remain."

A small lift in his shoe compensated for the half-inch difference, and he would use built-up shoes or inserts for the rest of his life. As a young man, after returning from overseas, he would golf and curl. Never once would anyone hear him complain about the discrepancy in his leg length or the war's impact on his athleticism. His disability never slowed him down until later in life, when osteoarthritis ravaged his hip and leg. He knew there were many wounded far worse than he and was also aware of the thousands who never returned at all.

On October 10, Mrs. Nearingburg received an encouraging letter from the Department of National Defence, informing her that her son was aboard a hospital ship bound for Canada. The letter stated he was being dispatched to his home District Depot unless a change became necessary due to his medical condition. They couldn't promise disembarkation leave; however, it was standard practice to grant leave provided personnel did not require immediate hospital treatment.

It would have been a long trip for his parents to meet his ship, especially in light of Alice's arthritic condition. This wasn't an issue because the facilities did not permit the public to proceed to the point of disembarkation. She was happy enough to know her boy was almost home.

He sent a final telegram home when he arrived in Halifax:

SHORT STOP TORONTO ON WAY LONDON FRIDAY TONS OF LOVE

With Johnny finally home, his mum removed a piece of paper from her purse, one she carried with her since the day Johnny headed overseas. It was a poem written by Nick Kenny, and the local newspaper included it in one of their editions. Alice knew she needed to cut out the poem when she saw it and carry it with her always. She may have felt the poem was written just for her, about her own Johnny, and would help keep him safe.

Day Unto Day
by
— NICK KENNY —

"KEEP AN EYE ON JOHNNY"
(A mother's prayer)

Verse

When her work is all done
At the close of the day;
She pleads for her son
As she kneels down to pray:

Chorus

Please keep an eye on Johnny,
This is all I ask of you.
He's still a little baby
With his shiny eyes of blue.

Please keep an eye on Johnny
For his mother and his dad;
Although he's sometimes naughty
He is never very bad.

It seems like only yesterday I held him on my knee;
Now he's in some distant land fighting for democracy.

We'll do our best to help him
While he's fighting over there;
Please keep an eye on Johnny
Is just a mother's prayer.

The poem Alice Nearingburg kept in her purse.

"What If"

Johnny's first stop in Canada was the London, Ontario Military Hospital, where he began his therapy and convalescence. It was only a sixty-mile drive from Galt, and no sooner had he settled in than a steady stream of visitors started arriving. The reunions with his family were bittersweet, especially with his mum, but it felt good to be surrounded by family.

Johnny's life changed forever when a young nurse by the name of Margaret Raney entered his world.

Margaret Raney was born and raised in Toronto. In June 1943, she was awarded certification in Home Nursing from the St. John Ambulance Association. Six months later, she received her Hospital Star from the Nursing Auxiliary section of the Canadian Red Cross, Toronto Branch.

Margaret became used to catching the eye of the many soldiers she treated. She was happy to help the men who returned but saddened because her first love was killed during the war.

Since his time in England, the shyness Johnny always felt around women had diminished somewhat. Still, there was something about this beautiful, blue-green-eyed, dark blonde nurse that once again made him feel a little shy, and Johnny was never one to make a big fuss around women.

During his treatments, Johnny discovered that while he was in England training to fight the war, Margaret studied and trained in nursing. In December 1943, she enlisted as a Voluntary Aid Detachment Army Nursing member. In September 1944, while Johnny was in the hospital in England, Margaret was posted to the Chorley Park Military Hospital, set up in the former Lieutenant Governor's House. The Canadian Government took over the premises and converted them to a hospital in anticipation of wounded troops returning to Canada.

Margaret was posted to the London Hospital for a short time. While assisting in Johnny's recovery, they became smitten with each other.

In January 1945, Johnny transferred to the Number 2 conditioning hospital in Brampton. At the same time, Margaret was dispatched to the Montreal Military Hospital. She served one month there, then was reposted, with two other women, to another Home War Establishment Unit at the Number 4 Conditioning Centre in Huntingdon, Quebec.

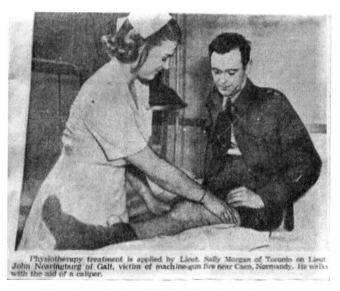

Physiotherapy treatment is applied by Lieut. Sally Morgan of Toronto on Lieut. John Nearingburg of Galt, victim of machine-gun fire near Caen, Normandy. He walks with the aid of a caliper.

Johnny undergoing rehab at the Number 2 Conditioning Hospital.

In May 1945, Johnny was still getting treatment in Brampton. He and other men on the ward posed for pictures to accompany a story about how troops were recuperating from their wounds.

The article ended up on the second section of the *Globe and Mail*'s front page on May 22, 1945. The pictures' editorial was about how the Army's Hospital builds up wounded veterans for civilian life. It included an extensive write-up on how the conditioning centre was speeding the recovery pace.

Johnny was now only an hour away from his family in Galt. While he recuperated in Brampton, the war in Europe ended. At the end of June, Johnny took his one-month debarkation leave. He returned to the family home in Galt for the first time since June 1942. He spent most of his time with his family. Still, the nurse who helped in London remained on his mind. While on leave, Johnny visited Gore Insurance to ensure he would still have a job when released from the hospital. With assurances his career would be waiting for him, he returned to the hospital at the end of July.

On August 27, Johnny was interviewed by Major S.R. Bull, the Army Counsellor. The officer needed Johnny to answer a two-page form from the Department of Veterans Affairs. Most of the questions concerned his prospects for future employment. After the preliminaries, Johnny told the major, "No offence, sir. I respectfully decline any further appraisal on the grounds that I have already arranged my future employment. There is no sense in either of us wasting our time. I'm sure there are thousands of other men who would appreciate what you are trying to do for them."[64]

With the Major's signature on the bottom of the form, Johnny was officially out of the army.

Following the war, Margaret moved home to Toronto. Over the next few months, each chance Johnny got, he would make the sixty-mile drive from Galt to see her.

Johnny and Margaret were married on May 4, 1946. By 1958 they were proud parents of three daughters, each of them born about six years apart.

The Gore Insurance Company offered the Nearingburgs the chance to move into a large, rambling old house on the expansive Gore grounds. Naturally, they jumped at the opportunity. The house was huge, and for years Johnny and his growing family shared the home with a lovely family from Ireland.

Each winter, accompanied by the family dog, Johnny would make a giant skating rink, flooding it late at night while smoking his pipe or sometimes a cigar. Many children and young local hockey teams would occasionally use it as an alternate practice rink.

Many Tuesday evenings were spent around a kitchen table or in rec rooms with a group of Galt friends who referred to themselves as the Rum Club. Some of them served with Johnny while he was overseas, including Dick Stauffer. They would play poker, other card games, and pool if a table were handy. A common thread among those returning from overseas was that this large group of rum club pals would focus on fun and camaraderie. They rarely talked about their experiences – the horror, noise, loss, or what would be referred to in the future as PTSD. Other times they just shared quiet conversations.

Johnny continued to work for Gore Insurance his entire life, retiring in 1984 as the Vice-President of Claims. Upon retirement, his staff presented him with a framed certificate with their names and pictures. The title below read, "John Nearingburg: A Respected Boss and Valued Friend."

With his work ethic and dedication, Johnny may well have climbed the Army ranks if he hadn't been wounded. Maybe he would have ended up being a general, as he told his mum in one of his letters home.

As a young officer, while training in England, he became accustomed to having comfortable quarters while stationed in various camps. He decided camping in civilian life should be no different. Camping life would not include roughing it. While Johnny attended many camps through the Galt Boys Club as a child, moving forward, he wasn't keen on tents or trailers. Instead, Johnny and Margaret purchased a lot at the edge of Lake Huron from dear friends. They built a beachside cottage in Southampton, Ontario, a few hours from Galt. It seems ironic that the place from which he later found so much joy throughout his life had the same name as a port in England: Southampton, the port from which he and thousands of other Canadians sailed at the beginning of Operation Overlord. If the Allies had lost the war, would Canadians ever have experienced the opportunity to enjoy a cottage on a lake?

During the summers, Johnny would drive his wife and children to the cottage, leaving them there for the week while he continued working in Galt. He would return after work on Friday night to join them for the weekend. To this day, family and friends still travel there throughout the summer months from various parts of Canada to enjoy the location's tranquillity.

Both Johnny and Margaret did their part to improve life in Canada and gave back to their community. Margaret volunteered for the Southampton and Galt Hospital Auxiliaries well into her adult life. They were living the Canadian dream; at the same time, they were helping in their communities. Both were involved with the Galt Humane Society, often taking 'Rescues' into their home. Johnny and Margaret also assisted troubled local youth needing guidance in their life. Johnny served as a proud, long-time member of the Galt Civic Service Club.

Music was prominent in the Nearingburg family, with pianos, guitars, and choir involvement being typical amongst Johnny's siblings. When the world-renowned jazz musician Winton Marsalis came to town, Johnny and his daughter attended the concert. As the trumpet player wowed the audience, Johnny leaned over and chuckled, "With a bit of practice, he might be quite good!"

Johnny also returned to his musical roots in the 1970s. Inspired by his daughter Patt, who joined the Galt Kiltie Marching Band. Patt played the clarinet, and Johnny rejoined the band as a trumpet player.

Although they did a bit of European travelling, Johnny never returned to Normandy, the site of the D-Day landings. He also avoided a return trip to Buron, where so many of his friends died. In 2019, his daughter Patt made the pilgrimage to the beaches and towns where her dad landed seventy-five years earlier.

No one ever heard Johnny complain about the lift he wore to compensate for the half-inch difference in his leg. He knew he was lucky to have had an excellent doctor in the Canadian Hospital, one who made sure he came home with both feet still attached. He understood there were a lot of other young men who weren't as lucky as he.

Did Johnny ever lay awake at night, thinking how his life might have changed if the doctors were unable to save his leg? While lying in traction, did he ever think it might have been easier if they just cut it off? Were there times throughout his life when he realized he might not have been so lucky if he was fighting with the regiment when they took such a beating in "Bloody Buron?"

Like the other men whose stories are told in this book, Johnny came home and made a good life for his family. The best description of him is that he was a gentle, honest man with a twinkle in his eye who loved the simple things about life. Birds at the feeder, the sun on the water, and weekly trips to the market were all precious reflections of his gifted life. By all accounts, Johnny was a generous, caring, and compassionate man who continued to do some of the things that make Canada such a beautiful nation. Even when he passed away on October 9, 2008, the family continued Johnny's legacy of giving back. Instead of flowers at his funeral, they requested people donate to the Poppy Fund, Humane Society, and Ducks Unlimited.

During the war, many of his letters home remarked about the beauty of some of the varieties of roses he'd never seen in Canada. His appreciation of gardens and flowers, especially roses, were some of the treasures he and Margaret shared for the rest of their lives. The gardens they grew together were colourful and beautiful, tended with loving care, and Johnny's siblings also carried on their mum's special appreciation of roses. The story of Johnny Nearingburg might have ended on a cobblestone street in France if he had not survived his "What If" moment. It would have concluded in the town of Buron on June 11, 1944, and the number of lives impacted by his loss is impossible to tally. Johnny's family was one of the fortunate ones. He was only wounded that day, allowing him to carry on being the loving son, brother, father, husband, and friend he was renowned for.

George Henry (Harry) Hildyard
999TH PORT OPERATING COMPANY,
ROYAL ENGINEERS

Inspired by stories from Harry's daughter, Marie Brown

Author's Note

I could say my meeting Marie Brown outside of St. Aubin, France was by chance, but it was deliberate on my part. Since beginning the quest of writing "Our Fathers' Footsteps," I have talked to hundreds of people, including Canadian families and the relatives of men from other countries, about the "What If" moments they experienced. This list includes people from Germany, Belgium, the Netherlands, the United States, and England. I searched for stories of ordinary men and women who put their lives on hold and went off to fight in World War II. They called it a World War for a good reason. After the war, men and women from around the world returned home, hoping the price they paid supported the values of freedom and democracy they so dearly fought for. Hopefully, this was the last war to end all wars. Sadly, this was not the case. Since the dawn of time, going to war has been an all too common denominator for settling differences. Unfortunately, atrocities around the world still continue to plague our society in one form or another.

Some people were lucky enough to have survived the war unscathed, and some returned with physical injuries that would heal in time. Others left pieces of themselves on the battlefields. Still, others suffered wounds that left marks in their minds' recesses from which they never recovered. Returning soldiers attempted to put their lives back together again. Something as simple as hugging their wife or meeting a child born while they were gone must have made them feel they had won the battlefield lottery. The tragic thing is, by a twist of fate or just plain bad luck, so many young soldiers never lived to have this opportunity.

One important aspect, often overlooked by those remembering our veterans, is the toll the Second World War had on the civilian population. The estimated civilian casualties who died in World War II were considerably higher than those killed on the field of battle.

While leaving the parking area near St. Aubin, France, I met an English family who made the pilgrimage to Normandy's coast. I spent a few minutes telling them about the book I hoped to write. Marie Brown quickly shared the story of her father. She told me how he let her mother, whose name was also Marie, know the invasion was on and where he thought they were headed.

It was a marvel how the Allies managed to keep the invasion a secret from the Germans. Still, there were rumours, and husbands managed to get word to their wives. In Marie's case, her father sent home a coded message. It was one line of the letter to his wife, telling her where he was heading: *"I hope our Margaret hasn't been caened again at school today."*

"Caened was used instead of *caned*, so my mother knew where he was going. He was on his way to Caen," she told me.

Would Harry be charged with treason if his letter had been opened and read by the censors? It seems the secrecy of the landings faltered as loved ones communicated with each other.

In May and June, before the D-Day landings, the *Daily Telegraph* crossword puzzles sent the planners for the proposed invasion into a panic. Over that period, *Juno, Gold, Sword*, and *Utah* were all answers for various crossword clues. These, of course, were the code names for the different beaches on the Normandy coast. Another clue was *Red Indian on the Missouri.* The answer, Omaha, was the code name for a beach where the US 1st Army would land. Ten days before the planned invasion, the word *Overlord* was the answer. Some words caused MI5 to investigate the author of the crossword puzzle. Mulberry was the name of the artificial harbours the allies would build along the coast. On June 1, while the troops were gathering in concentrated areas, the clue was "Britannia (he holds the same thing)." Britannia holds a trident. The other person known to carry a trident is Neptune. This answer was the code word for the naval operation of the landings. After an exhaustive investigation, MI5 concluded there was no espionage going on and that all the answers were merely coincidences.[65]

During our short beach conversation, Marie told me about another soldier whose family lived on the same street as the Hildyards. Marie's mother loved to tell the story of the soldier's wife running into the street, shouting, "They're going, they're going." His prearranged signal was to send home his kitbag full of dirty laundry.

As we departed to go our separate ways, I gave Marie one of the hundreds of business cards I took with me. It had the email address showing our fathers' footsteps on them. I hoped to hear from a few people if they were interested in telling their family stories. We wished each other well and headed off to see where our fathers had been 75 years earlier.

While touring the French and Belgian countryside over the next few weeks, I told the story Marie shared with me in St. Aubin about the signals the soldiers relayed to their families.

On the twentieth of July, a month after returning from France, I was thrilled to receive Marie's first email.

In her message, she wrote:

> *Your plan to write a book about "What Ifs" has given me much food for thought. I thought about your father and his "What If" and of the other lovely folk in your group. Did their fathers have "What If" moments?*

Marie went on to write:

> *On the journey back home, we covered many miles of dreary motorway. As the family began one by one to fall asleep, the quietness gave me time for reflection about my father and his life.*
> *My thoughts began to stray into areas I had rarely covered before in any depth, for our fathers are our fathers. They are 'just there,' and that is how we think of them.*

*Much as I knew about his life, my thought process began to look
back at it with a different vision.*

*"What if so and so had happened?" How would his life have been
different? My feelings strayed into several "What If" moments
and crossroads in his life. As the sun slowly dipped below the
horizon and we neared home, I realized I had had the opportunity to spend some quality time getting to know and understand
him.*

*For the "What If" idea you planted in my head at that time, I
thank you, allowing me to get to know my father better.*

*As a final "What If," what if we never met? This email would not
have been written. My father would have just continued being
my father, sitting in the corner reading his newspaper, and I
would have forgotten the turning points in his life.*

I was deeply moved by her letter and those that followed. Our
short conversation on the beaches of Normandy, 75 years after
both of our fathers landed there, is one of the reasons I began this
project. I wanted to tell the stories of those ordinary people who
were called upon and did their duty with the understanding that
they could be making the ultimate sacrifice.

It is amazing how similar and yet so different lives can be 6,126
kilometres apart. That's how far Hull, England, is from Winnipeg,
Manitoba.

Hull is 190 miles north of London. Its summers are short and
comfortable, and winters are considered long, very cold, windy,
and mostly cloudy. It seldom gets below -3 degrees Celsius in
winter or above 25 degrees during the summer.

By contrast, Winnipeg's average winter temperature is -20
Celsius. Canadians refer to this as a dry cold compared to the
bone-chilling damp weather of Northern England. In the summer,
Winnipeg can reach a sweltering +30.

The following is Marie's father's story.

Part One

Harry was born in 1905, the first child of George Henry Hildyard and Margaret Lavinia Best. If Harry had been much older, or if the First World War had gone on longer, he may have been involved in that horrific and devastating war to end all wars. Like millions of others, his family suffered, including the loss of uncles on both his mother's and father's sides.

In 1910 Harry became a big brother to his sister, Sarah Jane, who quickly became the family's pride and joy.

People have heard of the Spanish flu that ravaged the entire world. It started in April of 1918. Following World War I, it became one of the greatest medical disasters of the twentieth century. It was one of the first genuinely international pandemics, killing as many as twenty to fifty million people. Over 228,000 died in Britain alone.[66] The helplessness of a worldwide epidemic becomes much more personal when your sister is one of the victims.

Sadly, Sarah did not survive the deadly flu. After her funeral, the family feared they would be returning to further tragedy because Harry also contracted it. Fortunately, he survived. Was this the first of his "What If" moments?

In December of 1928, Harry married Marie Elizabeth Bell at St. Charles' Church, located on Jarret Street, Hull. They set up home at 116 St. Mark Street, near Dansom Lane, Kingston on Hull.

Finding gainful employment in Hull was a difficult task in the 1920s. Harry did have a job in the shipbuilding industry, but after the crash of 1929, Harry's role in the shipyard came to an end, just before their first child's birth.

In July 1930, Harry and Marie became proud parents to a son. In honour of Harry's uncle, who died in 1918 near the end of World War I, they named him Bernard Albert Hildyard.

Harry did manage to get work on occasion in the shipbuilding industry. Circumstances were difficult. Even more so with another mouth to feed. Marie gave birth to a daughter, Margaret Mary, in June 1932.

For the Hildyards, life went on. Food was scarce, and good-paying jobs were hard to come by. Like any good Brit, Harry remained hopeful, somehow managing to deal with the adversity he and fellow countrymen faced during the 1930s. He continued to keep a stiff upper lip around his family, telling them, "Life will get better soon. You'll see."

In 1935, Harry finally found full-time employment with Hollis Brothers and Company. They were an importer and manufacturer of wood products, specializing in woodblock flooring and parquetry work. They were also known for manufacturing custom mouldings and designer joinery.

When the First World War ended, Harry was just thirteen, and he knew the tragic consequences of war first-hand. With Germany's resurgence under their new Chancellor, Adolf Hitler, the winds of war were once again sweeping across Europe. Like the majority of people living in England, Harry was hopeful an ultimate showdown would never come.

In 1938, the fears of a nation, which lost close to a million of its citizens during World War I were abated. Prime Minister Chamberlain returned from Munich with a signed non-aggression pact between Germany and Great Britain. The British people were comforted, knowing they could sleep without the fear of bombs raining down from the skies. Many remembered too well the horrors of the Great War and the toll it took on the country. It is incredible how a simple signed piece of paper could bring such relief. This document helped relieve an almost palpable sense of dread and fear. The people of Britain hadn't felt this sense of relief since the signing of the armistice on November 11, 1918.[67]

While the country hoped that war could be avoided, precautions still took place. These included blackout drill rehearsals that became routine in early 1938. On September 1, two days preceding the declaration of war against Germany, these practices became mandatory. From that day until April 1945, the entire country went dark at night. During the first month of the blackouts, over 1100 people died in a variety of road accidents. [68]

Keeping Hull in darkness was necessary because of the value of its port. The city could be used as a beacon to lead German bombers to other locations inland. In September, when it was still light until after 8:30 pm, this wasn't much of a hardship. However, when darkness set in at 4:30 pm in the dead of winter, people became extremely depressed. Many were diagnosed with a syndrome called Blackout Anemia.[69]

One of the few hardships Marie complained about were the curtains: "They don't even want us to wash the blooming things. Look here, Harry, they even gave us a leaflet telling us how to clean them. It says here not to wash ordinary blackout curtains. Says it's apt to make them let light through. Here they go telling me to hoover, shake, brush and then iron. It says if I iron them, they'll be more light-proof."[70]

"I'm sorry, love, we all have to make some sacrifices," laughed Harry.

Harry's job at Hollis Brothers was as a Tallyman. His task ensured the wood and raw logs unloaded on the docks matched the ship's manifest. He would then make sure each factory area received the correct species and amount of timber required.

When the war started in 1939, Harry was thirty-four. What many considered the "phoney war" lasted for eight months. History books are not very kind to the French or English for the lack of effort that could have been made to stop the war before it escalated to the point of a world conflict. Some of those in power still believed Adolf Hitler would limit his actions. They were convinced peace could be negotiated with Germany by allowing them to control the significant gains of the territory they had already taken.

On May 10, 1940, any thoughts of limiting the German quest to control Europe ended when Germany invaded the Low Countries of Belgium and the Netherlands. That evening Neville Chamberlain resigned, and Winston Churchill became the new Prime Minister of England, leading to the end of the "phoney war."[71] On June 22, after a short fight with the Germans, the French signed an armistice in Compiegne, the exact location in which Germany surrendered after World War I.[72] Eighteen days later, the Battle of Britain began.

Harry's wife's brothers were called to active service. "Come on, Harry, time to get in the fight," they told him.

"I have a job to do here," he told them. "I'm doing my part at the mill and keeping fire watch. Besides, I'm thirty-five bloody years old. What would they get an old sod like me doing?"

Hull became a target for the Luftwaffe as soon as the bombings of England began. Most of the concentrated attacks came between May 7 and 9, claiming the lives of 422 people. By July 1941, over 930 civilians were killed.[73] When the war ended, the people of Hull had been under Air Raid alerts for over 1000 hours.[74]

Hull was subjected to 815 Air Raid alerts throughout the war and bombed on 82 occasions. Ninety-five percent of the buildings were damaged or destroyed, including twenty-seven churches, fourteen hospitals or schools, and eight cinemas. Much to the chagrin of the average working man, there were rumours that somewhere between twenty-three and forty-two pubs were destroyed. Only six thousand of the 91,000 homes were left untouched by the end of the war, leaving over 150,000 people homeless. 1200 people were killed in the bombings, and the list of injured and wounded treated topped 3,000.[75]

To maintain secrecy throughout the war, they seldom named Hull as a site suffering from continuous bombing. Instead, merely referring to it as a north-east coast town.[76] As a result, the population of Great Britain was unaware of how badly Hull was devastated. The destruction was so great that in August 1941, King George VI and Queen Elizabeth made a clandestine visit to survey the damage.[77]

During daylight hours, Hull became a target because it was easy to find. Hundreds of German aircraft flew above the city towards targets like the steel factories in Sheffield or the munitions plants in Manchester.[78] Over 7,000 residents of Hull began leaving their homes each evening when they suspected bombing would occur. This practice became known as "trekking." They would get out of their homes and trek to the countryside to sleep in the relative safety of nearby parks or the surrounding countryside.[79]

Winnipeg, Manitoba, had their "If" day to show Canadians what might happen if the Germans attacked one of their cities. The town of Hull where Harry Hildyard and his family lived faced the real horrors of the infamous German blitz

By the time Winnipeg experienced "If Day" in February 1942, Hull residents had lived with the bombings for nineteen months. During this period, thousands of people were killed or injured in the outlying areas. The nightly raids left few homes untouched by the devastation. Hull was the site of one of the first daylight bombings in June 1940, and this continued until March 1945.[80]

When the British Oil and Cake mill at the end of his block received a direct hit and burned to the ground, Harry decided it was time to get his family out of Hull. Even though their house was still standing, it would only take one bomb to destroy it and kill his entire family. Harry arranged for his wife Marie, and their children Bernard and Margaret, to take refuge in Beverley in East Yorkshire. He also ensured his wife's sisters and grandmother, who lived close by, were moved to the safety of the temporary residence. This location was twelve miles from the direct path of the German bombers.

Marie objected, but Harry insisted. "Sticking around here might not be safe. You heard Mr. Brown lost his sister Elsie, and her husband, just last week. They say it was one of the biggest bombs dropped so far. No, I think if you hang around Hull, it's not going to be safe for you or the children, my love."

He hated seeing them go, but staying on the enemy bombers' direct target routes was too dangerous. Moreover, Kingston on

Hull had some of the best docks in the entire country, making it one of the German Luftwaffe's prized targets.

British oil and cake mills at Hull. Located at the end of Harry's Street.

"Come on, Bernard. You'll be the man of the family up in Beverley. I need you to take care of your mom and sister, not to mention Auntie Nan and Auntie Betty, and we certainly can't forget Grannie Annie, can we?"

"But father, I want to stay here with you. I'm already twelve. Some of my friends have been helping out around here."

"I know, son, but I need to know you and the rest of the family are safe. I know I can rely on you. I can rely on you, can't I, Bernie?"

"Yes, sir," said Bernard reluctantly.

Knowing his family was safe made it easier for Harry to concentrate on his job. Keeping fire watch was a huge responsibility. The Hollis Brothers Sawmill was a mere 600 metres away from the Humber Estuary dock area. A fire at the lumber yard could quickly spread to this critical area. In March 1941, the Germans dropped

316 tonnes of high explosive bombs and over 77,000 incendiary bombs to set fire to properties.[81]

In late May, Harry knew it was time. He made the trip up to Beverley to see his family. Telling them his news would not be easy for him. "It's time for me to sign up," he said to his wife and children.

"Isn't our family doing enough?" asked Marie. "Bert's doing his job in the fire service in Newcastle. You're doing the same here. Who the hell knows where my brother Joe is. Somewhere in the Far East fighting the Japanese. My sister's husband is someplace in the deserts of Africa with the RAF. You've got two kids. What's to happen to them if you go off and get yourself killed," she cried.

His wife's heartache and anguish about Harry heading to war were the same concerns that thousands of other wives, lovers, and mothers felt about their menfolk leaving for battle throughout history.

Harry hugged and kissed all the women. He gave an all-encompassing hug to his daughter and a hearty handshake, and a tousle of his son's hair. Then Harry headed off to do his duty for King and Country.

9ᵗʰ Battalion, the Hampshire Regiment, helping to clear bomb damage in Hull.

Part Two

On June 4, 1942, at the age of 37, Harry volunteered for service. He wasn't a big man, just under 5'7", weighing in at ten stone, three pounds (143 pounds). Working for Hollis lumber had made him strong. One of his attributes was the ability to work smart. A lot of men worked just as hard or harder but would fag out in no time. Working smart allowed Harry to go on for hours. He could work all day and into the night if need be.

Harry enlisted with the Royal Army Service Corps (RASC) and was assigned a driver's job.

Harry Hildyard in Uniform, 1942.

In July, he joined the number 9 RASC training battalion in Alfreton, England. It was only eighty-three miles south of Hull. Still, it seemed like an eternity away. Before joining the Army, an eighteen-mile trip to Withernsea Beach on the North Sea would have been a long journey.

In August, he was once again on the move, this time to H Company of the Headquarters Battalion. By now, he was somewhat discouraged by how the army saw fit to use him.

One afternoon he said to Malcolm Langdon, one of the men in his RSAC unit, "So here we are, Mel. I've been in the army for what, four or five months. I've been given basic training as a soldier, and now I find myself posted to what is essentially a holding unit — sitting here on my arse waiting for a placement. I want to think they could put us to work based on a man's skill set and experience. But no, not this army."

"What do you expect, 'Arry,' said his bunkmate. "The army don't think like me and you. If they need us here, it's here we'll stay. If it's in the middle of the war in some godforsaken foreign land, that's where we'll be off to."

"I know," said a sullen Harry. "We're like the tin soldiers Bernie used to play with. He was the general and could put the soldiers anywhere he wanted. Now it's you and me who are the tin soldiers, and those faceless generals are the ones who put us where they want."

"You got that right, Arry. You remember that bloody poem they forced us to memorize in school, don't ya. The one about the Charge of the Light Brigade. How 'ours is not to reason why, ours is but to do or die,' or something along those lines."

"I remember it. I just hope the higher echelon don't expect us to be riding horses into the bloody battles."

"Don't you worry about that, 'Arry. If there are 'orses about, guys like you and me won't be looking over the head of the 'orse. We'll be takin care of what comes out of the arse end," laughed Malcolm.

In January of 1943, Harry's skills were finally recognized. He was not a snot-nosed eighteen-year-old kid. He'd been working since before most of the little buggers, many of whom were of higher rank, were even born.

As a result of his experience working in the dockyards in the late twenties, Harry ended up with the Royal Engineers. He was assigned the position of sapper (the equivalent of a private). He hoped to become a stevedore.

Royal Engineer's Hat Badge.

When people think of the Royal Engineers, they immediately think of men building roads and bridges. They imagine the exploits of men working behind enemy lines, perhaps parachuting into their destinations to blow up dams, factories, bridges and railway lines. There is so much more to them. If not for the concerted effort of the thousands of men like these and other logistics regiments of the allied forces, the entire war machine might have ground to a complete stop.

Engineers were involved in combat roles, fearlessly removing mines and obstacles from the beaches as Normandy's invasion took place. They were also responsible for unloading the ships when they landed in France after crossing the English Channel.

Those ships carried millions of tons of equipment and munitions required to continue the war effort.

The beginning of the movie *Gladiator* shows thousands of Roman Legionnaires in a camp, prepared to head to battle with the enemy. Have you ever wondered how all the tents were put up or how these thousands of men were fed? The same was true during the American Civil War. It wasn't engineers who did all this, but someone was responsible for ensuring all the equipment was prepared to go into battle.

Marie made a similar comment regarding another invasion. Before the battle of Hastings, the English caught the Vikings unaware when they invaded England. King Harold raced north to defeat them. The blood on the battlefield had not dried when word came that William of Normandy had landed in the south. Harold gathered his forces and raced to do battle with the Normans.[82]

Throughout history, men and equipment have needed to be moved from one place to another. They require food, weapons, water, and places to make camp. Most of these soldiers would have travelled on foot, so there was probably little time to stop for a rest. These armies would have required a support team. For the army of Great Britain during World War II, making sure the supplies continued moving was the Royal Engineers' responsibility, and Harry was a part of that support team.

In the 999th Port Operating Company, dozens of tradespeople worked on various tasks, similar to jobs done every day by tradespeople and stevedores in ports around the world. They did not have the lineage of famous regiments like the South Lancashire Regiment, whose roots go back to the 1880s. The 999th was established during World War II.

Most of the men doing the jobs were considered specialists. Some of these positions included; checkers, crane operators, railway clerks, and cooks. There were also trained soldiers in a pioneer section assigned to handle explosives and other duties, as well as stevedores like Harry.

Although referred to as a company, the total number of men in Harry's unit was more of a small battalion. There were over 360 men in the 999th Port Operating Company of the Royal Engineers.

In January of 1944, Harry was working his tail off on the docks of Leith, Scotland, on Edinburgh's outskirts. When he arrived in Leith during the winter of 1943, Harry had no idea it had also suffered the ravages of the German Blitz. Bombed-out buildings were evidence of even small cities experiencing their share of tragedy.

They were busy practicing the loading and unloading of tiny vessels called coasters, with tons of equipment, throughout the month. They also took part in regular military training during this period, including practice on the rifle ranges and other military drills. In addition, each month, the men would have regular medicals and routine military inspections. Most of these men were tradespeople. However, they were still in the British Army, where discipline and deportment were paramount. Therefore, physical training exercises were also a big part of their daily routine.

One day Harry commented to one of the other men, "Sure hope the civilian authorities don't hear what the army has us doing. All this drill and PT. They might want us doing this crap when we get back to Civvy Street."

"Oh, right, 'Arry, I can just see you doing jumpin' jacks first thing every morning," he laughed.

Halfway through January, the entire unit moved 170 miles north to Elgin, a small Scottish town on the coast, forty miles east of Inverness, Scotland. Upon arrival, they began intense military training, including learning how to defend their unloading areas should the Germans try to overrun any location they were assigned to.

At the end of each month, men were sent home to assist with the Home Front after being certified medically unfit for Beach Group Work. "I damn well wish they would send me home. I'm not cut out for this," came the comment from many in Harry's unit.

Since joining the army, most of Harry's accommodations were inside tents. Finally, metal Nissen huts (prefabricated steel structures) were constructed for temporary barracks at each location the company set up camp. In the cold, damp climate of Northern Scotland, the draughty units were not the favourite place for men to spend their nights. They were a definite improvement over the tents.

"Bloody Hell," said Harry when he heard they were moving yet again. This time it was another short jaunt to Carron, Scotland. In this location, some men in his company took part in simulated battle exercises. Others headed off to Glasgow for various training courses geared towards the work they would be involved with when Europe's invasion ultimately took place.

In February 1944, Harry was granted leave and headed home to Beverley. The 400-mile train ride from Northern Scotland seemed to take forever. Gazing out the railcar window as he travelled through Edinburgh and Glasgow, he again witnessed that no part of Great Britain had missed the bombings from Hitler's Luftwaffe.

When he finally jumped off the train in Hull, he hardly recognized the city where he grew up. It was tough to find a landmark because of the additional destruction since he left in June 1942. Before heading to Beverley to see his wife and children, he wandered some of the bombed-out streets. By some miracle, he found that the house he shared with his family was still standing. However, the devastation confirmed that moving his family out of the area had been the right thing to do.

Marie was pleased as punch to have her husband home for his leave. The other ladies, including Grannie Annie, didn't gush about it, but they were happy to have a man around the house, if only for a short time.

The children, on the other hand, were ecstatic. They were all over Harry as soon as he stepped across the threshold. Both were jabbering and asking so many questions Harry couldn't keep up with them.

"How long you home for, Dad?"

"When do you have to go back?"

"Can we kick the football around?"

"Did you see our house? Is it still standing?"

The rapid succession of questions wore Harry out almost as much as marching around the parade square. He managed to calm them down when he brought out his coupons for sweets he'd been saving.

Adults in England were forced to limit their consumption of many staple food items. Rationed goods included; ham, bacon, butter, milk, and sugar. Even tea was limited to only two ounces per week, along with a single egg. A big disappointment for Marie was that sweets were limited to twelve ounces every four weeks.[83]

"I have an announcement," said Harry. "Tomorrow I'm going to treat the entire family to a film at the Beverley Cinema. We can't go down to Hull because even before moving you here, the Luftwaffe must have destroyed at least eight of the theatres. You wouldn't recognize the place. I think we would be hard-pressed to find our way around. I hardly recognized the place."

"Father, can we go to see *The Son of Dracula*?" asked Bernie.

"I don't think it would be appropriate for your sister," said Marie.

Margaret piped up with her twopence worth. "I want to see *Lassie Come Home*. It's got Roddy McDowall in it."

Much to Bernie's disappointment, the family settled on *Lassie*. Harry would splurge for everyone in the house, including Grannie, Auntie Betty and Auntie Nan, to go to the cinema.

The following afternoon, Marie and the entire family dressed in their glad rags (best clothes) and headed to the cinema. The admission for all seven was forty-seven pence, and Harry used his rationing coupon to pick up some sweets before they went.

"I was guessing, with that sweet tooth of yours, the coupon for twelve ounces of sweets wasn't getting you through the whole month, was it? Am I right, my dear?" Harry teased before they went in to see the film.

"Well, there are three adults and two growing children in the bloomin' 'ouse. I could only say no so many times."

Marie quickly changed the subject. "Did I tell you how utterly handsome you look in your uni, Harry Hildyard?"

"Well, thank you, Mrs. Hildyard. You and the rest of the family look smashing as well, all done up in your Sunday best."

The rest of his leave was uneventful. Harry enjoyed his time with his family very much. Finding alone time with his wife in a busy household with two children and three older women proved challenging.

Back in Carron, one of the PT drills they took part in during March was log lifting. A large-diameter one was too heavy for one or two men. Yet, when they worked as a team, each man might only be responsible for lifting twenty to thirty pounds. The exercise reinforced the need for men to work together.

"I don't know about you, 'Arry, but I think we should be working more on carrying boxes of ammo. What the 'ell do they think our boys are gonna do? Throw these bloody logs at the enemy?" complained Malcolm, who was also posted with Harry's unit.

"Don't get your knickers in a knot, Malcolm. I don't think you were even holding up your portion of the thing," laughed Harry at the end of the day. Everyone's shoulder muscles were sore and chafed from supporting the log for hours on end. His arms and legs were cramped from running with the timber held above their heads.

In the latter part of the month, the unit began getting Typhus inoculations. The lack of definitive information about the prevalence of Typhus in Germany was a concern. Inadequate sanitation and hygiene problems could result in questionable water supplies. It was better to be safe than sorry as the boys prepared for the big one.

During this period, the weather was listed as fine by the company adjutant, except for the 29th. That day, while working on a battle exercise codenamed "Leap Year." Harry and one hundred other men in his company travelled to a training area in Kinloss on

Findhorn Bay, 168 miles north of Caron. As they were transported by truck to the exercise, all the men complained.

Harry said, "Can you believe this. Almost April, it's snowing, and it's colder than a witch's tit."

The following day the weather returned to average: not too cold, not too hot, neither brilliantly sunny nor overcast; just a typical day in Scotland. The "Leap Year" exercise ended with Harry and his fellow stevedores practicing unloading a Coaster onto smaller vessels and getting them safely to shore.

On April 19, the company was once again on the move. After a lengthy twenty-seven-hour journey, they arrived at Camp A7, Stakes Hill in Waterlooville, Hampshire. Their new camp was twenty-five miles from the port of Southampton.

Similar to other marshalling areas, the camp was sealed. This was done to minimize the risk that spies or the British public might realize the day of the invasion was getting closer.

The average soldier still had no idea when or where the invasion would take place.

Harry was pleased to get a letter from home when the mail came in and received quite a shock. It seems Marie had become pregnant during the moments of alone time they shared while he was on leave. "I sure didn't expect that," he whispered to himself.

Throughout May, the military training intensified. Proficiency using the British Army's Bren gun was an expected exercise that required a high degree of skill and stamina. Harry's unit practiced their marching and parade drills for a ceremonial parade in the latter part of the month.

Once again, the men of the unit grumbled. "With all the drills they're making us do, you might think they want us to be real soldiers," was one of the many complaints by the rank and file of the civilian soldiers. At the end of May, the men understood that everything they worked and trained for might soon be coming to a head.

Since January, there had been weekly dances and shows from the Entertainments National Service Association (ENSA). There were whist drives for the card players in the evenings, and each weekend Inter-Section football competitions were held. All of this stopped near the end of May.

On the 29th, every man attended a church parade. After the service, the new commanding officer of the 999th, Major Abson, gave the men a briefing. He went over their jobs for the coming days as they prepared to do their part for Europe's invasion.

The preamble to his instructions began on a serious note: "If I become a casualty during the landings, Captain Coles will assume command of the unit." There were no illusions about the possibility of there not being any casualties. Hearing their major talk about it so casually came as a bit of a shock.

Hearing the reality of the situation talked about so nonchalantly caused quite a stir amongst the men. "Hey, 'Arry," whispered Malcolm, "I heard casualties of the assault troops could be as high as one in three or worse. If we have anywhere near that many, it means me and you are gonna be okay. Which of these blokes is gonna be our third? I don't want to be standing too close to him when all hell breaks loose."

When the men quieted down, the major went through the rest of his instructions. He reiterated most of what they had spent the last months learning, including the numbering systems for the Coaster ships carrying supplies to the beachhead.

The official 999 Port Operating Company's official Top Secret Operational Order No. 1 included some of the following items:

The Commanding Officers Recce party will land at H Hour + 11 1/2. They will select the Coy bivouac area.
Three Coasters which will land on D Day will carry gangs for the first shift. Each ship contains 420 Tons of Extra High Priority Stores.
All ranks will be warned of the most severe penalties to be inflicted in cases of looting

or pilfering. Private purchases or barter is
forbidden.
On arrival in the Bivouac area, it is most
important that regard be paid to siting of slit
trenches so that they are in a defensive position
with correct fire plans for defence. PITT gun will
be defensively sited.
In the Bivouac, area personnel are forbidden
to enter any building. They must sleep below
ground with adequate blast protection. No fires
will be lighted unless authorized by an officer.
There must be enough slit trenches for every
man by evening on landing day.
On no account will any water supply be used
either for drinking or washing until passed fit
by an analyst of the Medical Officer or Hygiene
Section.[84]

Major Abson reiterated his concern about pilfering. "I don't
care what you're offered. Do not. I repeat. Do not try to make a
profit from your position."

The major continued going over the procedures they learned
during training, detailing various alarms and sirens they may hear
on the beaches. For instance, he told them what to do when an alarm
was sounded and the meanings of whistle blasts indicating enemy
aircraft. He again discussed the signals they would hear regarding
the suspected presence of any type of gas or other sprays.

During his briefing of the twenty-four operational items, the
situation became sombre as the commanding officer talked about
medical concerns and burials:

First Aid will be given at Beach Dressing
Stations. Severe stretcher cases will be sent to
Field Dressing Stations. (One on each beach.)

Both Medical Orderlies will remain in the
Bivouac area.
Burials will only take place in areas marked as
Burial Areas.[85]

Major Abson added, "Attending to the dead will not be a job for
most of you, chaps. I'm afraid there won't be time to grieve for our
dead, and the burial task will fall to the pioneers."

As he wrapped up his instructions, he ended on a lighter note.
"I left out item number fifteen, "One thing you men who will be
driving must remember. Those silly Frenchmen and the rest of
those mainland bastards drive on the wrong side of the road. So
just remember it is Drive on the Right."[86]

When all the orders and instructions were completed, the men
were dismissed for the rest of the day.

As they were standing in line for the evening meal, Malcolm
whispered, "Arry, did you hear?"

"Hear what?"

"We're going to be landing somewhere near Caen," whispered
Malcolm.

"Where the hell did you hear that?"

"Nye told me. He got it from the corporal who overheard a
couple of officers talking."

"I'll believe it when we land."

Even though he was suspicious about the information, Harry
sat down after supper and sent a note to his family. He filled the
page with questions about how they were getting on. He asked his
wife how she was feeling now since she was at least three months
pregnant. In the early stage of her pregnancy, her letters talked
about how ill she was with morning sickness. He wondered if the
food rationing was a contributing factor.

Harry inserted a coded note about where Malcolm thought
they were heading among the rest of his questions. He asked if
his daughter was doing her chores at home and paying attention
in school. *"I hope our Margaret hasn't been Caened again at school*

today." Harry purposely misspelled the word and capitalizing the C. He popped the letter in the post, hoping it would get past the censors, never giving the possibly treasonous letter another thought.

The first three days of June were splendid, weather-wise. On June 3, the 999th Port Operating Company headed to Southampton. Upon arrival, they embarked onto their coasters in preparation for their trip to the still unofficial beachhead in Normandy. While packing their gear, Prime Minister Winston Churchill arrived at the docks to wish all the troops "Godspeed."[87]

Harry and the men would not be travelling to France in comfort. They may have been less comfortable than most men who would be on converted passenger ships or ferries, but perhaps more tolerable than those making the crossings aboard the open LCI'Ls (Landing Ship Infantry Large) or the LCTs.

The coasters provided no accommodation for the Royal Engineers' men, so they slept under canvas tarps laid out on the hatches. Due to the poor weather, some men went below decks and slept on crates of ammunition. The crews of these vessels had small cabins, but there was no running water. The merchantmen serving on the ships were paid a few shillings each day to cover the cost of cooking and supplying their food. Although the Engineers didn't have to pay for their food, they were required to prepare their own rations.[88]

On June 4, the weather took a turn for the worse. The invasion scheduled for the following morning was put on hold for twenty-four hours. This meant that over 330 men of the Port Operating Company were sitting on various boats waiting to head across to the beaches of Normandy. Also sitting offshore were over 100,000 men on other ships of all shapes and sizes, waiting for word the invasion was on.

Finally, on the evening of the 5th, Harry's Coaster worked its way from its position outside of Southampton into the English Channel. They joined up with close to 7000 other ships, including more than 800 merchant ships loaded with supplies, like the one Harry was on.

Part Three

Tuesday, June 6, 1944, D-Day

When Marie was young, she recalled her father talking about sitting on the beach, watching all the ships arriving during the invasion. She envisioned him making his way to the beaches before the assault troops. In her mind, she could see him sitting in some hidden spot watching the show.

She now understands her father could not have been on the beach to watch the invasion as the sun came up on June 6. However, he did have a front-row seat for one of the most significant assaults of all time from the small coaster he was on.

When Harry saw the spectacle laid before him, he knew it would be difficult to describe the sights and sounds. Battleships, cruisers, light-cruisers and over 130 destroyers and destroyer escorts opened fire at 05:30. The noise was mind-numbing as the ships let loose broadside after broadside of shells from guns as big as sixteen inches. The flashes from the guns were blinding. This sensory overload was seared in his memory. Some of the echoes of the ships firing at the coastline may have come from as far as Utah Beach, which was over thirty-five miles away.

Harry continued to watch in awe as rockets were fired toward the beaches, as wave upon wave of LCAs made their runs to shore. Using a pair of borrowed binoculars, he watched in horror, as a great many tanks, with waterproof skirting, sank below the rough seas' waves as soon as they launched from their LCTs.

The advance of the attack boats was hard to watch. Harry observed LCAs filled with brave men, including Royal Engineers,

Commandos, and infantrymen, being hit by motor shells or exploding when the tiny ships struck against a mine.

From where he watched, it appeared as though hundreds of toy soldiers were strung out across the landing zone. Peering through the field glasses, Harry realized some men were motionless, while others were moving forward as shells exploded around them. He was sure all these men had just one thing in mind: staying alive.

By late in the morning, the beaches were littered with the hulks and remnants of landing craft. From where Harry watched, he had no idea German defences at Sword were not as strong as other areas along the Normandy Coast. He knew it was the British 3rd Division storming the beaches, including Commandos led by Lord Lovat and members of the Free French Army. Even though enemy resistance at Sword Beach was lighter than other beaches, the men landing there suffered upwards of 1000 casualties. From his vantage point, Harry couldn't see them, but all along the shore, lifeless bodies rolled in and out of the surf, like pieces of driftwood on the tide.

Royal Engineers cleared seven of the eight exit lanes by noon, and troops began moving off the beaches. Wave after wave of various crafts continued to pour ashore. By the end of the day, the British landed almost twenty-nine thousand troops on the beachhead.[89] While the men prepared their noon meals, the coaster's engines seemed quiet compared to the cacophony when the first naval bombardment began at 0530.

Just after sundown on what history would refer to as the Longest Day, Harry and the 999th Port Operating Company made their way to the beaches. Despite the seas not churning the same as during the assault landings, it was still rough. Four men were washed overboard from a coaster on the run to the beachhead. They were lost in the sea and presumed drowned. A constant enemy barrage of shells rained down on the beaches.

The soldiers tasked with unloading the ships were assigned to gangs. Two or three of these groups worked on each of the three coasters waiting to disgorge their priority stores.

As June 6 came to an end, it was time to do their part to keep the invasion moving forward. Eight gangs worked the first shift discharging the boats. Harry unloaded the Marcel, a Belgium-registered ship. The others, including the Northgate and Glengarrif, both British flagged vessels, had five groups working on them.[90]

Harry and the men worked throughout the night, praying the shells exploding around them would not find their mark.

The 999th Port Operating Company finished unloading 819 tons from the ships by 2300 hours on the seventh without losing any more men. Many of these civilian soldiers had now been awake for over forty-eight hours.

**Beach Group support troops digging in on
the evening of June 6, Sword Area.**

When the beach groups arrived late on June 6, they immediately dug defensive positions around the unloading zone. This included setting the company's three Bren-gun teams strategically to protect from any counter-attacks. With these in place, including slit trenches, the men could take refuge for the night. In addition, the shore party managed to get latrines dug in a safe spot. With the possibility of buildings on the beach being rigged with booby traps, entering any structure on or near the beach was forbidden by direct order.

Harry was relieved after completing a double shift. Stiff and bone-tired, he made his way to the bivouac area and met up with Malcolm. "Somebody told me we landed over 150,000 men yesterday.[91] The pubs back home will feel the pinch of all those lads being over here," joked his friend.

This was the last thing Harry heard as he fell fast asleep. He covered his body with a blanket from his pack, then rested his rifle against the wall of the slit trench in case the Germans counter-attacked. Finally, he set his helmet over his face to protect it from shrapnel.

They were close to Port City Ouistreham that had been liberated on D-Day by French and British commandos. The locks on the canal were still intact. However, the port was still too close to the front line to be used because it was only seventeen kilometres from Caen. As a result, it wouldn't be until August 21 before minesweeping of the Ouistreham Port could begin.[92] The initial goal from day one was the liberation of Caen. Once secured, it would allow the Allies to make use of their facilities.

When he woke at sunrise the following morning, he could hear the sound of battles taking place inland. The beaches were still being subjected to shelling and strafing from the enemy. They would be under intermittent bombardment every day until July 8.

June 8 was relatively easy. Harry was allowed to rest because other gangs had arrived to assist. The company unloaded an additional 126 tons from other boats loaded in Southampton.

On June 9, Harry and the men of his company were witnesses to a strange sight. While still under enemy fire from miles inland, they watched as several ships were lined up. In one case, the vessel required towing to its final resting place. By the end of the day, they were scuttled. This created a Gooseberry, a man-made breakwater to reduce the effects of the current to facilitate the unloading. The old transport and warships of allied countries were weighted with concrete before crossing the English Channel. The blockships off Sword Beach would make a temporary calm water harbour near Ouistreham. Each ship was rigged with demolition charges. Once set off, the vessel settled to the bottom. The hulls protruded about two metres above the high tide mark, instantly becoming a waveless area for the supply ships to be unloaded. Some of the boats sunk off Sword Beach included the HMS Durban, and the Sumatra, a Royal Dutch Cruiser.[93]

Scuttled ships at Ouistreham.

At the same time, the British were constructing a Mulberry harbour at Arromanches, while the Americans began building their temporary docking facility at Omaha Beach. They may not have been under the constant threat of snipers now because the Allied troops were miles inland, but there were periods of loud blasts of whistles each evening. The warnings and alarms would continue every five seconds to indicate another enemy aircraft in the vicinity. This went on until the all-clear signal came.

Harry's company participated in months of military training. However, they never took part in live-fire exercises like the regular infantry. Even men who survived the blitz in parts of England were getting jumpy each time the whistles blew.

The weather turned nasty on the 19th. A fierce storm, considered one of the strongest in forty years, resulted in unloading delays. The seas were heavy, with winds gusting between six and seven on the Beaufort scale. This translated to between twenty-five miles and thirty-eight miles an hour. Some of the Normandy beaches were subjected to waves cresting as high as twenty feet.[94] The storm continued for three days and reduced unloading to a trickle, with a mere 362 tons being unloaded. The Germans continued to send planes overhead, intent on destroying the artificial harbours. Heavy shelling of the beaches also continued despite the rain and high winds.

By the 22nd, the heavy winds caused the loss of equipment and supplies in transit and meant large-scale delays. By the time the storm passed, the American Mulberry harbour at Omaha Beach was virtually destroyed and was no longer capable of operating.[95]

As fierce as the German war machine was, there was a significant flaw. Re-supply lines were long, and Allied planes continued to destroy railways and bridges, making re-supply of German equipment difficult. In an attempt to disrupt the Allied supply lines, the Germans continued to shell the beaches, trying mostly in vain to target the supply ships. With no forward observers to help the Gunnars pinpoint targets, the shelling remained indiscriminate.

On the 22nd, the bombardments at Sword Beach finally paid off for them. It was after 1700 hours. The unloading of coaster 274 had just begun. In a never-ending circuit, amphibious boats unloaded tons of goods. Harry was nearing the beach after leaving one of the transfer vessels with its maximum three-ton load. Ferrying these loads from the coasters required a steady stream of the DUKWs, commonly called Duck boats. This versatile amphibious craft could travel in the water up to six miles an hour and up to fifty miles an hour on land.

Unloading from ships onto DUKW boats.

When he left the coaster, Harry called out to Dave Adams, one of the Royal Engineer sappers supervising the unloading of the coaster. "We'll be back for another load right quick, Davey." Harry's boat was close to shore when a shell struck the coaster, setting it on fire.

Harry had no way of knowing the fate of the man he just left. "I hope Davey's all right," he said to Malcolm when they began unloading the stores they were transferring.

The men of his unit stood together in the unloading area and watched as the ship continued to burn. "He's a good guy. Got a wife back home. I think he said her name was Minnie."

"I hope so, too," said Malcolm.

The company continued to discharge two other coasters. By the end of the day, they unloaded a total of 195 tons of equipment.

Most days, the crews unloading the vessels started work between 0600 and 0700 hours, usually ending around 1900. Occasionally, depending on the urgency or requirements of the stores loaded on the coaster, men might not finish their day until closer to midnight.

On the night the coaster was destroyed, they gathered in the bivouac area. Lieutenant Robertson approached. The group of men were just sitting down for their evening tea.

The protocol of standing when an officer entered an area was less formal in the field. Still, a few men began to stand for the officer. "As you were, men," he said. "I've got some bad news. The shell that hit the coaster this afternoon resulted in two casualties. I know he was well-liked by you chaps, so I'll just come out with it. Sapper Adams died a short while ago from the wounds he suffered. The other man aboard with him is being transferred to a hospital ship as we speak."

The mood in the camp became sombre. Other than the four men who drowned on the way to shore the first day, they hadn't lost another man. "I guess it was bound to happen sooner or later," said Harry. "I'd say we've been lucky so far. With all those shells and bombs landing around us, the whole lot of us making it off the beach in one piece is slim at best."

"That's for sure. By the looks of the casualties heading to the hospital ships, I get the feeling the boys on the front lines aren't having an easy go of it," said Malcolm.

One man passed a mug of tea to the officer. "Join us in a toast, sir? Here's to Davey. One of the finest Welshmen it was my pleasure to have known."

Everyone, including the lieutenant, raised their mugs. "To Davey."

Two days later, the company had one of its most productive days since landing. They worked late into the evening, with the last shift completing its task just before midnight. Even with heavy shelling by the Germans, the company unloaded over 2,960,000 pounds of supplies.

By June 30th, the 999th Port Operating Company was responsible for unloading a total of 13,859 tons (27million pounds) of equipment, rations, medical supplies, and ammunition.[96]

June was now history, and the new month began. Conditions remained the same for the men unloading the ships off the coast. The number of boats arriving with supplies slowed considerably during the first six days of July. By the evening of July 6, the company unloaded a little under 2300 tons from only five ships.[97]

Since landing on Normandy beach, the men who kept the war effort moving with the equipment they unloaded watched as hundreds of bombers passed overhead. Their job was to drop thousands of tons of bombs on the city of Caen and other strategic locations.

Despite all the explosives dropped on the Germans, their guns continued shelling the beaches and shipping areas. There were times when the explosions on the beach area continued through the night. The almost-complete air superiority of the Allies meant that enemy aircraft hadn't been harassing them or even been seen overhead since June 30.

On July 6, exactly one month since the British landed on Sword Beach, sporadic shelling of the area continued throughout the day. Shells would rain down for ten or fifteen minutes, stop for a few hours, then begin again, continuing intermittently for half an hour. Then the whole thing would start again. Even though the harassment went on throughout the day, Harry and the company's men continued to work through it.

The crew also began to load items back on the ships for the return trip to England. The first load consisted of forty tons of artillery shell casings.

After supper, the men, who completed their ship's discharge by 1415 hours, relaxed in the bivouac area.

"It looks like our boys finally gained the upper hand in the air. We ain't had an air raid drill since the end of June," said one of the men.

"Now you've gone and done it, 'aven't you," grumbled another.

"Done what?"

"Gone and jinxed us, that's what."

Another chimed in, "I sure wish someone could do something about the bloody shelling. It's getting on my nerves. Never know when one of them buggers is coming our way. They tell me it's the one you don't hear that kills you, but the ones you do hear still scare the devil out of you."

"Be glad you ain't down the road in Caen a few miles. We thought the blitz in Hull was bad. I've never seen so many planes in my life. There won't be a building standing by the time our boys go in there," said Harry.

Most of the men lived in places affected by the German bombing. They grew quiet as each conjured up memories and recollections of the attacks they witnessed in the early stages of the war.

A new shift began unloading the last ship of the day around 1950 hours. Harry left the group in the bivouac area and wandered down to the water's edge, and thought about his family as he gazed out to sea. Harry had received several letters since sending off his coded message, indicating all was well on the home front. Still, he was concerned about having left a pregnant wife and how she was getting on.

The enemy shelling tapered off during the supper hour, and then at 2115, it started again with a vengeance. It was one of the biggest barrages Harry witnessed, even worse than the day Davey Adams died when his coaster suffered a direct hit.

Explosions were going off all around him. Harry made his way up the beach to the nearest slit trench. Neither the officers nor men on the beaches knew for sure where they were being shelled from. The German 88s had a range of over ten kilometres, and for all they knew, they might have been coming from as far away as Caen.[98]

Forty minutes after the first shells hit, the bombardment finished. Harry rose from the slit trench and looked toward the bivouac area. There appeared to be over a dozen wounded men in the spot he had been before the shelling began. The final tally of injured soldiers was fifteen.[99]

Rushing to the area, he was shocked by the sight of so many wounded. It was sheer luck that not one man was dead. Medics were already on scene, treating the casualties. Most of the wounds were the result of shrapnel from the exploding shell. Harry figured every one of the men would have died right where they sat if it had landed any closer.

The smell of blood and explosives filled the air. Even in the darkness, bloodstains on the men's uniforms and dark, bloody patches were visible in the sand. The sounds of men screaming and moaning were a challenge to block out. The medics treated the disabled, then transferred them to aid stations.

Having survived the worst incident the company sustained, Harry took a deep sigh and offered up a small prayer of thanks.

The following morning he was back on duty unloading more equipment, and again the beach was subjected to enemy shelling. This time there were no casualties. There were no ships to unpack; instead, they continued to load an additional forty tons of scrap onto the boat they had begun filling the previous day.

The summer solstice came and went, and the sun was now setting almost the same time as it did the day they landed on the beach.

As the sun continued its downward arc to the sea, the sky grew darker as hundreds of Halifax and Lancaster bombers again appeared on a heading toward Caen. Moments later, Harry and the men on the beach listened as thousands of pounds of ordinance struck the city. The bombing went on for what seemed to be hours, and before the last bombers flew overhead, the first ones were heading in the opposite direction as they made their way back to England.

The 999th Port Operating Company was back in full operation on July 8, unloading 870 tons of supplies. It also marked the last day they were harassed by enemy shelling while on the Normandy Beaches.[100] It seemed that the Luftwaffe wanted one more crack at them as the enemy planes bombed the beaches in a final swan song that evening. It was more of a nuisance than anything, and the attack failed to injure anyone.

During July, they unloaded thirty-two ships, which carried over fifteen thousand tons (30 million pounds) of equipment and supplies from England.

On July 31, the company began moving to other areas to continue the job of supplying the troops. They were now responsible for dispatching the ordnance, medical supplies, and other equipment to the forces on the front lines.

There is an old saying attributed to Napoleon Bonaparte: "An army marches on its stomach." This is true during any war. With the advance of mechanized warfare, the other necessities the modern military needed to continue to move forward were petrol, oil, and lubricants (POL), and tons of ammunition.

During August, Harry and the men of his company kept busy moving the supplies forward. The POL was critical to keep trucks, tanks, and equipment running, and his unit shipped out almost four times as many tons of POL as it did ammunition.

As the calendar's pages continued to advance, Harry felt this job was no different from working on the docks back home. As the months wore on, the Port Operating Company continued to unload and ship thousands of tons of equipment.

When Harry first saw the city that had been bombed while still working on the coast, he couldn't imagine what it was like for the residents. He shook his head in sadness as he looked over the barren landscape of a once beautiful city. It was the home of William the Conqueror, who invaded England 900 years before. There was hardly a building standing. Sadly, he became aware that thousands of civilians never evacuated the city and died during those bombing raids despite being repeatedly warned.

Thinking back to the night he watched the hundreds of planes making their bombing runs on the city, he once again prayed that everyone at home was safe. He knew from his wife's letters that Hull hadn't been bombed at all since he arrived in France. It was the new threat that began just after D-Day that worried him. The

Germans were unleashing a new weapon. Fortunately for the Hilyard family, most of the V-1 flying bombs were dropping on the southeast corner of Britain, from Cambridge to Southampton

"Who knows where those buggers will drop," Harry said to Malcolm after reading about them in a copy of the *Times.*

Now that the Allies had overtaken the city of Caen, they finally had access to its port. Before they began unloading ships, they needed to clear the rubble from destroyed buildings on the docks as well as the roads leading to them. Cleaning up the sites became the responsibility of the Port Operations Company. During the cleanup period, there were times when German prisoners were ordered to help, while armed soldiers kept a sharp eye on them as they assisted with the unloading chores.

The size of the ships coming into Caen was limited by the depth of the canal at Ouistreham. In addition, the number of vessels was constrained by how many they could get in during high tides. After the Allies captured Dieppe, they began advancing quickly. This meant Caen was not used to its full extent for general cargo, except to keep troops based in Normandy fully supplied. Coasters continued to be used to transfer equipment up to Antwerp and to return surplus supplies to Britain. Goods like shell casings were salvaged and shipped home to be recycled into munitions.[101]

Finally, in November, Harry and the men moved from their canvas tents into billets, a welcomed improvement in conditions.

Shortly after being settled in their billets, the company was once again on the move. Their destination was Vaucelles, only 40 kilometres west of where they landed on D-Day.

Near the end of November, Harry received a parcel from home. Inside were a few treats his wife and relatives put together for him, including some boiled sweets, mint candies, and hand-knitted gloves. "My Marie has always been a whiz with knitting needles," Harry told his mates.

There were also magazines and handmade cards from the children. Along with the package came the great news: he was again a proud father of another daughter.

Each day he had waited eagerly for the mail. So when he finally received the good news, he was overjoyed. "Malcolm, I've got another daughter. Marie says both she and my little girl are doing just great."

"Good for you, 'Arry. I couldn't be appier for ya. What's her name?"

"Marie. After my wife. We thought I would be getting another son. His name would have been Michael."

His wife's letter went on to say:

She was born at home, Harry. Nan and Betty were here to help me. When they told me we had another little girl, I was quite shocked. They asked me what her name was. Well, we never thought it would be a girl, did we? Only had a boy's name picked out, didn't we? Nan and Betty realized we were unprepared for another little girl because we hadn't thought of a name.
It was Nan that said, "I think you should give her your name. She is your gift."

Christmas Day 1944 wasn't a holiday for the men of the 999th Port Operating Company. Knowing his family was safe in England and that he would have a new daughter waiting for him was gift enough for Harry.

Harry was still in France, along with 395 other men from the company. Even though the war in Europe was further away, they loaded and unloaded ships for the entire month.

"Merry Christmas, men," said one of the duty officers as they started the day at their usual time of 0730. "Since it's Christmas, you only have to put in a half-day. So you can knock off at noon today."

While generally pleased with the idea, one of the men couldn't help himself and piped up, "Thank you very much, Uncle Scrooge."

The duty officer left without comment.

One of the other men then quoted the final line from Charles Dickens' *A Christmas Carol*. In the high-pitched voice of a child, he said, "God Bless us, Everyone!"

"Well said, Tiny Tim," laughed Malcolm.

When the laughter died down, the men wished each other a Merry Christmas and talked about how much they missed home. They went on about the incredible feasts they would have next Christmas and spoke longingly about memories of Christmases past.

"I don't imagine the Germans will put up the white flag for Christmas, will they?" Malcolm said.

By December 31, 1944, the 999th Port Operating Company had discharged over 106 thousand tons of equipment and supplies. During the same period, they loaded more than ten thousand tons for return to England. FN

As the war continued through Belgium, Holland, and eventually into Germany, Harry continued his job as a stevedore. It wasn't the kind of heroic story history books would spend a significant amount of time telling, but his role was vital.

Since the Germans' final day of shelling while still on the beaches, they had not been subjected to further enemy attacks. There were no attempted escapes by the prisoners assisting with the unloading process. Their captives appeared resigned to the fact that they were out of the war. Many seemed happy not to be standing in the way of the juggernaut heading on a one-way course to Germany. The officers felt that many of their prisoners wondered about the German war machine. Would Germany have been more successful if they had a similar amount of equipment rolling through the ports day after day?

In February, Harry saw his beautiful daughter for the first time. It was only a picture, but he treasured it. The picture showed his wife, a proud-looking mother dressed in her most beautiful outfit, including a fur shawl Harry had bought for her one Christmas when money wasn't as tight.

Marie Hildyard and Harry's daughter, Marie.

His daughter Marie was propped on a chest, looking nice and warm in a knit coat, complete with hood and leggings with built-in booties. Baby Marie appeared content. Her mother clutched her close with one hand while the other held on to his daughter's tiny fingers.

To the proud father, his daughter was a thing of beauty. He was positive her eyes were looking directly at him.

He tucked the photograph in his battle dress pocket close to his heart and vowed, "I'll keep you right here next to my heart until we get a chance to meet."

To him, it was a sacred vow. It would stay there until he finally made it home. With the Allies now crossing into Germany, he knew the picture shouldn't have to remain in his pocket much longer.

During the first months of 1945, Harry`s company began moving eastward through France and Belgium. In early May, the 999th Port Operating Company moved from Diksmuide, Belgium, to Oosterhout, Holland.

That is where Harry was on May 7, 1945. At 5:10 that evening, the church bells began ringing, and air raid sirens began to wail. In Oosterhout, located in the middle of Holland, people flooded onto the streets. Celebrations immediately started throughout the city.

"Do you hear that, 'Arry?"

"I sure do, Malcolm. Do you think it means what I think it does?"

"It sure does, boys," said Joel Bywood, their section commander. "It's official. The war is over. I'm so happy you boys made it out of this mess in one piece. The same can't be said for a lot of lads who were in the thick of things. Never forget about your contributions. Old Monte wouldn't have put the Germans on the run if you men hadn't kept our boys supplied with all the bullets and bombs. So call it a day and go celebrate. You've earned it."

Then he added, "tomorrow there will be a parade. Most of you will be in it. Unless told first thing in the morning you are on duty, you'll be expected to be there. Behave yourselves tonight."

Harry was excited by the prospect of heading home to meet his new daughter. The excitement was short-lived. After being given the day off following the celebrations, the 999th returned to work like any other day. With civilian help, they checked and loaded equipment and supplies designated for the locals who had endured horrible conditions for the past five-and-a-half years. For the next nine months, Harry worked with the army to help bring order back to Europe and feed thousands of starving civilians and refugees.

Even though the hostilities had ended, the Port Operating Company stayed busy. Stevedores were now supervising civilians as they unloaded the ships.

As the months dragged on, the company continued their work, although they did enjoy recreational and training days. They also unloaded and sorted lorries full of enemy equipment.

"Why the hell do we get stuck doing all this work, 'Arry?" Malcolm asked.

"I don't know, Malcolm. I guess somebody has to. At least we're getting a paycheck and three squares a day, unlike the poor buggers we've seen scrounging through our garbage piles."

At the end of August, for reasons unknown to Harry and his mates, the civilians decided to strike. The soldiers carried on despite the interruption.

Harry and other members of his unit were finally moved into some billets. Even here, they were required to clean them out of any enemy equipment before they could move in.

In October, Harry was posted to Hamburg, Germany. The city was in shambles. Harry was positive it had suffered far worse than his hometown of Hull.

The order for Harry to report to company headquarters finally came.

Geoge Henry Hildyard is standing on the left. He never could get the beret to sit right.

"We're sending you back to England, Hildyard," said the duty officer.

"Does this mean I get to go home?"

"Not quite yet. We need men to help with the clean-up of London. It's still a bloody mess."

It was a much smoother trip home when Harry crossed the channel than when he came across sixteen months earlier on a small coaster.

From November until February 1946, Harry helped return parts of England to some normalcy. Once again, he spent his nights in a tent, this time in Purfleet.

While he and others like him worked either on the docks in Tilbury or helped clear away the rubble from various parts of London, they also helped repair hospitals and schools.

In a letter home to his family just after Christmas of 1945, Harry wrote:

> Well, at least they gave us Christmas day off this year. Not like last year when we worked right through. It shouldn't be much longer now. They are starting to send some of the boys home. I do wish they had called my number. I could have been home for the holidays with you and the children. I'm sure it won't be long now.
>
> They won't give us any extended leave, so I guess I won't be home until I'm home for good. Give Margarett and Bernie and little Marie a big hug for me. I'm sorry I wasn't there to help celebrate her first birthday.

Harry's military career came to an end as they slowly mustered him out of active service in February 1946. In March, he received a medical inspection. The doctor declared him physically fit. Then another transfer took place, this time to the 1043 Port Engineering Company.

In Greenford, Middlesex, England, on May 1, 1946, he received his notification of imminent release. Once again, he was transferred, this time back to his original unit of the 999th Port Operating Company, to receive his discharge.

"Permission to speak," said Harry to the major, who was filling out the papers.

"Go ahead."

"Well, sir, it seems like there's a hell of a lot more papers to be filled out now that I'm leaving the Army than there was when I signed up."

"No doubt about it, Hildyard. Throughout the war, there were daily memos and lists of the tonnages we unloaded each day. On top of that, there were intelligence reports, diaries, and casualty reports on every man jack in the army. I don't know how we found time to fight the bloody Germans. That's the army for you," laughed the major as he gave a final stamp to Harry's release form.

Harry's name, rank, and address were listed on the form. It showed he was a Timber Tallyman previous to enlisting and received a trade qualification in the Royal Engineers as a Stevedore II. In the line enquiring about his military conduct, the major wrote a single word: *Exemplary*.

The testimonial from the major made Harry proud. The major told him that his report would be going into Harry's permanent record. "Based on what I've heard and seen, your service has been exemplary. You have proven to be a trustworthy, reliable, and hard-working soldier. By all accounts, both sober and conscientious. I see you have passed your D II trades qualification as well, so I'm also making a note of that."

"Thank you, sir. I hope to use my trade qualification to get a good job when I get home."

The last thing the major said after Harry gave him a final crisp salute was, "You should be proud of the work you did. You'll be heading home to a place fit for heroes."

When Harry finally met his daughter for the first time, she was sixteen months old. He fell in love with the bundle of joy as soon as he saw her.

Part Four

The last statement the officer made couldn't have been further from the truth. A year after defeating the Germans, England in general, and Kingston on Hull in particular, were still skeletons of their former selves. Bombed and burned-out buildings were everywhere. The rubble of these buildings was gone, carted away. Now there were only empty spaces of land where the once-proud structures stood. The schools around Hull stayed closed for an entire year after the war. They only started up again shortly before Harry returned.

One of Harry and his extended family's blessings is that all the men returned unscathed from their military service. This was quite a feat, considering how many families lost loved ones. Some families had lost two or more brothers during the five-and-a-half years of war. There were also entire civilian families killed during bombing campaigns throughout England, Europe, and other locations the tentacles of war touched.

While home on leave in February 1944, Harry took his son Bernard over to Hollis Brothers. At the time, Bernie was still only thirteen years old and wasn't eligible to start work. Bernie returned to Hollis in July after turning fourteen. To get there, he used his dad's Hercules bicycle. Harry originally purchased the bike when he began working at Hollis years before the war. At the time, the Hercules Cycle and Motor Company claimed it was the largest bicycle company in the world.[102]

As he had been introduced at the factory by his father in February, Bernie had no trouble being hired as an apprentice joiner (carpenter) when he returned after his fourteenth birthday. He was working his way towards becoming a fully qualified tradesman by the time Harry returned home. Bernie trained for the next seven years before getting his journeyman's ticket. He would work with Hollis Brothers for the rest of his career.

Harry hoped that having served his country and with his son working for the company, he might have a leg up when applying for his old job. The problem was that men who had been discharged much earlier than Harry filled most of the available positions he was trained for.

Harry ended up being like thousands of other veterans who lost their place in line while fighting for their country. It was especially difficult for those remaining in Europe as the Allies tried to put the broken pieces back together again.

For the men who returned after Europe's occupation, the welcome home the Major alluded to never materialized. "If this is how they treat the heroes, I'm sure as hell glad we didn't lose the war," said Harry to his family at supper one night.

The comment came after another day of reporting to the docks with hopes of getting a day or two worth of work. Employment on the docks became casual labour. The men would turn up each day, having walked a long way to get to the wharves, then gather around the foreman each morning with the hope of being chosen to help unload the ships. The foreman would stand on his soapbox to select his crew, an unfortunate situation for many, as it tended to lead to favouritism.

Those not chosen would turn on their heels and head for home. Although there is no sign of the word in any dictionary, slang or otherwise, the process had a unique terminology. For some reason, it was known as "Dinting." The wives would watch their menfolk head out each morning. They knew he hadn't been one of the chosen ones when he turned up at home early.

Of course, no work meant no pay. A lot of families weren't merely working poor; they were destitute.

Many women would begin making bread early in the morning. Then, having mixed the flour and yeast in the pancheon (a large bread-making bowl), they would take it to the pawnshop to swap for money. During the day, the dough would rise. When the man of the house came home at the end of the day after managing to get work and with some money in his pocket, the women would go back to the pawnshop. After paying a fee, they would retrieve the bowl of risen dough, head home, and continue to bake the bread.

Harry's life was challenging throughout the 1950s and 1960s. Besides the lack of work, it seemed that the unions would call a strike just as there was an opportunity for more work. The strike might only last a day or a week, and no work meant no pay.

Although Harry was a qualified driver in the military, he hadn't owned a motorcar before the war and never did. On more than one occasion, he was overheard saying, "Why do we need a car? Work is just a couple of blocks away, and we can take the bus or train anywhere else we need to get to."

One day in the 1960s, Bernie showed up in a small car he had purchased. Before long, Harry thought it wasn't so bad after all, especially when his son would show after work for tea and to share an evening with his mom and dad.

"How would you two like to take a ride out to the country?" he would ask.

Harry never needed to be asked a second time, saying to his wife, "Come on, Marie, grab yer coat; Bernie's going to take us for a drive in the country." In a matter of minutes, they were on the road. They took great pleasure in stopping at a country pub for a pint on the way home from their outings.

Remembrance Day was never a national holiday in England. Workers may have stopped to observe two minutes of silence at eleven in the morning, after which it was straight back to work. At home on November 11, Marie recalls that they would always listen to the ceremonies on the radio in the early years. When they finally purchased a television, they would watch broadcasts of the services.

One of Harry's indulgences following the war was the soccer pools. He would faithfully fill out his forms, then on Saturday at teatime, he would check to see how his teams faired in vain hope his picks would make him a winner.

On occasion, he would take a trip to the local racetrack to watch the horses. Other than the football pools, he was never much of a gambler. However, he occasionally liked to put a quid or two on a horse that caught his fancy.

Never one for reading novels or fictional accounts of stories, Harry would buy two papers each day. Then he would spend the evening reading them from the headline straight through to the last page.

Harry Hildyard with Marie on her wedding day.

In 1962, when she was just eighteen, the young girl, born while Harry was serving in France, got married. What if Harry had been on the Duck boat instead of Davey, or if he had been amongst those injured when the shells hit the beach? How would the family have managed without him? Who would have been there to walk his beautiful daughter down the aisle?

Marie told me, "I cannot remember going without. They must have been amazing at covering their problems up and away from me," she said. "After all, everyone was going through the same thing. I grew up having a happy life."

One of the happiest memories Marie has to this day was a couple of trips to the seashore. They would make their way to the coast by bus to stay in a caravan on the beach. "How mom managed to get all that gear for a week on a bus is a wonder. I thought I had died and gone to heaven," she said.

Like many World War II veterans, Harry never graduated from high school. In those days, the three Rs were still the backbone of any education. Harry was a whiz at numbers. When his daughter was first married, he helped her understand the intricacies of both money and payments. She took those lessons from her father to heart throughout her married life, "hence no debt," she told me.

Harry finally earned his Docker's book (regular work) in the late 1960s. By then, jobs were drying up on the docks because the age of containers had arrived. These encapsulated units allowed for more efficient cargo movement and less pilferage, and over time, fewer and fewer dock workers were required.

With full-time employment, and all their children gone, Harry and Marie had the opportunity to travel. They surprised their children by announcing they were taking a trip to the continent. Travelling abroad meant all the hassles associated with international travel. These included passports and currency for the places they would visit, something neither had needed before.

To the amazement and shock of the entire family, they went on a coach tour through France, Belgium, and Holland and even managed to make it home. "Bet the kids never thought we would make it back in one piece," laughed Harry as they arrived home from their first trip. "Hell, I made it home the first time I was there. At least this time, there was no one dropping bombs and trying to kill me."

They did so well and enjoyed themselves so much during the first trip that they ended up doing more travelling over the next few years. One of their excursions included Italy, Austria, and Spain.

Harry Hildyard at the Colosseum in Rome.

When not travelling abroad, they enjoyed excursions to the south of England, especially London and some seaside resorts such as Torquay and Bournemouth. In addition, Harry and Marie embarked on numerous holiday trips around Britain by both coach and train.

Harry took an early retirement package in 1969 at the age of sixty-four. His golden handshake came to about £5000. At the time, it would have been in the range of 11,700 Canadian dollars, considered a staggering amount. This would be worth approximately $65,000, or little more than a year's wages in today's numbers.

When he celebrated his sixty-fifth birthday, Harry's new life was good. "I have a loving wife and family, and we've money in the bank for the first time in our lives. And soon we'll be on another trip to Spain. What more could a bloke ask?"

Three months after their Spanish vacation, on June 4, 1971, Harry unexpectedly passed away, just two-and-a-half months shy of his 66th birthday.

"He was gone. Just like that. No goodbyes to anyone," said Marie. Fortunately, the money from his golden handshake left his wife secure for years to come.

When we met, Marie still had images of her father watching as the beaches became littered with the hulks and remnants of landing craft. In her mind, she saw her father sitting on Sword Beach as British Commandos rushed ashore.

"What If"

Think about Harry's "What If" moments throughout his life. There were numerous times the incredible memories of a young girl growing up with a loving family might never have happened.

Harry survived the Spanish flu following World War I. There was the chance of being killed by an errant bomb in Hull during the Blitz. Perhaps he could have been mortally injured while helping to keep the supplies flowing for the troops fighting in Europe. A slight misstep at any one of those moments in time might not have changed the world. Indeed, it would have changed life for those who loved him for the man he was.

Harry never told his family how lucky he considered himself to have survived the war. Did he ever wonder what might have happened if it was his coaster the waves swamped as it came ashore on the evening of D-Day? If so, would he have been another of those who drowned?

Did he consider himself lucky to have been on the DUKW when the German Shell hit the ship he was unloading, killing Sapper David Adams? The British D-Day cemetery in Hermanville-sur-Mer is where David is buried. He was thirty-three years old. Engraved on his cross is the inscription, "Beyond the Shadows, but always in the sunshine of our memories."

What about the night fifteen men were shredded by shrapnel from the German shell? If he had been in the bivouac area at that moment, would he have been one of those maimed or perhaps killed by the bomb?

These were a few of Harry's "What if" moments during the war.

For Marie, many emotions surfaced in the process of telling her father's story. None more so than when she removed the picture from the family album and found the photograph her mother sent to her father in February 1945. Most people intend to record important information on the back of a photo, perhaps a note to document the people or location in the image. In this case, it was the handwriting on the back that brought tears to Marie's eyes: "Love to Daddy."

Back of the photo of Marie and her mother from 1945.

The other item recorded was the exact date the picture was developed: February 5, 1945, when baby Marie was less than three months old.

Marie tried to imagine what her father would have felt when he received the picture he carried around in his breast pocket for the rest of his time in the service. It was only three words, but they must have meant so much to the man who was so far from home. She wondered why she never saw the back of the picture before. "What If" she hadn't decided to send a copy to me? She may never have seen it. Who looks at the back of a picture in an album anyway?

Finally, I think back again to the email I received from Marie after my return from France and the not-so-chance encounter we had in a parking lot above the beach.

"What If' her dad was on the beach on D-Day morning? His story would likely be different. He would have had a front-row seat to history. Perhaps he might have witnessed Lord Lovat being piped ashore by Piper Bill Millin. He played "Highland Laddie," one of Lovat's favourite tunes as they disembarked from the landing craft. He would also have witnessed the Free French Army as it once again set their feet on native soil if he had been watching from the beach as young Marie imagined.[103]

Now, seventy-five years after the invasion, it seems more apparent what Marie's dad did during the war. Marie was only 22 when her father passed away and may have taken his tale about D-Day more literally than intended. With the help of the war diaries and personal stories, she finally knows more about her father's role during World War II, seventy-five years ago.

I feel the conclusion of Marie`s first email bears repeating. It is one of the reasons I wrote this book. It is why I want to continue writing about the anonymous men and women whose stories have not yet been made known. In her email, she said:

> As a final "What If," what if we had never met? This email would not have been written. My father would have just continued being my father, sitting in the corner reading his newspaper, and I would have forgotten the turning points in his life...
> ...and his story would never have been told.

Royal Artillery
Charlie Nelson

Duke of Wellington
Ralph Nelson

East Yorkshire
Ted Nelson

The Nelson Brothers
DUNKIRK

Inspired by memories of Marie Brown

May 1940

Whel Marie and I finished working on her father's story, she passed on another about her father-in-law. She told me she could not give me chapter and verse but assured me the following information is factual. She is the only living person who heard the story directly from her father-in-law and his brothers about their evacuation from Dunkirk. They talked about their experiences with fantastic humour, and their yarn telling was outstanding. Later in life, these brothers maintained a powerful bond. They saw each other regularly and made their homes in Hull, not far from each other.

Marie's husband's grandfather, Pietro, was one of three brothers who left Italy in the early 1900s. Life was hard in the small village on the toe of Italy, where they lived. Like thousands of people around the world, their dream of living in America was about to become a reality. His older brothers left Italy on an earlier ship, and Pietro Malvasio would follow.

The passenger ship young Pietro travelled on, docked in Hull, England. However, as an immigrant heading to the United States, he needed to get to Liverpool before continuing his journey.

How they met isn't known, but Pietro was introduced to a young woman along the way, and his plans changed. Pietro married Martha Panitzke, the daughter of another immigrant. Martha's father was of German-Polish descent and became a police constable with the Hull Constabulary after becoming a naturalized citizen.

The young couple became the proud parents of three young boys: Charles Peter (Marie's future father-in-law), James Ralph, and Edward Lewis, all of them excellent English names.

In 1913, after their third son's birth, Pietro left for America, intending to find his brothers and a place to live for his family. Martha and their sons would soon follow.

Whether because of the First World War or events family members never knew about, Martha and her sons never left England. Family folklore says there were tickets purchased for the boys but never used, and Martha had to raise her three sons on her own. As the 1920s arrived, life became incredibly hard for a single mother with three sons. The two younger ones spent time in one of the many homes in England dedicated to caring for orphans and children of destitute families.

As they grew older, one of the only opportunities for regular employment for these young men meant joining the armed services. Charles (Charlie) joined the Royal Artillery, James the Duke of Wellington's Regiment, and Edward (Ted) the East Yorkshire Regiment.

When they signed up for the service, the three men decided they needed an English-sounding surname. After discussing the options, they settled on Nelson. In their minds, there wasn't a nobler name for a military man. No one in the family is sure if they ever made the change officially, but they became known as the Nelson Brothers from the day they enlisted.

All three served for several years, and each of the boys spent part of their military career abroad. In the mid-1930s, they all left the service, found civilian jobs, and settled into life in the working class, but each remained a reservist.

The outbreak of World War II altered the brother's plans. The army recalled reservists, and it wasn't long before each of the brothers returned to active service. As experienced soldiers, they were among the first to go to France as part of the British Expeditionary Force (BEF).

Charlie already had two young children; his third child, Peter, was born in January 1940. Like Marie Hildyard, Charlie's wife raised three young children on her own as her husband went off to war.

James Nelson and the Duke of Wellington's Regiment went to France shortly after England declared war on Germany. Until the end of the "phoney war," they never saw much action until the Germans invaded the Low Countries and France. The Germans finally invaded, and as they advanced with their Blitzkrieg, the Allies began to retreat. James Nelson's Regiment acted as the rear guard for the retreat to Dunkirk.[104]

Edward's East Yorkshire Regiment was part of the 2nd Battalion, 3rd Infantry Division. They were also in France as part of the BEF. When the time came, they were amongst the regiments who fell back to the beaches in good order. They would be one of the last Battalions to leave Dunkirk when the Germans attacked.[105]

The third brother, Charlie, served with the Royal Artillery. Like other regiments, they were forced to depart when the Germans made their assault on the allied forces. This resulted in the retreat to Dunkirk.

On May 24, one of the major "What If" moments of World War II included Adolf Hitler hitting the stop button on the advance of the German panzer columns. Why did he issue the halt order? No one knows for sure, but Hitler had fought in that part of France in World War I, and he worried that the terrain was too muddy for tanks. After the panzers halted, the Luftwaffe planned to pulverize the defenders until the slower-moving German infantry divisions caught up to finish the job.[106]

There was speculation but no proof that Hitler's halt order resulted from a belief that Great Britain would be more willing to make peace, especially if England's pride was not wounded by seeing its army surrender.

In the end, no matter how much planning or how many ships or how well the RAF could have protected the skies over the evacuation area, none of it would have mattered if Hitler had continued with his Blitzkrieg toward the channel.

The evacuation of Dunkirk is considered a miracle. The initial plan called for the removal of approximately 45,000 men from the beaches over two days. However, due to a series of "What

If" moments, Operation Dynamo was a complete success. They evacuated over 338,000 men, 140,000 being French, Belgian, and Polish forces, between May 27 and June 4, 1940.

The men who pulled out from Dunkirk were picked up by Navy vessels and hundreds of civilian fishing and pleasure boats, skippered by ordinary citizens. "What If" they hadn't answered the call for help?

One of the other miracles during the evacuations was a reunion. Initially, it may not have been a "What If" moment, but more like a "What Are the Chances" moment.

With the Nelson Brothers in different regiments in three different parts of France and Belgium, what are the chances these three could find each other amidst the throng of over 300,000 men? The odds of the three brothers meeting up were on the low side of less than impossible, but somehow they did. One can only imagine how shocked they must have been.

Charlie saw Ralph's regiment as they entered the area. After asking his sergeant's permission to look for his brother, he searched the ranks as they filed onto the beach.

Charlie ran down the line of soldiers, calling for his brother. "Ralph! Ralph! Has anyone seen Ralph Nelson?" he called out. Finally, from the middle of the column, he heard his brother call back.

"Charlie. Over here!" he called as he stepped out of line. They embraced each other, thrilled to see the other was alive and gave each other a hearty slap on the back.

"Have you seen Teddy?" Charlie asked.

"No, the Snappers (the nickname for the East Yorkshire Regiment)[107] haven't shown up yet. I heard they were bringing up the rear."

"Ain't that just like our little brother? Always the last one to show up for anything."

"Well, just be glad he's not with the 51st Highlanders. I've heard word that the whole lot of them have been ordered to stay behind.

They are supposed to slow down the advance to make sure the rest of us get the hell out of here."[108]

The brothers kept looking for the East Yorkshire Regiment. Their patience finally paid off when they began to arrive on the beach. This time, both brothers ran up the line to see if they could find their little brother.

Ralph spotted him and called out, "Over here, Charlie! I found him!"

Together for the first time since leaving England with the BEF, each was relieved to find their brothers were alive. During their reunion, German planes made strafing and bombing runs on the causeway, where the larger ships were loading the troops. Throughout their lives, the brothers teased each other incessantly. Even on this occasion, no matter how desperate or foreboding, nothing would keep them from harassing or pestering one another.

"What the 'ell are you two silly buggers doing standing around here?" Teddy asked.

"Just waiting for you, little brother," said Charlie.

"Just wanted to stop by to say you look like bloody hell. Not quite the sharp-dressed soldier I would expect from a man in the East Yorkies. Helmet all askew, no spit and polish on them boots," chided Ralph.

"Well, if that's all you've got, the both of you can just sod off," laughed Teddy.

With their humorous banter finished, they knew it was time to get serious. There were thousands of men on the beaches. Many were in long columns waiting for evacuation onto the larger ships.

"We've got to get ourselves out of here. It looks like the queue to get on the bigger boats is pretty long. I'm not waiting in a bloody plodding lineup while the Germans keep shooting at me. I've got to get back to Alice and the kids in one piece. I'm going to swim out to one of those boats getting close to shore. I suggest you two do the same thing."

It was a gut-wrenching experience for all of them, but they knew it was time to leave. After a quick slap on the back and a few words of encouragement and wishes of good luck, they dropped their gear and prepared to go. Charlie was the most capable swimmer and said he would head past the boat closest to shore while the other two swam toward it.

"Whoever gets home first, make sure you let Mum know we were all together here," was the last thing Charlie shouted as he headed into the water.

"Let's go, little brother," said Ralph.

Ralph didn't realize Teddy hadn't made it into the water until he climbed aboard the small pleasure boat. When he realized Teddy wasn't with him, he scanned the beach where several bodies lay scattered about. Ralph couldn't tell if one of them was his little brother. He wanted to head back, but the boat's owner told him they needed to leave immediately, and if he went back, he wouldn't be waiting for him.

Taking another look at the figures lying prone in the sand, Ralph feared his brother might be dead. He realized if anything happened to Charlie, he'd be the last one to be able to look after the families at home. Ralph sat on the deck of the small thirty-foot boat with his head in his hands and cried for his brother as the overloaded little boat turned and headed back to England.

Teddy didn't die on the beach. Instead, he suffered a wound to his neck. When the Germans found him, they took him to one of their surgeons, who operated on Teddy and saved his life. This was the good news. The bad news was that he would spend the rest of the war in a POW camp at one of the many Stalags throughout Germany. It would be months before his family found out he survived, only to become a POW.

Edward (Teddy) was one of the 40,000 men who never made it back to England until after the war. Unfortunately, the list of casualties included 11,000 men who died and never made it home. The retreating forces left their heavy equipment, including tanks, on the beaches and roadways of Dunkirk.

Both Peter and Ralph made it home in June. They told their mother about the ordeal and how they were with Teddy on the beach but were afraid he didn't make it back. They didn't know for sure if he had been killed or captured.

In November 1940, Martha died in an explosion at the boarding house where she lived, without knowing her son's fate. The following year, on the anniversary of her death, Peter and Ralph placed a notice in the paper:

Nelson. Martha. *In loving memory of our dear mother, who passed away on November 14, 1940. Not forgotten by her sons Charlie, Ralph, "Teddy" (POW), also daughter-in-law Alice and Grandchildren.*

After the war, the brothers held a joyous reunion. When they gathered together on family occasions, their stories would have everyone in attendance bursting with laughter until tears rolled down people's faces. Their prime sense of humour was laughing at themselves and not taking things seriously.

There are other "What If" moments for the Nelson Brothers and their families after surviving the Miracle of Dunkirk. Those "What Ifs" all have names. They are the children of the three Nelson Brothers who would not have come into this world if they hadn't survived those terrifying moments less than fifty miles from England.

There is also the question, "Does everything happen for a reason?" Charlie was the only brother who had children at the time of Dunkirk, including his youngest son Peter. What would have happened to his young son if Charlie had been among those killed as the BEF made their way from Dunkirk during the evacuation? He would have grown up fatherless, and his life may have taken a different path.

In 1944, Charlie's wife gave birth to a fourth child, a young girl named Patricia. This is significant because if it wasn't for Patricia, the picture of Marie Hildyard in her wedding dress in 1962 might never have been taken. She probably would have married, but perhaps not that day or to the man her father would walk her down the aisle to be with.

Patricia Nelson and young Marie Hildyard grew up as best friends. They would play in empty fields, places where factories had stood before the war. Sometimes they played inside the bombed-out church where children shouldn't have been hanging about. Patricia and Marie would have a marvellous time standing at the front of the empty church. Below the remnants of its arched ceiling in the chancel area, both pretended they were on a grand stage at a London Theatre.

As they grew older, their thoughts turned to boys, and it wasn't long until Marie fell in love with Patricia's older brother, Peter. So was it destiny, fate, or something meant to be that led to the picture of Marie and her father on her wedding day in 1962?

Marie said to me, "There's a what-if. If Charlie hadn't survived Dunkirk, that picture wouldn't have been taken. Patricia, the youngest, wouldn't have been born in 1944. She wouldn't have gone to the same school as me. I wouldn't have met her brother. We probably wouldn't have married and produced my children and six grandchildren, and so the 'What Ifs' make themselves known yet again."

John (Jack) Hedley Hamilton
"A" COMPANY 7ᵀᴴ PLATOON,
THE ROYAL WINNIPEG RIFLES

Inspired by stories from Anne Hamilton and her father's journals.

Part One

T his story is about Jack Hamilton, who also served with The
Royal Winnipeg Rifles. Both he and Gerry Levers were from
Manitoba, but their backgrounds and life stories are different.
Gerry came from the city. Jack was from the town of Brandon, 133
miles due west of Winnipeg.

I met Jack's daughter, Anne, during my pilgrimage to Normandy.
It was not Anne's first visit to the beach where her dad landed so
many years before. Jack and Anne never walked those beaches
together, even though her dad returned to Normandy twice. The
first time was for the 30th anniversary of the landings. The second
was for the 45th anniversary of the invasion with 75 members of
the "Little Black Devils" in 1990. This tour would take the participants from Normandy to Nijmegen in the Netherlands on the
border of Germany. He did such a fabulous job telling his stories
that she must have felt he was right beside her when she attended
the 75th anniversary.

Anne travelled to England before the rest of our group
from Canada. When the time came to meet us in France, she took a
ferry from Portsmouth and crossed the Channel just like her father
did 75 years earlier. Ferries are not known traditionally for luxury
accommodation. Still, the trip was far better than what her father
would have experienced. The weather was not perfect, but the
ferry was not subjected to the half-gale-force winds the thousands
of ships encountered on their voyage to Normandy on the night of
June 5, 1944.

I had told the group heading to Normandy about my project,
Our Fathers' Footsteps. Before I left for France, Anne contacted me
to find out more about the book's concept. I explained the premise

and asked if she would be interested in having her father's story included.

After checking with her brother, they agreed to provide information for his story. It is an honour to try and do Jack's life justice. My impression of this man is that he went willingly into harm's way and made a difference when he returned. Prior to Remembrance Day in 2012, Jack was quoted in the *Westman Journal*, a Brandon newspaper. *"Just don't call me a hero,"* he laughed. Later in the same interview, he said to the reporter, *"Getting a letter from the Department of National Defense was the best thing that ever happened. The Army made a man out of me."*[109]

He was one of the average young Canadian men who headed off to war. At the time, he was not officially considered a man by the government, nor would he be until he reached the age of twenty-one. After the war, Jack was a man who kept a promise he made after the heat of battle. He returned to Canada and helped to make his nation a better place. The following is Jack's story.

John Hedley Hamilton was born in Brandon, Manitoba, on August 30, 1922, the eldest of five children. Like many boys named John when they were born, it seemed everyone was soon calling him Jack.

His father immigrated to Canada in 1907 from Neilston, Renfrewshire, Scotland. His mother was a local girl who lived seven miles southwest of Brandon.

Between 1921 and 1941, Brandon, the second largest town in Manitoba, averaged just over 16,500 residents. This small city in the middle of the Canadian prairie is only 80 miles from the Saskatchewan border.

1924 saw an improvement in the economy of Jack's hometown, which had languished, much like the rest of the country, after World War I. In 1926 Jack's father moved the family to another property in town and relocated his dairy business to their home.

Slowly, times improved for the family. However, one afternoon before Jack was old enough to go to school, his father took a nasty fall, resulting in broken ribs. With his dad laid up, Jack was forced into being the man of the house, with multiple responsibilities, including milking the cows. In addition, he now had a baby sister, and his mom was expecting another child in 1929.

Fortunately, Jack's father wasn't off the job for long. Time off is a luxury you cannot afford when running your own business, so it wasn't long until his father returned to work. Bound up tightly to help his ribs heal during the cold winter, Jack had no choice but to travel with his father. His job was to turn the key on and off as required on their Model T Ford truck. His father had difficulty managing this simple task with his broken ribs, meaning that Jack needed to assist with deliveries.

In the mid-1930s, the City of Brandon fell on hard times. They never declared bankruptcy, but the Province did step in to control the finances. Any money the city council wanted to spend required approval by the Province's oversight board. Another hardship for the town came in the summer of 1937. At that time, 4,000 transients lived there, and the city felt obliged to feed these people twice a day.[110]

In 1934, Jack's mom gave birth to the last of her five children. His father managed to keep them all fed. However, this meant twelve-year-old Jack's responsibilities increased around the home and family business. It may have been these obligations that began to put the chip on his shoulder that he confessed to carrying for years.

Jack admitted many times he wasn't an outstanding student. He never really liked school and even ended up repeating the tenth grade. He never did graduate, something he would come to regret later.

During school, he got his first paying job. He began delivering newspapers during his lunch hour for the *Brandon Sun*, often not returning to class until 1:30. He was still providing papers when Britain's Prime Minister Chamberlain declared, "Peace for our Time." The foreboding headlines meant that Jack sold all his extra papers to earn some extra money. He made sure to look after his regular customers on his four-block route, ensuring they still got the dailies they paid for.

Jack began working as an office boy for the Canada Credit Bureau in 1939. In September, Jack bought one of the *Sun* papers. The front page was dedicated to stories about Canada's declaration of war on Germany. By early 1940, there was not enough work at the credit bureau to keep Jack employed. His boss felt he was a good worker with strong ethics, so he recommended him for a job with the Olympia Candy Company.

The company changed its name and focus in the early 1940s, shortly after Jack began working there. They were now a full-fledged food distribution company called Olympia Wholesale. Between April 1940 and October 1942, he worked there in a variety of positions.

While he worked hard, for some reason, he always felt he was hard-done-by. Perhaps seeing his friends and fellow workers head off to war began to weigh on his conscience. He had obligations at home, and the extra paycheck helped put food on the table for the family of seven.

The company's business picked up. They were soon supplying the army bases throughout Manitoba with a variety of products. Jack's workload also increased. With the change in focus, Jack needed to work harder to keep up with the demand because so many men were going off to join the army.

He didn't know why. Perhaps it was the conflicting obligations he felt about home, work, and the war. Whatever it was, the chip on his shoulder kept getting bigger. He had no problem telling anyone who would listen, "I'm a self-proclaimed miserable son of a gun."

Jack wasn't one to get into fights, but if challenged, he wouldn't have backed down or walked away from it; even so, he was never sure if he possessed what it would take to be a soldier.

In April 1942, the Canadian government held a plebiscite about conscription; eighty percent of Canadians outside Quebec voted in favour. Eventually, only 12,908 conscripted soldiers were sent abroad to fight. A tiny number compared with the hundreds of thousands of Canadian volunteers, including French Canadians that ended up overseas. Only 2,463 of those conscripted soldiers reached the front lines before Germany surrendered in May 1945.[111] The majority of draftees did their military service in Canada.

Part Two

In October 1942, Jack received a letter from the Department of National Defence telling him that the army was still looking for good men. It may have been the excuse he needed. A few days later, Jack went to sign up. After volunteering his services at the recruiting centre, he was sent to Fort Osborne Barracks in Winnipeg for his medical.

Following the First World War, the main building of Fort Osborne became a convalescent hospital for men returning from the war. At the outbreak of World War II, the southern barracks became home to the Winnipeg Grenadiers, the 2nd Battalion Princess Patricia's Canadian Light Infantry (2 PPCLI) and C Battery of the Royal Canadian Horse Artillery.[112]

Jack passed his medical tests without issue: no flat feet, no heart problems, and no concerns with his eyesight. He was a healthy, fit twenty-year-old Canadian, just the kind of man the army needed. After completing his medical, he was told to report back on January 2, 1943.

Jack Hamilton in uniform, 1943.

Jack's posting was with the first battalion of The Royal Winnipeg Rifles, the Little Black Devils. Inscribed in Latin on their regimental regalia are *Hosti Acie Nominate — named by the enemy in battle.* According to the regimental history, the regiment was still known as the 90th Rifles during the Northwest Rebellion.

After the Battle of Fish Creek in 1885, a captured Metis fighter said, "The Red Coats we know, but who are those little black devils?" During the battle, the 90th battalion wore the traditional green colour of a rifle regiment. From a distance, the Metis fighters thought the enemy were wearing black uniforms.

The Royal Winnipeg Rifles hat badge.

From then on, the 90th Rifles became informally known by the unofficial nickname, "Little Black Devils." This name followed the regiment as it became The Winnipeg Rifles and, eventually, The Royal Winnipeg Rifles. Their hat badge proudly displayed the regiment's battle honours, including the South African War, Ypres, the Somme, Vimy Ridge and Passchendaele.[113]

During the period between his medical and reporting for duty, Jack continued to work at Olympia Wholesale. By the time he was ready to report, he was the head country shipper. They liked Jack's work and assured him his job would be waiting for him when he returned from the war.

In December 1942, Jack celebrated Christmas with his family as usual. Since the declaration of war in September 1939, the headlines of the Brandon newspaper told grim stories about the war. The news improved with reports of the Russians winning their first victory against the Germans at Stalingrad. Around the same time, news came about the allies landing in North Africa under the command of a general named Dwight D. Eisenhower. It seemed the allies were slowly closing in on Rommel's Afrika Korps.

"Maybe this horrible war will be over before you have to go," offered his mom.

"Not likely," answered Jack. "There's still a heck of a lot of Germans occupying countries all over Europe. Our boys took a pretty good beating at Dieppe, and I'm sure they'll be wanting to make another push to the continent one of these days."

While Jack counted inventory at the end of his final shift just before the New Year, a few men he worked with, Bill Wright, Elmer Kidd, and Jack Anderson, stopped to wish him well.

"Keep your head down over there, Jack," warned Elmer.

"Don't go trying to be a hero," said Bill.

"Yeah," Elmer continued, "There was a piece in the paper the other day about all the Canucks who won the Victoria Cross in the last war. Almost half of those heroes received their medals after they were dead. Like Wright and Anderson said, keep your head down and don't go playing the hero."

"Okay, I won't," Jack said.

"Won't what?" Bill asked, "Keep your head down or try not to be a hero?"

"Both," he assured them.

"One other thing. Don't go getting yourself a commission, and become an officer," advised Elmer.

"Why not? I'd make pretty good officer material," Jack replied.

"Because the enemy always tries to shoot officers first. If they kill enough of them, their troops have no leadership, and everything goes to hell," laughed Jack Anderson.

"Remember what happened on the Plains of Abraham. Both generals died of their wounds. We might all be speaking French today if Montcalm hadn't died. N'est-ce pas? Didn't they teach you anything in school?" Elmer asked.

"Yeah, yeah, I learned about the history of Canada in school." History was one of Jack's favourite subjects. "The bottom line is, don't be an officer; don't be a hero and keep my head down. Any other advice from you, gentlemen? Don't forget, even if they do make me an officer, it's not like they're gonna make me a general."

"Who knows, Jack? Enough guys ahead of you get knocked off; they might make you an officer, it's what, only five or six more steps 'til you're a General," laughed Bill.

This was Jack's last conversation with his co-workers before heading off to basic training. On January 2, he reported for duty at Fort Osborne.

Fort Osborne Barracks, Manitoba.

During his first weeks of training, Jack still carried the giant chip on his shoulder he'd been carrying around for years, but it didn't take long for drill sergeants to knock it off.

After a couple of weeks at Camp Osborne, Jack was shipped to Debert, Nova Scotia, to begin training with the rest of his regiment. With the chip on his shoulder gone, it wasn't long before he was getting along with everyone. His hard work earned him a promotion to the rank of lance corporal. Besides learning all aspects of being a rifleman, Jack was also trained to use the two-inch mortars each platoon carried to support the men.

Belgian 2-inch mortar team in training, Wales, United Kingdom.

Around this time, Jack realized that the army had already made a man out of him. He hadn't come from a military family. However, it seemed that the army life agreed with him, and he began to think joining up was the best thing to happen to him.

Both his old boss at the Credit Bureau and the owners of Olympia Wholesale told Jack he was a good worker. Yet, it was the training staff at Debert who seemed to recognize something special in him that no one else ever had. One afternoon during basic training, he was ordered to report to headquarters. Somewhat nervous, Jack reported to his commanding officer as instructed. Approaching the office, Jack wondered what he might have done wrong and whether he might be about to catch hell.

Nothing could have prepared him for what was about to take place.

Upon arriving, he was told to take a seat and to wait for the major.

"Major? Darn, I really must have put my foot in something," he thought as he nervously waited while standing at ease in the clerk's office.

When told to go in, Jack marched smartly to the officer's desk, came to a halt, and offered a proper salute.

"As you were, Hamilton; have a seat."

"Can't be too bad," he thought. "If I'm about to get my backside chewed, he wouldn't be offering me a seat."

As he sat, Jack saw what he figured was his personnel file lying on the desk. When he settled into the chair, he decided to nip whatever problem there was in the bud.

"Excuse me, sir. Am I in some kind of trouble?"

"Quite the contrary," offered the major. "Your test scores have been outstanding. Therefore, we want to send you to an Officer Training course. The recommendation has come from your platoon commander. What do you think of that, Hamilton?"

Jack was dumbfounded. Moments earlier, he was worried about catching hell for God knows what; now they were sending him to Officers School.

He heard himself say, "It sounds terrific, sir. Thank you." Meanwhile, the little voice in his head reminded him of what Elmer teased him about before he left: "They shoot the officers first."

"Don't thank me just yet. Let's see how you make out over there. That will be all. See the orderly for your travel papers, and good luck."

Jack stood, gave the major a regulation salute, executed a precise about-face and marched out of his office. As he opened the door, he turned back and said, "Thank you again, sir."

Jack made the trip to the OTC and couldn't wait to tell his family back home. When he arrived, he found the accommodations were undoubtedly much better than those in Debert. All the men training to be officers referred to the place as "Camp Utopia." The training was a tough go, but he loved it and spent the month of June taking courses on being a proper officer.

In the end, there was one minor issue. Jack never could figure out why they hadn't spotted the problem before they sent him off to OTC and wasted everyone's time in the first place. The day he met with the major, his file was on the man's desk. It turned out his failure to graduate from high school came back to ruin his chances of being promoted.

Disappointed by not becoming an officer, he was afraid the chip he'd had on his shoulder might begin to fester and grow again. The thing is, Jack was turning out to be the kind of man he wanted to be. He shrugged off his disappointment and returned to train with the rest of the LBDs in Debert.

"According to Elmer, I might just have dodged a bullet," he said to himself.

In August, he was granted embarkation leave in advance of departing by ship to England, and Jack used his furlough to head home by train. He spent his days visiting with family and friends. During his leave, Jack also made time to see his grandfather on the farm. Finally, he made a point of going to see his old co-workers at the Olympia Wholesale Co.

He was now only a month shy of turning twenty-one. Dressed in his uniform, he joined his former co-workers for a drink at the Prince Edward Hotel

Barroom of the Prince Edward Hotel, 1913.

In 1912, a new hotel was built in Brandon. Supposedly, some of the brick for the façade of the Prince Edward Hotel was imported from Belgium. As the construction phase neared completion, the hotel owners ordered interior furnishings from Europe. They failed to make it to Brandon. Local folklore claims some of the hotel's furnishings were lost off Newfoundland's coast when the Titanic sank in April 1912.[114]

Although the interior furnishings may not have come from Europe, the Prince Edward Hotel was still an upscale place for the City of Brandon. Jack, in uniform, never did buy a drink that night.

When his pals heard he wouldn't become an officer, Elmer said, "Consider yourself lucky, Jackie boy. Remember what we told you about the enemy. Put pips on your shoulders, and the enemy will put a bullet right there." Then he gave Jack a stiff poke in the middle of his forehead.

The Queen Mary pulled out of Halifax at the end of August and headed to New York to pick up thousands of additional troops. On the 27th, she pulled out of New York for the trip across the pond. Jack quietly observed his twenty-first birthday on board the Queen Mary with over 15,000 troops and 900 crew members.

When launched in 1934, the owner-built ship of the White Star, Cunard Line, was designed to carry 1,957 passengers and a crew of 1,174.[115] Close to 13,000 troops, plus doctors and nurses, were stuffed into every nook and cranny of the ship, making conditions crowded, to say the least. Except for the crew and medical personnel, everyone aboard was on their way to fight with the Allies. The comfort of the troops was not the army's concern. Realizing that many of their families may have come to Canada in steerage class accommodations years ago was not lost on these men heading toward Europe. There weren't sufficient bunks for all aboard. This meant each man was required to sleep on the open deck at least once throughout the journey.

Living on the Canadian prairies with the ability to see for miles in any direction did not prepare Jack for the ocean's vastness. Days passed with endless seas extending to the horizons.

Many of the men on board were afraid they might cross the path of a Wolfpack of German submarines. During one of his nights spent on deck, Jack spoke to one of the Queen Mary's crew members.

"Aren't you afraid of U-Boats? We don't even have a convoy with us. We're all alone in the middle of the ocean."

The crewman looked at him. Then, in a calm voice, he replied, "We're too fast for the U-Boats. Mary here can do better than twenty-eight knots an hour. She got as high as thirty-two knots when she did her speed trials."[116]

"What the heck is a knot?" Jack asked.

"Well, for you land-lubbers, it would be over thirty-two miles an hour, making us about twice as fast as a German U-Boat running on the surface. If the U-Boat is submerged, she might be able to get up to eight or nine miles an hour."[117]

"Besides," explained the crewman, "we do all kinds of zigging and zagging on our trips. Those subs will never catch us — Mark my words, but I guess you should be glad you weren't on our trip in December."

"Why's that?"

"Rogue wave damn near capsized us when we were 700 miles from Scotland. Someone told me the wave crested at ninety feet."[118]

"Thanks a lot. I'm sure I'll sleep much better, knowing that."

The ship travelled north toward Iceland then skirted the coast of Ireland. They finally arrived at the port of Gourock, Scotland, the day after Jack's birthday on August 31. Other than being overly crowded, it was an uneventful trip. There were no submarines sighted, nor were there any big waves threatening to capsize them.

Jack hardly had time to get his land legs back before loading onto a troop train bound for Camp Whitley in southern England, close to 500 miles away.

He wasn't at Whitley long and would soon be with the battalion at Gosport. Before joining the rest of Manitoba's men, Jack was given a small taste of what England's people faced during the blitz.

When the air-raid sirens sounded, he followed the men out of the barracks and joined them as they jumped into the slit trenches.

Over the following nine months, Jack and the rest of the RWRs moved from camp to camp for various training exercises. Most were within sixty miles of Southampton, the same place thousands of men would be concentrated in preparation for heading across the channel to France in May 1944.

One of Jack's most memorable moments was spending a night immersed in the history of England. While on a scheme (battle-field exercise), the regiment bivouacked at a centuries-old estate on the Salisbury Plains, dating back to the sixteen hundreds. He was in his glory. Jack knew about the wars fought in England over the years, including the War of the Roses, the Hundred Years War, and the English Civil War involving Oliver Cromwell in the middle of the 1600s. So when he heard he might be bunking down inside of a home where Cromwell himself might once have visited, he was in awe.

Unfortunately, all the furniture and pictures in the elegant two-story building had been removed. Still, it was easy for Jack to imagine the splendour of the place in its heyday. The men spent the night sleeping on straw-filled sacks on top of the finely polished oak floors. Jack had loved learning about those wars in school. Never in his wildest imagination did he see himself camping out in the middle of historic battlefields or sleeping in the home of a man who helped shape England's history.

During one of their schemes on the Salisbury Plain, a pal of his took a memorable picture. Jack inscribed a note on the back and sent it to his mom and dad in Brandon.

While out on their route marches, laden with full packs, mortars, and rifles, they would occasionally get a twenty-min-ute break. During his respite from the hike, Jack would pull out his cigarette papers and fine-cut tobacco, roll a smoke, and then light it up using his flint lighter. Its brass fuel tank could use the fuel from any of their vehicles. By the time he finished rolling his

Jack Hamilton, somewhere in England, January 31, 1944.

Somewhere in England 1943.
Out on a scheme doing our own
"mess tin cooking." Given rations
for this meal consisted of raw
cod fish, raw potatoe, raw
carrot, raw turnip, cooking fat,
bread & marg. and a piece of
pie for desert.

From left to right: Rfn. Hamilton,
Brandon man.; Rfn. Bandwick J.,
Brandon man; F/Cpl. Sakolinsky J.,
Brandon man.

Had a lot of fun on this
platoon scheme - lasted about
a week - a real picnic!!

cigarette and smoking it, they were ready to head off on the next part of the grind.

Since his arrival in England, Jack's mom and dad had regularly sent him half-pound tins of tobacco and two hundred cigarette papers. It was a cheap treat, only costing his folks a couple of dollars plus shipping. Of course, they sent other gifts of the edible kind at the same time. "There's nothing like the taste of home," he would tell his chums as he shared the home baking. When their care packages arrived from Canada, the others would reciprocate by sharing their bounty.

Occasionally he received a carton of two hundred "Tailor Made" cigarettes. These came directly from the manufacturer for the same two dollars his folks were paying back home for the loose paper and tobacco. There were no taxes on these cigarettes, which accounted for the low price. The catch was that they were only available to overseas service personnel.[119]

Besides route marches, target practice with all types of weapons, and map-reading exercises, the unit practiced house clearing exercises in Southampton's burned and bombed-out parts. "Get used to the smell of charred wood, gentlemen. It won't be the worst thing you encounter over there. You can be sure of that."

The instructor for the house-to-house fighting drills made it clear: "If you break a leg, you won't be of help to anyone. At least here, the streets are clear and void of rubble. Where we're going, the walls of buildings and homes will be spread across the entire road. There may also still be shelling in the towns and villages, leaving debris on the streets. Enemy and civilian casualties may also hinder your progress.

It was hard work, but each man understood that once they were in Europe, the lessons they learned in England could save not only their lives but those of their pals.

It wasn't all training for war while Jack was in England. When it came time for leave, Jack made a four-hundred-mile trip up to Paisley, Scotland, to visit his aunt and uncle, John and Margaret Hamilton.

Jack had never met his dad's brother's children because his father immigrated to Canada thirty years earlier. Still, there was a tight connection with the ancestral family. His aunt and uncle encouraged Jack to bring friends during his furloughs, so he often took several buddies. During those visits, a marvellous time was enjoyed by all. They would skate at the rink, go to a movie, or tour about in a car as far as the family's limited amount of petrol would allow.

Several men joined Jack on his journeys to Scotland, including Ray St. John of Prince Albert, Osborne Doak, another Brandonite, Tony Hubert from Dauphin, and Tom Cratty from Rosetown, Saskatchewan. He even took a guy from D Company, Don McIntyre of Regina, because he was Doak's chum. During training, he also made friends with Bob Mitchell from Montreal, who was in B Company. The others never held it against him, and he tagged along on a couple of trips.

Those joining Jack on his trips were grateful to get away from the constant training in the southern part of England. It gave them an appreciation for the historic sites they saw and the magnificent Scottish landscape.

"Don't know when we'll get home once the show starts," said Osborne as they headed back to Southampton after an enjoyable trip to Paisley. "Me and the boys want to thank you for letting us tag along. By the way, your cousin sure is cute. I sure wouldn't mind seeing her again."

"That's just about enough out of you, Doak," laughed Jack. "Keep talking like that, and I'll never take you up there again."

"Well, how about her friend Eileen Houston? She's a looker too," Cratty jested.

"At least she's not related to me."

At the end of May, the regiment left their last camp in England. They marched twenty-six miles in battle order to an area called the New Forest in Cranbury Park in Hiltingbury, England.

None of them were sure this was the actual event they'd been training for, but all the soldiers hoped so. Other regiments, such as the Seaforth Highlanders, the Loyal Edmonton Regiment, and the PPCLI, had been fighting in Italy since they'd landed on Sicily's shores in July 1943. Everyone agreed: "It's our turn to take the fight to those Nazis."

Part Three

June 1 – 5, 1944

These days were, for Jack, much the same as those of Gerry Levers. Both men were in A Company. One of Jack's other recollections was working on a sand table while the company was cut off from the rest of the world. During these exercises, the company officers would outline where they would be attacking, using sticks to make drawings in the sand. Everything was rehearsed and repeated so often that each man would not have to think about his job if the landing didn't go according to the plan. Men would instinctively know what to do, no matter what the circumstances were.

The Royal Winnipeg Rifles, waiting to embark for the invasion of France.

Even during the final briefings, the actual locations they might be landing were not revealed. A straight line represented the imaginary coastline.

"We will land here," the officer would proclaim as he pointed his stick to a point in the sand. "From there, we will head southeast to here." Another X was marked. "Finally, we will turn and head to the west and south. We will join up with the units of the British Army here." One final X was marked. "Then, you can sit down with your counterparts from jolly old England and have yourselves a spot of tea."

The men attempted to relax during their stay in the embarkation camps. Some played cards, some lazed around in groups. For others, there were betting pools. Jack and other soldiers put down some of their remaining English pounds and guessed where they might be heading. There was even a category for "just another exercise." Seeing all the men and equipment in the staging area, Jack wasn't going to put his money on that one.

"Here's five pounds," approximately twenty dollars Canadian in 1944, a great deal of money considering he was only making around $1.50 a day. "Put it all on the Dutch Coast. I figure that's where we're going for sure," he declared as he laid his money down.

With operational secrecy still being maintained, Jack boarded the Llangibby Castle with the rest of A and C Companies, still unsure of their destination.

On the afternoon of the 4th, they knew it was the real thing, but the men were disappointed when told the invasion was on hold for twenty-four hours due to the poor weather. Despite the ship's size, the men on the Llangibby Castle felt the effects of the stormy seas.

"It could be worse," said Jack.

"How do you figure, Hamilton?" Doak asked.

"It could be snowing."

Embarkation on the Llangibby Castle.

They still didn't know where they were going. Those who placed bets on the possibility of it being an exercise were out of the game. Each man was both apprehensive and excited about heading into combat for the first time.

Tom Cratty reminded his pals from the 7th platoon, "Make sure you chaps keep your heads down. They've told us time and again not to stop if someone goes down. However, if you promise to take me back to Paisley when our jobs are done, I might make an exception for you, Jack."

Osborne Doak piped up. "Hey, Jack, just remember I'm from Brandon too. I'd hate to tell the folks back home you didn't help me."

Finally, at 2100 hours on June 5, the Llangibby powered up and headed out to the channel. With the sealed orders for the mission open, they learned the name of the coming scheme. Operation Overlord was underway. The location they were heading for was the beaches on the coast of Normandy. Each squad, section, and company once again went over their tasks. Each section leader had a map detailing their objectives for the first day.

"Any idea who won the pool? I wasn't even close," said Jack after the briefings and hearing letters of encouragement from Eisenhower and Montgomery.

Answers of "Not me" resounded amongst the men.

"I picked France," claimed Cratty, "does that count?"

"I think you needed to be a little more precise," said Tony Hubert.

The sailing was awful. The men became so seasick that no matter how many motion sickness pills were issued, they made little to no difference.

Part Four

June 6, 1944, D-Day

The regiment was in their battle dress uniform as each man geared up for battle. The jacket and pants were both made from khaki-coloured wool. The tunics' shoulder insignias indicated they were with The Royal Winnipeg Rifles. Below it was a small patch telling the world they came from Canada. The other cloth swatch on their shoulders was a French-grey, rectangular patch. It identified the men as part of the 3rd Canadian division.

Jack's gas cape was rolled up on his belt, and he ensured his shell dressings were tucked securely under the netting of his new invasion helmet. Since leaving the encampment area, the men had lived in their uniforms and were well aware they could be in them for at least forty-eight hours or longer once they landed.

Still, the officers made it clear they were to report any effects of being in their uniforms or boots for too long. One of the maladies they needed to watch for was trench foot, a serious condition that caused the feet to blister, become blotchy and then dry out. This would cause the skin to flake and peel off, producing a great deal of pain, numbness, and itching.[120] Jack figured sore feet might be the least of his worries and was more concerned about a bullet to the head.

Since coming aboard the Llangibby Castle, the men unpacked and then repacked their Haversacks (small packs). Jack wanted his kit as balanced as possible. Inside his Haversack were: mess tins, a holdall with his towel, soap and razor, eating utensils, and personal items. In addition, his small pack included the twenty-four-hour ration packs, a cardigan sweater, his beret, an extra pair of boot laces, and a couple of packages of his tailor-made Sweet Caporal smokes. There was also an extra pair of wool socks. Jack often commented, "When the heck are we going to get a chance to change our socks?" Unless they had a completely dry landing, he would want to put on a dry pair as soon as possible. This would help eliminate the dreaded trench foot that historically had caused so much pain and trouble for the soldiers of the Great War.

Back in the staging area, before loading onto the ships, he had organized his large pack. It was stored in the regimental vehicles, which would be landing after the allies established a beachhead. It contained his leather jerkin, a cap comforter, a towel, boot brush, dubbin and polish, a pair of canvas shoes, more boot laces, an extra pair of boots and anklets, more smokes, and a housewife (a sewing kit including needles, a thimble, buttons for their battle dress and shirts, and different threads for darning socks, gloves and other woollen items, all wrapped up in khaki cloth).[121] Inside the other pack was a summer vest, three more pairs of socks, and underwear.

All the other items needed to do battle, including extra ammunition, were attached to his web belt. In the front pouch, Jack and most of the other men carried two additional Bren-gun magazines. This extra ammunition was critical because the platoon's Bren-gun would make up thirty percent of their platoon's firepower. Other items attached to his belt included his spike bayonet and his gas mask respirator.

Jack ensured his water bottle was full. He helped others get their gear up and onto their shoulders and confirmed all their webbing was tightly fastened. Then they took turns securing their entrenching tools. Jack's was a shovel, while others carried small picks slung under the strapping.

Jack's kit weighed between seventy and eighty pounds. Lastly, Jack picked up his Enfield, a bolt action rifle fully loaded with a ten-round magazine. He also carried a bandolier with fifty rounds of rifle ammo. He was now ready to take his position in line for loading on the LCA.

Dawn was breaking as they prepared to load onto their LCA. Standing on deck, Jack beheld the breathtaking image of some of the thousands of cruisers and craft of all kinds. "Hey, boys," he called to the men in his section as they loaded onto the tiny boats. "Isn't that a sight to behold? I'll wager another five quid there's never been anything like it in the history of humanity."

"You're sure loose with your money these last couple of days, Jack," suggested St. John.

Before he could answer, the ropes holding their LCA were slowly released. Their craft, with the entire 7th platoon of A Company, descended to the sea. Just as the little craft settled onto the chop, a wild wave caused their landing craft to smash against the side of their mother ship. The collision knocked out one V8 engine. At this point, Jack was unsure whether they could still make the run to shore with only a single engine. The skipper of the little landing craft persevered, doing a great job getting them on their way toward shore.

Most of the men were hunkered down on the benches. The naval bombardment had ceased. There was no sound other than the engine and the pounding waves against the front ramp. LCTRs began sending salvos of rockets toward the shore, creating a thick mattress of explosions when they hit the landing area. As their LCA advanced, elements from the 12th, 13th, 14th, and 19th field regiments began firing their self-propelled (SP) 105 mm guns directly from their LCTs towards targets on the beaches.

The sounds of shelling would have made it almost impossible to hear what anyone had to say. Rifleman Andy Mutch was deathly ill during their trip across the channel, becoming worse as they circled in the water in preparation for the run-in. Somehow Andy had managed to climb onto the gunwale of the boat.

Shells began exploding around the landing craft. It was already taking on water from the heavy seas crashing over the bow, so the men began removing their helmets and madly started bailing.

Some twelve hundred yards from shore, the boat's skipper finally noticed Mutch and began yelling at him. "Andy! Andy!

Mutch, Rifleman Mutch!" The nearest man stood and tried to get Andy off the side.

Before they could coax him down, the LCA was rocked by a good-sized wave, and when the sea finished washing over the landing craft, Andy had disappeared. The man who stood to grab him screamed in anguish. "We haven't even hit the beach, and we've already lost Andy," he cried.

There was no time for anyone to mourn. They were only a thousand yards from the shore, and machine-gun fire began peppering the boat's front ramp. The boat's pilot tried to get all the power out of the remaining engine. Many on board were positive she would sink before they reached the shore. If they floundered, Jack knew they would be sitting ducks and might have to swim for it. He just prayed he could keep his head above water.

Jack's platoon was set to land on the right flank of A Company. On the far right, the Americans were landing on the beaches of Omaha and Utah. On the Canadians' immediate right, the British were landing on Gold Beach. The Canadians' objective was to join up with British soldiers on the left side of Gold Beach. On the left side of Juno, where the Canadians were landing, another British contingent was assaulting Sword Beach.

The wind and rough seas meant that the LCA operator came toward shore so far to the right he couldn't see the rest of the company. Metal obstacles embedded in the sand prevented their boat from making a dry landing. The skipper, concerned with the mines attached to the barriers, stopped well short of dry land to unload the 7th platoon.

Jack saw the coxswain give the signal, and the ramp lowered. His heart jumped to his throat as the front of the amphibious craft's ramp disengaged and dropped.

The interior doors flung open. From an area near a lighthouse, machine guns began shooting directly into the opening. The first man in line was Rifleman Phillip Genaille of Beaconia, Manitoba. Jack was standing immediately behind him when Genaille took a full burst of bullets to his stomach. He crumpled to the deck, lying motionless where he fell. Jack figured he must have died instantly, though there was no time to check.

Jack and the others leaving the boat needed to step over their fallen friend as they headed toward the end of the ramp. It didn't register with him that he would have been the one with his midsection ripped open if he was first in line.

As he jumped into the waist-high water, he could see an almost continuous arc of the tracer rounds coming from the lighthouse directly in front of where they landed. By some miracle, none of those bullets struck him. After taking only three or four paces on the beach, Jack was knocked unconscious from one of the German mortar shells raining down and exploding all around him.

Jack was left where he fell, while the others made it farther up the beach and managed to take cover behind the dunes. Due to the lack of heavy weapons, the platoon bypassed the lighthouse and began moving inland. 7th Platoon's Lieutenant Battershill advised other forces of the situation. It would be up to them to neutralize the lighthouse position with tanks or self-propelled guns.

With only map references to guide them, it took the 7th platoon hours to catch up with the rest of A Company. Nevertheless, they managed to link up with them before they got to Sainte-Croix-sur-Mer, then moved with the rest of the company toward Creully. When they stopped for the day, the 7th platoon established their defensive position and settled in for the night.

The water had risen during the time Jack was knocked unconscious. One of the reasons for landing when they did was to take advantage of the tides. Low tide arrived in some areas of Normandy coast at 0530 hours and began to rise after that. At some of the beaches, it rose up to three feet per hour. At Omaha Beach, the difference between low and high tide was eighteen feet, with the high-water mark arriving just after ten in the morning.[122] The Allies needed to begin the assaults shortly after low tide so Engineers could blow up the obstacles so the LCAs could make it to shore. In addition, the tide had to be rising for the landing craft to unload troops and depart without danger of being stranded by a receding tide, allowing them to return to the troop carriers for another load.[123]

When the Canadians landed on Juno Beach just before 0800 hours, the water had reached approximately four-and-a-half feet above its low point. Jack figured he must have made it higher onto the beach than some; either that, or he wasn't unconscious long. The chilly water of the channel was up around his knees. If he had been there any longer, he might have drowned while lying motionless.

He came too with the realization he'd been hit on the bridge of his nose by flying shrapnel. In an attempt to cover his wound, Jack removed one of the field dressing bandages from his helmet's netting. He found the dressing too bulky to tie onto his face, and covering it up made it difficult to breathe. He gave up trying to put on the bandage and threw it aside. Rivulets of blood continued to flow from his wound onto his lips, giving him both salty and metallic tastes. The flow of blood continued to drip down his face and onto his uniform.

Landing so far to the right of their intended location meant no medics were around to lend him a hand. Maybe they were too busy to assist a guy who was only knocked out cold with what looked like nothing more than a bloody nose. If they came by while he was unconscious, they might even have thought he was dead. He was sure there were far more pressing cases for them to triage.

When he first became aware of his surroundings, he saw the dead bodies of Canadian Scottish soldiers lying beside their bicycles. They were supposed to have been the support company, landing after Jack's platoon hit the beach. Soldiers who died in the water rolled in and out with each wave as it lapped onto the shore.

The beach's sand ahead of him was stained dark in the places where they fell, and their uniforms were caked with blood and sand. In a fleeting moment, Jack noticed others who had not bled at all. These men must have died instantly, he thought. The bandage Jack threw away was smeared with his own blood. As he looked towards the dunes, he could see hundreds of red poppies.

They reminded him of the poem he learned in school, written by Lieutenant Colonel McRae during World War I. He began to recite the first lines:

"In Flanders Fields, the poppies blow,

Between the crosses row by row."[124]

Someone tapped him on the shoulder. "You okay?" the soldier asked.

"I'm not sure. How do I look?"

"Well, your nose is as big as a plum. It's still bleeding too. Do you think you can make a go of it?

"Hurts like the dickens, but I think I'll be all right," sighed Jack.

"What do you say we get some of these walking wounded and get back into the war?"

They rounded up four other men, all of whom were ambulatory, into a small section. Then, using one of the maps and a compass, they commenced their inland journey. By the time they headed off, they were four to five hours behind the rest of the unit.

As they moved off the beach, one of the others stammered, "Spooky, ain't it?"

"Sure is," Jack replied. "There's a strange calm to the whole area. I hear gunfire and explosions up ahead. Guess that's where we need to go."

As they moved forward, they kept a close eye out for snipers. The entire time, Jack kept wondering if the enemy was lurking close by. Was there movement near the barn on the left? How about the big tree five hundred yards ahead on the right? Was the wind moving the branches, or was someone with a scope taking a bead on them? It was extremely stressful.

They heard the constant sound of mortar fire and shelling just ahead of them throughout the day. By the time they found where it was coming from, the battle was over. Walking through St. Croix-sur-Mer and Banville, they discovered the troops preceding them had liberated both towns. As they made their way forward, they came across a lot of German casualties. There were several wounded men from the regiment who were waiting for medics and stretcher-bearers. The small group finally caught up with the rest of the RWRs on the outskirts of Creully around 2100 hours.

The castle at Creully would eventually become General Montgomery's headquarters. The BBC would also broadcast from this location until July of 1944. Creully was also where Montgomery would entertain Churchill, De Gaulle, Eisenhower, and King George VI when they arrived in Normandy following the invasion.

Being reunited with the men of the regiment was comforting. The hours he and the small section of walking wounded spent on their own was disconcerting.

The regiment's original objective called for them to be farther inland by this point. Unfortunately, the stiff resistance encountered along the way slowed their advance. In the end, the colonel was happy to have reached the second objective assigned to them for the first day of Operation Overlord.

It was a costly day for the RWRs, who suffered over 130 casualties. This number didn't include Jack because his face wound was never officially reported.

When he arrived to join the others, Jack heard how decimated Captain Gowar's B Company was. It shocked him to learn the captain left the beach with only twenty-eight men and four stretcher-bearers. During the first assault wave, Gower landed with an oversize company consisting of over 164 men and twelve sappers.

The battalion was already getting replacements from the 14,000 men who landed throughout the day. At 1800 they were joined by five officers and seventy-eight other ranks. All these men went to help reinforce B Company. Goward learned his company would be used in a limited capacity the following day.

When Jack arrived, he reported to Lieutenant Battershill. "Lance Corporal Hamilton, reporting for duty, sir."

The lieutenant didn't look at him right away but said, "You're a little late, Hamilton, but good to have you here. We were a little late to the party ourselves." Then the officer looked up and saw Jack's face.

"Jesus Christ, Hamilton, your face is a mess. Are you all right?"

"From what the other guys told me, it seems to look worse than it feels."

"Well, it sure does look nasty. Get yourself over to the RAP and get it looked at."

Under the glow of a flashlight, Captain Caldwell, the Medical Officer (MO), dressed his wound. "It's okay, Hamilton. It was just a glancing blow by the looks of it." The diagnosis of the MO would turn out to be incorrect. Over the next month, the wound healed, but a large lump remained.

In the Winnipeg Rifles War Diary, Colonel Meldram made the following remarks:

> It is desired to make a special note of the services rendered to the Bn (Battalion) during the first day of operations by our MO (Captain Robert M Caldwell) and the Bn RAP staff — and the assault sec of 14 Canadian Field Ambulance u/c Capt. Henry Dixon. Not only were the wounded cared for with skill and dispatch, but confidence was developed, and morale increased accordingly. A very special note, too, should be made about the general tone of the Bn during this day called D — 6 Jun 44. Not one man flinched from his task, no matter how tough it was — not one officer failed to display courage and energy and a degree of gallantry. It is thought that the Little Black Devils, by this day's success, has managed to maintain the tradition set by former members. Casualties for the day exceeded 130.[125]

Before bedding down for the night, Jack sat with Osborne Doak and heard what took place with the platoon when they headed inland and how they skirted the lighthouse. "We didn't catch up with the rest of the company for quite a while. They thought we'd all bought it when we didn't show up right away."

As they talked, Jack and Osborne prepared a meal from their 24-hour rations packs. "When you're this hungry, I guess even this slop can taste good," Osborne said to Jack.

"Sorry, Jack," he continued, "I didn't even see you go down. I was so busy trying to stay alive after seeing Genaille go down on the boat, then having to step over the poor kid. Once I hit the beach, I just tried to get to the dunes as quick as I could."

"No worries, Ozzie. I promise I won't tell anyone back home you left me there to die," laughed Jack.

The little bit of rest the company enjoyed was interrupted at 0200 hours when an enemy patrol attempted a counter-attack against the RWR's position.

The Rifles repelled the attack and were able to take nineteen prisoners. They killed a German officer in a volley of fire while he tried to make a run for it. During this short battle, the battalion didn't sustain any casualties.

Part Five

June 7 – 8, 1944

The following two days might be some of the darkest days in the history of The Royal Winnipeg Rifles.

At 0615 hours, Jack and the rest of his company headed toward their first day's objective. Codenamed the Oak Line, near the town of Putot-en-Bessin, they advanced accompanied by a six-pound field gun.

By 1600 hours, the battalion consolidated their position around the town, but sniper fire pestered them throughout the day. At Putot, A Company positioned itself to defend a critical bridge. The crossing would be needed to get heavy tanks and equipment further toward Caen as the invasion force moved forward. The Company's responsibilities included defending the route toward town from any counter-attack.

Road sign near the railway bridge at Putot, 2019

The first German counter-attack began at 2100 with enemy troops and tanks, which Jack and the men of A Company managed to repel.

Shortly after, Sergeant Richardson took Cratty and McIntyre with him, heading out on what they referred to as a termite patrol. They would silently approach enemy positions, inflict as many casualties as possible, then retreat to a predetermined safe location. At one point, they walked right into a German patrol, taking them by surprise; they killed or wounded ten enemy soldiers. The Little Black Devils' sergeant suffered wounds during the short exchange of gunfire. Cratty and McIntyre managed to get the sergeant behind their lines after withdrawing from the fight. At 2200 hours, the regiment was finally brought up to almost full strength when the rest of the reinforcements arrived.

Throughout the rest of the night and into the early morning hours, the Germans continued to fire toward A Company's position in hopes of getting return fire. Any shots fired toward the German lines would allow them to pinpoint the RWRs and launch their counter-attack.

At 0400 hours, Jack's company heard enemy tanks on the other side of the railway. As the sky grew brighter, the Germans began their attack, supported by artillery and mortar fire. First, they attempted to cross the railway bridge directly in front of Jack's platoon. Then, as tanks moved forward, one of A Company's anti-tank groups managed to knock the tracks off one. Next, they made a direct hit on an enemy armoured car. Knocking out these two pieces of equipment stalled the enemy's advance.

Around noon the battalion came under constant sniper fire, and more enemy soldiers began to infiltrate the rest of the town of Putot.

The rest of the day would not improve, and by early afternoon three companies were completely surrounded. Enemy mortar, artillery and MG 42 fire began concentrating on the company's light machine-gun positions. Those taking refuge in slit trenches were taking direct fire from the Germans. The constant salvos meant that not even the Bren-gun carrier could get ammunition to the men, all of whom were running low.

Between returning fire toward the enemy and keeping his head down, Jack again wondered whether he would survive the next ten minutes, let alone see the next day. He'd seen at least a dozen men from the company killed or wounded.

At 1400 hours, with the Battalion surrounded, the Colonel ordered a barrage of shells to be fired, including smoke rounds to cover the area, hoping the companies could return to the regimental lines. As the smoke shells fell, Jack and his section members made a hasty retreat and were among a handful to make it back to the Battalion HQ.

After catching his breath, Jack inquired about some of his friends. "Hey, Ozzie, where are the other guys?"

"I saw Cratty and St. John a few minutes ago trying to get some more ammo. By the looks of it, there isn't a lot available. Haven't seen Tony yet."

Colonel Meldram's War Diary from June 8 included the following statements:

> During the morning, our losses had been heavy, but a great many of the enemy had been accounted for. The enemy attacked with at least two coys on each of our coy positions, with a vast superiority of automatic weapons.
> As soon as the coys had withdrawn, arty (artillery) was brought down on the town, but this did not dislodge the enemy who had now surrounded the BnHQ area by fire.
> The remnants of the Bn held on until 2000 hrs when a barrage, by 4 regts arty, was laid down, starting from the BnHQ and moving up to the South side of the railway.

The Canadian Scottish Regiment put in an
attack on the village supported by the 6th Armd
Regt, which restored the situation. [126]

At 2300 hours, the regiment fell back toward a small farm
on the outskirts of town. Those who managed to retreat through
the smoke during the afternoon were the lucky ones. Company
commanders Hodge and Gower were both missing. Three of the
regiment's companies came close to being wiped out. By day's end,
the RWRs suffered over two hundred casualties, including more
than one hundred wounded. Another one hundred and five were
killed or missing.

Stretcher-bearers worked fearlessly throughout the battle
under direct fire from the enemy. The MO, Captain Caldwell, also
came under fire in the forward positions as he attempted to treat
the wounded.

"Guess we dodged the bullet again today, Jack," said Ray St.
John when they were finally settled in for the night.

Jack was still concerned about the whereabouts of his friend
Tony. "We sure did. I sure hope Tony is all right."

A while later, Jack realized he'd lost his haversack. There was
nothing in it that would be of help to the enemy. His lighter and
Sweet Caporal tobacco and a book of poems by Robbie Burns were
in the kit. He'd received the book as a gift from his Aunt and Uncle
while visiting them in Scotland.

"Don't imagine I'll be needing a book of poetry, but I sure could
use a smoke. Got any, Ray?" Jack asked.

A couple of days later, Jack learned just how bad the situation
turned out for some of his friends. The Germans captured twenty-
four men from the RWRs during the first part of the counter-attack
at Putot. They were all taken to the Chateau D'Audrieu, including
Jack's company commander, Major Hodge.

There were witnesses to the events at the Chateau. They
said that the first prisoners were brought in around two in the

afternoon. Three men at a time were taken into the command post, where they speculated the Canadians were being interrogated. After fifteen minutes, the prisoners were seen being escorted to the woods behind the courtyard. A few moments after being led away, the estate's gardeners heard three evenly spaced single shots, then watched as the German escorts returned without their prisoners.

Entrance to a wooded area where Canadian soldiers, including Major Hodge, were murdered.

According to another witness, at 1430 hours, thirteen more prisoners received short interrogations, then taken to a corner of the grounds. These men were lined up facing the chateau with their hands above their heads. Under the direction of their officer and using automatic pistols, the German soldiers shot their prisoners.

About an hour after the executions, a German officer entered the kitchen, smoking a British cigarette. He looked at one of the staff and said, "English cigarette, good cigarettes, Tommies Kif-Kif, with my revolver, that's who killed them." According to the same witness, the soldiers were ordered to carry out the executions to help morale.[127]

On the same day, many other men captured during the fighting around Putot were escorted back to the German lines for interrogation and disbursement to POW camps. In the early evening, the prisoners were allowed to rest and given food and first aid by their captors. Early the following morning, they were told to take a break at the side of the road. During the rest stop, a German Officer from the 12th SS must have decided taking prisoners was too much work and occupied too many troops. He ordered the men to be executed on the side of the road.

In all, the SS were responsible for the murder of over fifty men of The Royal Winnipeg Rifles.

June 9 – 30, 1944

The entire invasion of Normandy became bogged down after the initial success of the landings. By June 9, the RWRs were still only ten kilometres from the beaches where they landed.

The Royal Winnipeg Rifles, advancing through Normandy.

After the blow they received at Putot, the battalion regrouped a few miles back toward the beaches in an orchard outside the town of Secquiville-en-Bessin, finally settling in after 0500 with their defensive positions established.

Sergeant Cronk moved throughout the defensive lines. "Hamilton, Cratty, you're up. Time for chow."

"Don't have to call us twice," said Jack.

"Make sure you fill up your water bottles at the same time."

Jack and Tom relished their first hot meal since landing in France. "Sure beats those emergency rations," quipped Tom.

"Good to get some clean water too. I emptied mine the first night," explained Jack. "I ate the crackers out of both packs, the chocolate bars, the porridge, candies, and soup too. I didn't even cook it. I ate the stuff right out of the packs while sitting with Ozzie. Oatmeal was a bit dry, though," laughed Jack.

"I bet it was."

When they finished their meal, Sergeant Cronk announced, "I want you and your section to get settled in your defensive positions. Then take turns getting some rest."

"I'm sure that'll be easy," said Tom.

Both men managed to sleep. It wasn't restful, but they fell asleep for a short period.

By 1700 hours, more RWR reinforcements were arriving. The only thing Jack found familiar about them was their shoulder patches. He didn't recognize a single man.

Cratty pointed to one group as they arrived. "Those guys don't even have any entrenching tools. Guess they'll be digging their slit trenches with their helmets."

During the first few days after the company had moved to the orchard, enemy aircraft flew over and dropped anti-personnel (AP) bombs. They were also bombarded by artillery shelling targeting their location.

The men in Jack's platoon were given a chance to go to a well at the farmhouse to clean up for the first time since landing.

After dark, patrols were sent out to locate enemy positions. During these sorties, the men blackened their faces and carefully made their way around the area. Their goal was to establish enemy positions and not to engage with them unless there was no choice.

During the day, German aircraft made survival questionable as the planes strafed the regiment on several occasions. When the company's anti-aircraft guns let loose, Jack and the boys were forced to cover their slit trenches to avoid being injured by shrapnel.

At eight-thirty one morning, Jack witnessed an aerial fight between two RAF Spitfires and two enemy aircraft. The entire platoon cheered when the Spitfires shot down the enemy planes.

By June 15, enough weapons and replacements had arrived to return the regiment pretty well back to full strength. The regimental quartermaster did equipment checks. The armourer made sure all rifles and Bren-guns were in good working order.

The battalion was on the move again, this time to the town of Lasson, less than four miles from where they began. They were now just under five miles from the point where their next major offensive battle would take place — the Carpiquet Airfield.

On June 21, Ray St. John returned to the company area after being up at headquarters. "You boys better look lively. We got a couple of bloody Generals up at HQ."

"You can't be serious," replied Cratty.

"I kid you not. I saw the brass with my own eyes. Two of them. Crerar and Keller."

"Guess they haven't heard it's dangerous out here. What with mortars, 88 mm's, snipers, and Tiger tanks all around, not to mention hundreds of enemy troops. What could go wrong?" Jack wondered aloud.

While sporadic fighting, which killed enemy combatants, occurred at each area the battalion stopped, there also moments for reflection and remembrance. The villagers of various towns were friendly with the soldiers. HQ's officers were concerned that there could be enemy spies amongst them. As a result, interaction with civilians was kept to a minimum.

"Some of those people seem pretty hungry, Sergeant. Would it be okay to share some of our rations?" Jack asked.

"Just make sure you guys keep enough for yourselves."

Shortly after sunrise on the morning of June 27, Major Fulton was approached by several of the villagers of Lasson, who requested permission to tend the graves of the men killed during a night patrol. They were buried the previous day in a short service conducted by Captain Horton, the regimental padre. Major Fulton granted his permission, and by breakfast, flowers covered the graves. The civilians also placed white wooden crosses marked "Died for France" on them.

"Guess these folks do appreciate what we're trying to do here," mused Ray St. John.

Patrols were still taking place each evening. On the night of June 22, Jack and St. John joined Lieutenant Battershill. They moved toward the enemy positions, setting up traps. They hoped they would take the enemy moving into the area by surprise the following day. Nothing came of the ambush, and the patrol returned to camp without having fired a shot.

When possible, on Sundays in late June, Captain Horton held Protestant services, and Captain Steele, the Catholic padre, would conduct services for the Roman Catholic members of the regiment.

"While having these services, it's hard to realize there's a war going on, don't you think, Jack?" Doak said.

"You're right, Ozzie, but it only takes a couple of shells coming in to give you a quick reminder of what we're doing here. I'm amazed at how many of those rounds are duds."

"I wonder if the Germans know?" Jack asked.

No sooner had they finished the conversation when the enemy began shelling the battalion. As the bombs fell, the men jumped into their slit trench, ensuring they kept their heads down. During the barrage, Jack heard a loud thud behind them. When the bombardment ended, they lifted their heads and found themselves staring at an unexploded twenty-pound shell.

The rest of the men in Jack's platoon figured Jack was living a charmed life.

Saturday, July 1, 1944

It was hard for Jack and the other RWRs to believe that they'd been sitting in Southampton just one month ago, getting ready to begin Operation Overlord. Since landing, the regiment experienced more than four hundred casualties, including KIAs, the men murdered by the SS, those taken prisoner, or wounded and transported back to England. Not all the casualties were part of the original assault waves who landed in the LCAs before 0800 on the morning of June 6, but a vast majority were. Some arriving on the evening of June 6, and others from the unit's reserves had also become statistics.

The weather was sunny and warm, but forecasts for the next several days called for clouds and showers. These conditions would be less than ideal to allow air support for their next objective. The third Canadian infantry division needed to capture the Carpiquet airport. They could then make their final push toward the City of Caen. The original overly ambitious plans for Operation Overlord called for British and Canadian forces to be in Caen by the evening of June 6.

On July 2, Captain Horton and Captain Steele once again held church services for the regiment. As forecasted, clouds rolled in, and rain continued throughout the day. During the afternoon, Lieutenant-Colonel Meldrum returned to camp with news. He told his men that the RWRs would be under the 8th Brigade's command for the coming operation. On D-Day, the 8th Brigade landed at the Nan sector of Juno Beach. The Queen's Own Rifles of the 8th came ashore at Bernières-sur-Mer, suffering staggering casualties, losing more men than any other regiment. The Regiment de la Chaudière from Quebec were also involved with the upcoming operation. They were in the follow-up wave to the QORs and the North Shore (New Brunswick) Regiment (NSR). These regiments were also part of the initial waves, landing less than a kilometre away at Saint Aubin-sur-Mer at 0810 hours.

The assault of Carpiquet, code-named Operation Windsor, was set to begin at 0500 on July 4. After breaking camp on July 3, the RWRs moved out in Troop Carrying Vehicles (TCVs) toward their start point (SP).

Jack, accompanied by his corporal and another rifleman were assigned to the 7th platoon's mortar section. It was the first time he was tasked with this position since his training in Nova Scotia. Their job would be to fire high explosives or smoke bombs as required to support his company's advance as they attacked the airfield.

Despite being continually bombed by the allied forces in the preceding days, the Germans were entrenched in well-placed locations. The 12th SS Panzer Regiment had 88mm artillery pieces. Fifteen German tanks had taken up defensive positions in the aerodrome area.

The convoy hadn't travelled far when a shell from an 88 hit the first transport truck. Then the Germans opened fire on the rest of the convoy.

Jack and the men with him hopped over the side of the truck, taking refuge in one of the hedgerows. They were keeping their heads down, but the shelling grew more intense.

While Jack and Corporal Jim Ashcroft were taking cover, an 88mm shell landed right between them. They looked at the projectile — another dud — the second time a shell had failed to detonate when it landed next to him.

Jack snorted, "I guess that one didn't have our names or number on it, Jimmy. I've been thinking ever since we landed, if those bombs don't have your name or number on it, they won't kill you."

Ashcroft looked at Jack, made the sign of the cross, and then looked toward the heavens. He offered a quick *Hail Mary* while Jack recited the *Lord's Prayer*. They knew there would be other men who might not have been so lucky when the shelling began. They were probably lying in ditches somewhere, hugging Mother Earth, saying prayers to any God who would listen.

Colonel Meldrum's war diary at the end of the day on July 3 reported the events as follows:

> D and B Coys reached their areas safely, but the enemy shelled the road near St. Mauvie and caused casualties in A Coy. Sgt. Lavallee, the transport Sgt., was wounded by shrapnel. A Coy continued in the TCVs while C Coy and the BnHQ marching personnel under the 2 IC carried on foot. Both coys came under mortar fire 300 yards west of Marcelet and the whole Bn area was shelled and mortared constantly during the rest of the day and night with more casualties. The Bn was in position at 1745 hrs. At 1920 Brig. Blackader visited the Bn, and at 2100 hrs, the CO gave his orders to the coy commanders. These orders were given while mortar bombs were landing very near to the BnHQ.[128]

Tuesday, July 4, 1944

Operation Windsor would be backed up by an impressive array of guns and equipment, including squadrons of tanks from the Fort Garry Horse and the Sherbrooke Fusiliers. Each squadron consisted of a troop with four tanks. One of these was a Firefly, a Sherman tank fitted with a seventeen-pound anti-tank gun capable of destroying a German Tiger tank.[129]

The operation also included Crocodile Tanks, capable of spewing flame from their barrels like flame throwers. There were also flail tanks, another of the specialty-built tanks designed by

General Percy Hobart. The flail tank could set off mines up to four inches below the surface in a swath nine feet wide. These specialty tanks and others were known as Hobart's Funnies.[130]

Besides the tanks, the advance would be supported by 760 artillery pieces plus the sixteen-inch guns from two British battle-ships stationed off the coast. A total of thirty-six medium machine guns and sixteen two-inch mortars were split between the four regiments.

The artillery barrage began before 0500, almost one month after the ships began shelling the beaches for the initial landings. 2,000-pound shells from the British Navy, sixteen miles away, flew overhead. The 760 artillery pieces were firing at the airport to support the advance. Closer to the line of advance were a large number of self-propelled seventeen- and twenty-five-pound guns. There were also twelve Sherman tanks lined up track to track, laying fire down towards the enemy.

During the initial stages, the supporting barrage landed far too close for C Company's comfort. Fortunately, none of the men were injured by friendly fire.

Major Lockie Fulton, the Officer Commanding D Company, would later remark, *"It was the worst shellfire he ever experienced in the entirety of World War Two."*[131]

The shells passing overhead sounded like nothing Jack had ever heard. Above the roar, he heard Rifleman Davis, one of the other men in his mortar section, yell, "Ever heard anything like this?"

"Not since I've been here, thank goodness. It reminds me of standing between the railway tracks back home and having an express train pass you on both sides."

At 0530 hours, A Company headed off from the SP. Jack's company needed to move through two kilometres of wheat fields and then cross the airfield's open tarmac. D Company's objective was the number one hangar on the left. A Company's destination was the number three hangar on the right. Even before passing the SP, both companies took casualties from constant shelling. The enemy lobbed salvos of mortar and directed artillery fire at the advancing Canadians. It became worse as they approached the edge of the airfield. Afterwards, one padre recalled, "everywhere you could see the pale upturned faces of the dead."[132]

The enemy mortar and artillery batteries had plenty of time to zero in on their target areas in the lead-up to the battle. The Germans knew the airfield was a strategic location for both sides. It was less than a mile from the outskirts of Caen, which meant they were defending it with every weapon available.

Shrapnel from the shells began landing on the tarmac of the airfield. Jack heard Alex Kuipers, one of the men moving forward with him, yell out, "Sounds like a Manitoba hailstorm, eh, Jack?"

Jack agreed with his description but didn't bother to respond. As they began crossing the field, Jack could see the company suffering many more casualties.

B and C Companies followed in reserve after the initial assault. Advancing in a line called abreast formation with their bayonets fixed, they would make their way through the three-foot-high wheat. If they came across a casualty, they would stick the wounded man's rifle in the ground as a marker and then carry on.[133]

Remains of hangars at Carpiquet Airport after Operation Windsor.

Jack and his mortar section made it to the edge of the runway. There was little to no protection next to the plowed section of dirt or grass next to the airstrip. Enemy machine guns began firing from inside the hangars as A Company moved closer to the runway's edge.

This is how Jack described his ordeal at Carpiquet:

The attack went in at daybreak, and we weren't in very far when we started to suffer many casualties. I had the platoon mortar section (2" mortar, two riflemen, and a corporal). We had both HE (High Explosive) and smoke bombs for our mortar. I was on the alert for orders to lay down either one type of fire or the other, but they never came back to us, for we had so many wounded or killed that there was a severe breakdown in communications. We were all hugging mother earth. Our area had no protection on a plowed strip of grass area by the runway of the airport. I prayed I would live to see another day as the mortars exploded and machine-gun fire ripped the earth all around me. At one point, I raised my head to see what kind of protection I could give to the advancing troops.

At the same moment, a German sniper must have been getting a bead on the side of my head. The bullet hit my Sten gun and shattered it. I received two lashes across my right arm and shoulder. It appears the bullet was a coated lead-filled round, and it splintered into pieces, with some fragments hitting the bridge of my nose and into my right eye. There was so much blood gushing from my face and upper arm that the corporal with me figured I was likely dying.

When he realized Jack was conscious, the corporal cried out, "Jesus, Jack, your face is a bloody mess. Thought you were dead for sure when that bullet cracked off your Sten. There's nothing more for you to do here. See if you can make your way back and get yourself looked after. By the looks of it, the attack isn't going quite the way they drew up the plan."

Jack never did find out what happened with the sniper. He shed his equipment and began to work his way back to find aid as he was trained. He couldn't see out of his right eye, but for the most part, his facial wound did not feel any worse than the blow he'd taken on the beach. His damaged arm was a different matter. He figured once the medics treated him, he would again be back in the fight.

When he reached the wheat fields, he came across Lieutenant Jack Mitchel from D Company. The air was rent with steel, with the Germans pouring all they could down onto the RWRs. The Canadian guns were duelling back with all the firepower they could muster.

"You okay, sir?" Jack asked. Then he figured it was a stupid question after seeing the shrapnel sticking out of the lieutenant's right arm.

"Buggers got me with one of their mortars, I think. Got you, too, did they?"

"Yes, sir, this is the second time."

In his memoirs, Jack said:

I don't believe Mitchel and I would ever have got back except for our Regimental Sergeant Major Mickey Austin driving a stretcher-bearer jeep accompanied by G.W. Sinclair from the battalion aid station. They picked up the two of us and rushed back to our RAP.

After the RSM acknowledged the lieutenant, Jack said, "Lance Corporal Hamilton, sergeant major."

"You were on the mortar section this morning, right?"

Jack just nodded. The jeep rushed them back to the RAP, located at the farm where they were two days earlier.

When they arrived, medics covered his face with bandages. Once Jack was ready to leave in the ambulance, the sergeant major stopped to check on him. Jack couldn't see him because of the dressings on his face but recognized his voice. He called out, "You and Sinclair saved our lives. If you hadn't come along in the jeep,

I'm not sure the lieutenant and I would have made it back. Thanks, RSM Austin."

"Glad you made it, Hamilton. You get patched up, and we'll see you back soon, I'm sure. Who knows, we might be in Germany by then, but the way the Germans are fighting here today, it might take us a while."

Then he was on the way to the Bayeux airport, where they were evacuating the worst casualties back to England by plane. Once triaged, the medical staff determined Jack didn't need to be air-lifted and placed him amongst the wounded in the field hospital tent. The medics told him he would be taken back to Bernières as soon as space became available in a transport vehicle.

While waiting to be evacuated to the beach area, someone offered him a half slice of bread. "You bet," he said. "I've been living on rations for a couple of weeks. I'm sure even a half slice of bread will taste terrific."

Along with the bread, he received a half mug of hot malted milk. "You'll want the hot milk to wash down the sulpha tablets," suggested an attendant he couldn't see. "The sulpha will help to stave off infection."

The man was right. He would need something to wash them down. There were two Alka Seltzer-sized tablets. Even with the hot milk, they were a challenge to get down. The attendant also gave Jack a shot of morphine. It kept the pain at bay, and his thoughts began to get foggy as he drifted in and out of consciousness.

The RWRs fell back to the starting point just after 1300 hours on July 4. There had been 132 casualties in all: forty-six men were dead, and eighty-six were wounded. The men from New Brunswick didn't fare any better, suffering the same number of casualties as the boys from Manitoba. German shelling was responsible for the terrible beating Canadian tanks took. The flame-throwing tanks proved useless in getting the enemy out of their pillboxes.[134] During the battle for the airfield, many of the Canadian tanks were destroyed

Major Lockie Fulton went into the airport battle with only one hundred men in D Company, almost thirty men below full company strength. By the time he reached hangar number one, he was down to less than a platoon and was the only officer left. The only other man left above the rank of rifleman was a corporal. All of his other officers and non-commissioned were either killed or wounded.

Throughout the battle, the RWRs were shelled by guns from across the river. The Germans observed the entire action from the towers of the Abbaye D'Ardenne. Sections of this building, less than four kilometres from the Carpiquet airport, date back to the twelfth century.

Major Fulton continued to request that supporting artillery take out the German guns throughout the morning, but it never happened. After returning to the Canadian lines, all he said was, "*It was a mess.*"[135]

Constant enemy shelling and strafing from the air by the Germans on July 5 and 6 inflicted another sixty-two casualties on the RWRs. Then on the evening of July 6, the battalion closed down their BnHQ. The Queens Own Rifles took over their positions as the RWRs pulled out to prepare for operation Charnwood.[136] However, the battle for the Carpiquet airport would not be over until July 9.

While the struggle for Carpiquet was still going on, Jack was resting in a makeshift school-turned hospital. While lying there, he learned that his pal, Tom Cratty, died in the middle of the wheat field on the airport's edge. According to the other men, he was killed in an explosion from a German mortar shell.

Jack was devastated by the news of his friend's death and cried unashamedly. "He was a great guy," he told the man in the cot next to him. "Took him up to Scotland with me a couple of times to visit my aunt and uncle. I think he was smitten with my cousin's friend."

Part Six

Friday, July 7, 1944

Early that evening, Jack was taken by a DUKW boat out to the Dutch hospital ship Queen Wilhelmina for the trip back to England. When he arrived in Southampton, Jack was loaded onto a hospital train destined for Leatherhead, a seventy-mile journey from the coast. This was close to some of the locations he'd trained at during the lead-up to D-Day.

The hospital area suffered from the constant harassment by Hitler's newest weapon, the V-1 Rocket, first launched against London on June 13, 1944, a week after the D-Day landings. During the first V-1 bombing campaign, up to 100 deadly new bombs fell in London every hour. Over 80 days, more than 6,000 people were killed, with over 17,000 injured and a million buildings wrecked or damaged.

As the V-1 approached its target, the buzzing noise could be heard by persons on the ground. Then, at a preset distance, the engine would suddenly cut out, and a momentary silence followed as the bomb plunged toward the ground, followed by an explosion of the 1,870-pound warhead.[137] Locals began referring to the rockets as Doodlebugs and Buzz Bombs.

One of the men with Jack was Nick Shadlock, who knew him from letters his parents sent. Leaning over to Jack, who still had bandages covering his eyes, Nick said, "I know you can't see this, Jack, but there isn't a stitch of glass in the windows of this hospital. Except for the doors, all the openings are covered."

"Must be from all those doodlebugs we heard about on the train."

Jack's introduction to the English hospital was less than favourable. The treatment was rough, and he felt that the doctor possessed no bedside manner. Maybe seeing so many injuries over the past month had sucked away his compassion. At least he was placed in a bed beside his new friend Nick after the doctor's initial examination.

"How are you doing, Jack?" Nick asked.

"I thought it was going to be good here. The first nurse I saw when I got off the boat in Southampton was okay. She took one look at me and called out, *'Oh, Johnny Canuck. You're homeward bound.'* She must have figured my eye was gone because if it was, they would've sent me home PDQ."

"Then we get in here, and I'm not sure what to think. I don't think the doctors at this hospital have much time for us colonials filling their wards. After he removed the bandage, he took one look at my face. Then that cold-blooded limey doctor who doesn't look old enough to have graduated from grade school pulled out the piece of shrapnel stuck in my nose."

"I don't think I screamed any louder when I got hit. I darned near hit the ceiling from the intense pain of his callous act."

"Guess you can't put in a complaint to the medical association," laughed Nick.

"I'm afraid you're probably right."

Jack wasn't the only one screaming during his stay in the hospital. One of the men in his ward was a former tank commander. After being hit by a shell, his tank was incinerated. The explosion threw him from his turret position and killed his entire crew.

During the six nights Jack stayed in the Leatherhead hospital, doodlebugs continued their assault on the area. Having lost his tank crew and surviving the ordeal left the poor commander a panicked wreck. Jack figured the man might have lost his mind. As the doodlebugs came over, the man would scream and cry, waking the entire ward.

It didn't take the army long to send a telegram to Jack's mom and dad, advising them he'd been injured. There was no information on the extent of his injuries. It only said he was reported wounded on July 4.

The first telegram the family received was disturbing. Like thousands of other telegrams sent to families in Canada, information the government clearing sections posted about casualties never seemed complete. The exceptions were the messages from the front lines that confirmed a soldier was killed in action (KIA). His family was unaware of the extent of his injuries and added to the worry about Jack's condition. "How bad has he been hurt?" they wondered. "Has he lost a leg or an arm?" They desperately needed to know what happened to their son.

After six days, Jack was transferred by ambulance for a fifteen-mile trip to the Number 18 Canadian Hospital Unit in Horley to the EENT ward (Ear, Eye, Nose, and Throat) for the start of his repairs.

Jack had confidence in his new doctor the moment he met him. Captain Murdoch would save Jack's right eye. The first thing he said to Jack was, "If you let me, I think I can save your eye." It would take seven operations to remove as much of the shrapnel as possible. Captain Murdoch even escorted Jack for another sixty-mile trip to the Canadian Hospital at Basingstoke.

On July 18, while undergoing one of many operations, his family received another telegram from the Director of Records in Ottawa:

MINISTER OF NATIONAL DEFENCE WISHES TO INFORM YOU THAT H105035 ACTING LANCE CORPORAL JOHN HEDLEY HAMILTON PREVIOUSLY REPORTED WOUNDED IN ACTION NATURE OF WOUNDS NOT REPORTED WOUNDS RIGHT ARM AND RIGHT EYE STOP
WHEN FURTHER INFORMATION BECOMES AVAILABLE IT WILL BE FORWARDED AS SOON AS RECEIVED

Even the second telegram didn't answer his family's questions. The wording was vague. Again they wondered if he'd lost an eye or an arm. Yes, they knew he was alive, but the DND's message kept them wondering how bad his injuries were.

At the hospital in Basingstoke, the doctors experimented with a giant electromagnet to extract ferrous metal from patients. Jack's shrapnel in his eye was lead. The soft metal did not react with the machine because the fragments were non-magnetic.

"Doc, I want you to know how grateful I am for everything you're doing for me. If I was still under the care of the pipsqueak English kid who pulled the metal out of my nose, I'm sure he would have already given up. He'd have pulled out my bad eye and put in a glass one, or I'd be wearing a patch like some mythical pirate," said Jack.

"There'll be no glass eyes or patches for you, Hamilton."

Captain Murdoch travelled to London to see if there was any more to be done for Jack, consulting with doctors who treated soldiers during the battles in North Africa. They cautioned about removing objects deep within the eye, fearful that the patient could lose sight of his eye entirely.

"I know it's not one hundred percent, Jack, and you've told me about still seeing black spots in your field of vision, but it beats the alternative."

"I appreciate everything you've tried. A guy couldn't ask for more. I'm happy and fortunate to have lost only a third of my vision, thanks to you."

When he arrived at the Canadian Hospital in Horley, they operated on Jack's arm. He was fortunate the bone wasn't broken. The other good news was the tendon hadn't been severed. For the operation on his arm, he went into the O.R. at ten in the morning. He regained consciousness at two that afternoon.

Six weeks after the operation, the ward nurse came in one afternoon to remove the bandages. The men in the ward liked her. She was both pleasant and kind to each man, regardless of his rank. The Nursing Sister, from London, Ontario, was one of the few to refer to the men by their first names.

Jack was saddened when the bandages came off. "Oh my, Sister, will you look at this. Nothing but skin and bone. All my muscle is gone."

"It's all right, Jack. You still have your eyesight, and with a little work, you'll be getting the muscle back on your arm in no time. I'm sure of it."

"Well, it still looks like there are flies all over the place from the shrapnel in my eye, but at least I can still see out of it," agreed Jack.

Then he looked directly at the nurse, "Can I tell you something, Sister?"

"What's on your mind, Jack?'

"After I got wounded up in Carpiquet, I made a vow. I swore if I ever made it back to Canada, I'd do everything I could to be a good citizen and give all the help I can to our Vets."

"Good for you, Jack. I'm sure you will."

Jack began occupational therapy (OT) immediately. In September, he transferred from Basingstoke to the Canadian Convalescent Hospital in Farnborough. While recuperating there, he was given hours of physical therapy to strengthen his arm.

Jack spent the next five months getting his arm back in shape. When finally released, he received medical categories for his damaged right eye and another for his arm. The doctors deemed him unfit to return to the RWRs. He was sadly disappointed by his medical classification. The idea of returning to the regiment kept Jack working hard during his recuperation. He kept hoping he would be with his unit when the Germans surrendered.

During his time in the hospital, he'd been keeping track of the regiment's movements. He knew they recently crossed the Rhine with the 7th Brigade and fought a battle near Louisendorf, Germany. He was now sure it was only a matter of time before the war was over.

When he finally returned to duty, he was posted to the Canadian Infantry Reinforcement Unit (CIRU) at camp Aldershot. While there, he was promoted to corporal. Jack was assigned as a store's man, complete with a tradesman's rate of pay.

"This is a lot like the job I did for Olympia Wholesale back in Brandon before the war," he told his sergeant when he reported for duty.

Sitting on his bunk while reading the paper in March of 1945, the area where the shrapnel entered his nose on D-Day morning began to feel odd. He reached up, absently scratching the itch as he continued to read; then, something dropped onto his paper. "What the heck is that?" Leaning forward, taking a closer look, he shouted, "I knew it. I knew it. They didn't get the darn thing out."

His bunkmate was busy writing a letter home but looked up to see what Jack was excited about, then asked, "Didn't get what out?"

"The shrapnel in my nose. It's been there since June 6. It never did feel quite right. Ever since the MO fixed me up, there's been a lump right here," he said as he touched a finger to the spot.

"I thought you just broke your nose at some point, and it never set right."

"No. Look at this." He showed the piece of metal on the newspaper to his pal. He then tore off a portion of the paper to wrap up his memento of D-Day and carefully tucked his souvenir away in his wallet.

In January 1946, eight months after the war, most Canadian troops had already returned home. Before Jack left, he was given one last leave. He headed back to Scotland to say goodbye to his aunt and uncle. They were sad to hear about the fate of the men he brought along on his previous trips.

Cratty, of course, had died the same day Jack was wounded. During the battle of Putot, Tony Hubert became a prisoner. Jack found out that he had managed to escape from a railway car and fought with the Free French Marquis resistance forces until he met up with his regiment. He was with them as they made their push through Belgium and Germany. While working in the CIRU at Aldershot, Jack found out that Tony had also been wounded. He recovered in a hospital north of London before returning home.

On September 6, Don McIntyre was wounded, not far from Montreuil, France, as the regiment advanced toward Calais.

Bob Mitchel was fortunate to have survived, considering the terrible toll B Company took after landing on the beach at Normandy and the Carpiquet airport battle. However, he was also wounded during the push from Holland to Germany on February 16.

Ray St. John was wounded on September 25 on Caen's outskirts as the RWRs attempted to overtake Vieux Coquelles. One month later, on October 25, Lance Corporal St. John was killed in action during bitter fighting in a series of house-to-house battles. He died in the town of Boerehol, eleven kilometres inside the Netherlands border.

Five of the six men he took to his uncle's home in Scotland had been either killed, wounded, or taken prisoner. The only one to come through unscathed was Jack's pal from Brandon, Osborne Doak. Jack's aunt, uncle, cousins, and friends were all overcome with emotion as he told them about the loss of his friends.

There was a cablegram waiting for Jack when he returned from leave. This time it was sad news from home. His grandpa on his mom's side had passed away while Jack furloughed in Scotland. Jack felt terrible. He was upset by the fact he didn't have an opportunity to say goodbye to his grandfather. He thought about this good man, who was deeply loved by his family, particularly by the grandchildren. All of them spent summers at his farm.

A week later, Jack boarded the RMS Queen Elizabeth, the sister ship to the Queen Mary. He had vivid memories of his maiden voyage to England just two-and-a-half years earlier. Jack had lost many friends during the thirty months he had spent overseas. Jack tried to block thoughts of the bad times during the voyage home. Instead, he conjured up memories of the good ones he shared with the men who had become his brothers in arms.

It turned out that this was the second-to-last voyage the troopship Queen Elizabeth would make before returning to Southampton, England, for refit. She would return to the private sector after being released from Government Service. During her career as a troop transport, RMS Queen Elizabeth carried more than 750,000 troops across the world's oceans. When the war in Europe ended, she began repatriating the troops. She also brought thousands of war brides back to North America.[138] Once in dry dock, a massive refit would take place to return her to the majestic liner she was built for preceding the start of World War Two. On October 16, 1946, she began her maiden voyage as a beautiful luxury liner. In the years to come, she would carry celebrities like Gregory Peck, Vivien Leigh, Laurence Olivier, and Elizabeth Taylor, to name a few.[139]

"What If"

If you count Jack's "What If" moments, there are at least five. If he was first off the LCA, the bullets that tore up Genaille might have riddled Jack's belly with lead. There were at least two enemy shells that failed to explode when they landed beside him.

In his memoirs, Jack wrote about unexploded shells. He spoke about enemy shells having a soldier's number on them:

Had occasions where 88mm shells landed amongst us and didn't explode thanks to workers faithful to the allies in the munitions plants in Czechoslovakia.

He referred to them again after his close call before Carpiquet:

It either had a faulty fuse, or if it was filled with something other than explosives by someone faithful to the allied cause, and if that was the case, that worker saved two allied soldiers in one episode.

He was fortunate to avoid capture at Putot, like so many of his company. They were then murdered by the SS in various locations.

Another incident took place as the Germans took RWR prisoners to Caen. Jack didn't hear about it until after the war when men from German prisoner-of-war camps were liberated.

According to Captain Gower during testimony following the war: "On June 11, pilots of four allied forces Mustang aircraft must have mistaken the column of prisoners for German soldiers and strafed them with friendly fire. When the smoke cleared, ten

Canadians were dead, another thirty-nine were wounded, and some of those casualties would later die of their injuries."[140]

Finally, "What If" the sniper who took a bead on him hadn't only shattered Jack's Sten gun? Did Jack move his head at just the right moment, causing the bullet to miss by mere inches? Did one of the shells exploding in the area throw off the sniper's shot? None of the reasons matter. Jack survived.

I wish more veterans had taken the time to tell or write their stories for families as Jack Hamilton did. Writing his story would not have been possible without the information he left for his family.

Jack was interviewed several times by local papers in Brandon. He made it clear to a reporter from the *Western Journal* in 2012 that he didn't consider himself a hero.[141] However, though not wanting to be considered a war hero, Jack returned home to be a good and proud citizen, as did so many other young Canadian men. Over the next seventy-one years, until passing at the age of ninety-four in 2017, Jack kept the promise he made when he thought he would die after the battle of Carpiquet.

After arriving on the RMS Queen Elizabeth, filled to the gunnels with returning soldiers, he loaded onto a CNR train coach bound for Winnipeg. One of his recollections after arriving in Winnipeg was the food. Since joining the army in January 1943, he experienced some meals that were better than others. In the end, there was nothing like the food you grew up loving to eat. In Winnipeg, having fresh milk, eggs, real bread, and tasty meats was like a slice of heaven for those returning soldiers, including Jack.

Jack arrived home in late February, after yet another train trip. It was not the nicest of times weather-wise on the prairies. His mom met him at the train station in a taxi and took him home to see the rest of his family. After spending a few days at home with his mom and dad, it was time to go out and pay his respects to his Grandfather. They were close as Jack grew up, and he regretted being away and missing his Grandpa's funeral.

He left Brandon and travelled to Roseland, outside of town, on a sleigh drawn by horses. This method of travel made the cramped quarters he experienced over the past couple of years seem luxurious.

With his duty to his family completed, Jack returned to work for the Olympia Wholesale Company. However, less than a month after returning, one of the sales representatives quit the company. Soon after, Jack was promoted to the sales department, taking over the man's territory as a travelling salesman. He spent entire weeks driving around in the company's four-door Ford, making 150 calls per week and covering close to 1000 miles to do it. Over the years, during those travels along the rural roads and visiting Manitoba's small communities, Jack had plenty of time to ponder how close to death he came during his "What If" moments.

In July 1946, Jack got a pleasant surprise. After work one evening, when he returned home, a package was waiting for him from the Canadian Military Headquarters in Ottawa. Inside the box were the contents of the small kit bag he lost during the battle of Putot on June 8. The items included the book of poetry given to him by his aunt and uncle. A Bible issued to all Protestant members of the forces, and a stainless steel mirror complete with a metal nail file. There was also his Zipper leather pocket wallet, with his dog tags inside. One was a sterling silver dog tag with his home address engraved on one side. On the other were his name and service number. His mom and dad bought him those dog tags a week before he headed overseas. A Parker fountain pen and pencil, complete with a leather case containing the writing instruments, and paper were also among the returned items. Finally, there was his flint cigarette lighter.

He was amazed that these personal treasures had found their way to him after more than two years. "How is this even possible?" he asked his folks.

"I guess getting you a fancy silver dog tag made it worth the price we paid for it. Of course, you know your brother and sisters chipped in for it too," his mom told him.

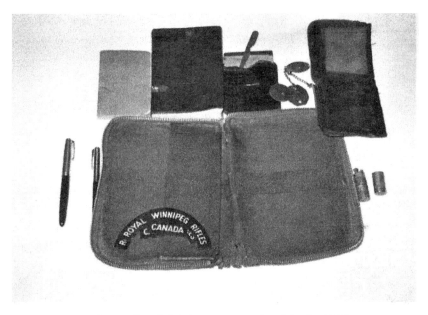

Jack Hamilton's kit bag, returned to him in 1946.

In 1947, Jack joined the Royal Canadian Legion. As a Legion member, he would continue to sell poppies each year for the next sixty-five years. He also served on various executive committees of the Royal Canadian Legion for forty-five years. Unlike other veterans who stayed away from Remembrance services, Jack stood front and centre for all of them, often as a member of the Legion's colour party.

Jack was also a proud member of The Royal Winnipeg Rifles Association, which allowed him to keep in touch with many men who survived the war. Considering the number of casualties the RWRs suffered, it was a miracle that all five boys from Brandon who joined up with the Little Black Devils managed to make it home safely.

It took Jack a while to meet the woman with whom he would spend the rest of his life. Jack and Isabel met in 1950 while skating at the old Brandon arena. At first, he watched Isabel from afar as she glided effortlessly around the rink, then found out that his cousin Marion seemed to know the smooth-skating beauty. "Who's the fine-looking lady?" he finally asked his cousin.

On May 12, 1951, Jack and Isabel were married in Brandon's First Presbyterian Church. They spent the next fifty-seven years together until Isabel died of cancer in 2008.

Like many families of their generation, they lived in the same house for over forty years and raised two children in the home. Their daughter Anne was born in 1954, and her brother David completed the family in 1957.

According to Anne, her father was a gentle, decent man who loved life and dedicated himself to whatever project he put his mind to. She described him as self-effacing. He never called attention to himself and always remained modest about his many accomplishments.

When I began writing about Jack and adding the dialogue to his story, I envisioned him using his share of cuss words. However, when she looked at the rough draft, Anne told me, "He never would have sworn. Regardless of the circumstances. I never heard him utter a cuss word my entire life. He probably didn't even swear when he was shot."

One of the hobbies from which he got a considerable amount of joy was tinkering and fixing things about the home, some of which weren't on a small scale. He ended up going well beyond tinkering and constructed a homemade tent trailer. Despite the time he spent sleeping in open fields and slit trenches, he enjoyed camping with his family. In the beginning, the family roughed it in a burdensome canvas tent, but he soon tired of having to fold and store it when they returned home after the trip.

His homemade trailer weighed so much that the small family Rambler had difficulty keeping up to speed, slowing to a snail's pace to get up mountain roads in the Canadian Rockies.

Jack continued to take his children to the family farm that held such fond memories for him as he grew up. A trip to the Roseland district was such a long drive for his children, much of it over dusty country roads and loose gravel. "You think this is far," he would tell them, "you should have been here when I came out by sleigh back in 1946. Now that was a long, cold journey."

Jack never complained about the injuries he sustained during the war or about the spots in his field of vision. So, it was quite a shock for the family when what was supposed to be an afternoon of fun with them ended up causing him such pain.

It happened while they were enjoying a favourite Canadian pastime. Jack and his family were tobogganing on North Hill on the outskirts of Brandon. He loved to sit on their sizeable grey sleigh with his children as they slid down the hill until a bumpy run injured his back. It was rare for his family to see him admit to being in pain or even being sick. Even though his back was in bad shape, he refused to take anything for it. Unfortunately, the injury sidelined him and took the joy of tobogganing away from him. Even during this painful ordeal, Jack didn't let a cuss word escape his lips.

On top of his dedication to The Royal Winnipeg Rifles and the legions, Jack was a dedicated employee. He continued to work for Olympia Wholesale for 29 years. Over time, the company changed its name to Canada Grocers. He left in 1972 because the company went bankrupt.

Jack spent another twelve years with another wholesale food company called Codvilles. He retired in 1984 but continued with his Legion work until he passed away in 2017.

On April 14, 2015, Jack received another honour when the local legion named one of their meeting rooms after the man who dedicated so much of his time to this group's efforts. It seems fitting because of the vow he made after being wounded in Carpiquet. Jack did become a good citizen and continued helping our Veterans throughout his life.

ROYAL CANADIAN LEGION
MAY 2015   VOLUME XXXV: 5

"JACK" HAMILTON MEETING ROOM

Branch #3 Royal Canadian Legion Executive Members on April 14, 2015 honoured our Veteran "Jack" Hamilton by naming the meeting room in our lower level the Jack Hamilton Meeting Room. Comrade Hamilton has spent many years ensuring that Canadian, Royal Canadian Legion and local history be preserved for future generations.

Proclamation of the Jack Hamilton Meeting Room.

One of Anne's funny recollections is the return of wholesale goods. Dented cans and outdated packaged food with the labels removed would be returned to the suppliers for credit.

If the cans had no brand identification, the company was able to keep them. These unlabelled cans were made available to the staff to be taken home and used. When he brought them to the house, Jack would store them in a basement pantry. Anne's job would be to choose a couple of the mystery tins to accompany the meat for supper. She would shake the cans hoping for some clue as to what they might contain. Creamed corn? Spaghetti? Green peas? On occasion, she would make the wrong choice. Sometimes the can of choice would be completely wrong, and her mother would end up opening a container of dog food. Jack's wife would shake her head and send Anne downstairs to try again.

Jack did end up in curling and bowling leagues and even took up golf after retiring. He and his wife enjoyed gardening. As a grandfather, Jack kept his grandchildren entertained by opening up his workshop for their projects. He made their crazy ideas into reality.

This demonstrates that, like so many other men who had volunteered to serve their country during World War II, Jack returned to life as a civilian with great pride in his country. He went on to be the kind of man who helped make Canada a place often considered the best place to live and the envy of people around the world. He was a good father, grandfather, and friend.

In 1974, Veterans Affairs chose Jack to be a representative at the 30th Anniversary of the landings at Normandy. Also joining him were three other men from The Royal Winnipeg Rifles: Garth Combs, wounded on June 14, 1944; George Haycock, a soldier who made it through the war without serious injury; and Cal Minaker, a Sapper who was wounded on August 28, 1944.

Fifteen years later, he joined with seventy-five other Winnipeg Rifles to mark the 45th Anniversary of D-Day. During this trip, they spent time in the Brighton and the Sussex area in the south of England. This is where the RWRs spent much of their time. The trip concluded in Nijmegen, the Netherlands.

Several years later, Jack turned down a second sponsored trip because he did not feel physically well enough to attend.

In 2010, through his ongoing connections with the RWRs, Jack was contacted by Fredrick Jeanne from France. He was researching the role of Canadians on D-Day for his book *Hold the Oak Line*. Jack and Fredrick, or Freddie, became friends. They spent an entire weekend together as Jack showed Freddie his souvenirs and pictures, telling him more about what the Canadians did during the first month of the battle of Normandy. After their conversations, Jack donated his pack and tunic to the Overlord museum in Normandy. Anne and I were at the museum during our time in France. Inside a case, in front of an exhibit showing men from The Royal Winnipeg Rifles, is Jack's uniform, complete with shoulder patches, topped off with his beret and hat badge. His haversack with his service number and initials on the back are also on display.

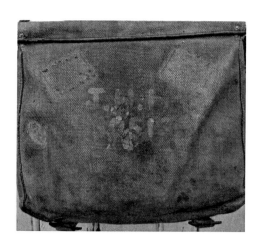 

Jack's Haversack returned in 1946, and his uniform complete with a wound stripe on the left sleeve.

In 2014, the French government awarded Jack the title of Knight of the National Order of the Legion of Honour for his participation in France's liberation. During an interview after receiving the honour, he told the reporter:

"It's considered a civilian honour. This isn't an ordinary medal. It's the Legion of Honour, a French order that is the highest decoration in France and awarded to those who deliver excellence in civil or military conduct."

He went on to say:

"It really speaks quite a bit to the French. They consider it equal to the Victoria Cross in honour."[142]

After he received the award, I wonder if Jack thought about the men from the Olympia Wholesale Company. I guess they were wrong. Not all those who were awarded a medal like Jack died before receiving it. He still didn't consider himself a hero.

Just before he died in July 2017, Jack was honoured once again; this time, the Quilts of Valour – Canada Society recognized his contributions.

During his interview with the Brandon paper in 2012, Jack declared:

"I thank God every day I get upright. The number of casualties in the first and second world wars was horrific – a terrible loss of life. The cost of our freedom was terrible."[143]

In August 2017, shortly after Jack passed away, the family received a letter summing up his life on one page:

From Murray Tallont, Brandon, Manitoba.
Dear Family,
Dawn and I wish to express our sincere condolences on the passing of your loved one and our Comrade, John "Jack" Hamilton.
Good people in life are few and far between. Jack was one of them.
His dedication to the Royal Canadian Legion and The Royal Winnipeg Rifles Association is well known by all.
Gentleman Jack, well dressed, well mannered, well-spoken, quiet, but when he made his statements, well listened to.
Jack was a very special individual to myself. He reminded me of my father and uncle. All were involved in W.W. II. Their service to their country, and their families, the 1st priority always were in front at all times.
All three were involved with the Royal Canadian Legion and a lot of other organizations. They always gave of their time, whether asked or not.
By today's standard, they were "A special type of person," something that seems to be fading away by today's standard.
We thank your family for all the services he did for his country and the time you all allowed him to be away. We often forget in

a lot of things that the families left behind are not recognized. Without the family supporting people like Jack, who knows what might have happened.

Both of us loved history, be it military or otherwise. Over the years, we exchanged books, read them, and on returning, had many decent discussions about them.

Over the years, Jack spoke of his wartime experiences, including his wounds and some of the saddest stories one would ever want to hear. I felt privileged to be allowed to listen to them. He was a very special friend to me.

In closing, I thank you all for allowing Jack to be all that he could be. "Old soldiers don't die; they just fade away." He was a very remarkable man.

There is one last thing that pays tribute to the life of Jack Hamilton. The emblem of The Royal Winnipeg Rifles is engraved on his headstone, along with his name, dates of birth and death, and a fitting epitaph: "GENEROUS OF HEART, CONSTANT OF FAITH." To be remembered like this is a fitting finale for Jack Hamilton.[144]

Reflections and Conclusion

Normandy, June 2019

Unlike my father seventy-five years ago, I was not crossing the beach with machine-gun bullets ricocheting off my landing craft, nor were mortar shells bursting all around. I didn't have to jump into the frigid waters of the channel to wade ashore while landing craft assault boats were being blown out of the water by mines and shells from miles away. I put my hand in the cold waters but never dipped a toe in the Channel. I didn't have to leave a friend lying in the sand for fear of being shot myself.

I left my quiet home on the outskirts of Edmonton, Alberta, at nine o'clock in the morning. Nineteen hours later, I walked onto the same stretch of beach it took my father two years to reach.

In fairness, the planning for my walk on the beach had been in the works for ten months. I travelled with eleven other people from across Canada, all having connections to Normandy and D-Day. The logistics for putting a trip like ours together is micro-scopic compared to the years of planning required to accomplish Operation Overlord.

During the war, travel time for a soldier was long and monotonous, including two or three days by train from Winnipeg to Halifax. This was followed by an Atlantic voyage bearing no re-semblance to passage on one of today's luxury liners. Then there were another three-and-a-half days sitting on a ship being tossed around by bad weather in the English Channel. Finally came a two-and-a-half-hour stint in a landing craft. Bobbing up and down like a cork made many soldiers feel as though they would die of sea-sickness before the enemy had the chance to shoot at them.

We thought we were hard done by when it took us three hours to collect our bags, clear customs, and pick up the rental cars.

Then, using a GPS, not a map, we made a four-hour trip directly to our objective: a two-story house, occupied by the Germans on June 6, 1944, in the town of Graye-sur-Mer, which would be our home for the next two weeks.

For D-Day's 75th anniversary, the owners gave our group the use of their home for our entire stay. It was only the first of many incredible gestures by the people of a town whose existence dates back to the ninth century. This small village still appreciates what Canada's soldiers did all those years ago.

Twenty minutes after arriving, I walked from the house where we were staying onto Juno Beach, the same place my father and thousands of Canadians landed, and hundreds died. The first thing I noticed was how difficult it was to walk on the dry sand. I imagined attempting to run across the beach with sixty-five to seventy pounds of equipment weighing me down. Each step was a struggle, with my foot sinking to the ankles each time I moved forward. I wondered how much of the sand would have been as dry as the part of the beach I walked on or if the rain and choppy seas would have made it firmer.

The hands of time have changed the beach from seventy-five years ago. Dunes still hide the positions where the gun emplacements were located. There are no longer any tank traps, barriers, Hedgehogs, Belgium gates, barbed wire, nor mines sitting on top of steel bars embedded in the shoreline. Stepping to the waterline, then looking both left and right, I realized I was one of the few people on the beach for as far as I could see. There was a tranquillity to the area. These beaches had seen enough tragedy on one day to last for the rest of eternity.

I noticed the bright red poppies, unaware at this point how Jack Hamilton talked about the poppies in his memoirs. As someone from Alberta, I couldn't help but see the abundance of wild roses along the trails on the backside of the dunes. They were in full bloom and were much larger than the ones back home.

Over the next twelve days, no matter where we stopped or with whom we spoke, we were treated with respect, dignity, and friendship by people most of us had never met before. We were welcomed into people's homes, one of which was a spectacular Chateau where I spent the night. This residence had been in the family for generations, built well before the idea of a country called Canada was even a dream.

Several villages held banquets of appreciation for us, showing Canadians continuing respect for our fathers' efforts to help liberate their towns.

One of the most sombre moments for me was seeing the headstone of L. Chartrand at the Beny-sur-Mer Cemetery. He was one of the men my father wrote about in his letter. Even now, as I write this, my emotions creep to the surface. Seeing his headstone reinforced how close I came to never being born. I am more confident than ever that being wounded saved my father's life.

Close to this headstone is a second one bearing the same last name. There are no first names on the gravestones, only initials, their rank and the day they died. I knew the first Chartrand headstone was the man my father talked about. Despite both their first initials being L, the second one was for Sergeant L. Chartrand. The monument for the first L. Chartrand has his parent's names engraved on it and his hometown of Camperville, Manitoba. The Sergeant's marker only lists his service number, rank and the day he died. Were they related? Would their families have received the dreaded telegram on the same day?

During my time there, I took random photographs of several other headstones. Then, while writing Jack Hamilton's story, I thought I recognized the name of the young man killed when the doors on the landing craft swung open. He was the one Jack stepped over as he made his way off the landing craft.

Headstone of P.A. Genaille. Killed before Jack got off the LCA.

Three sisters and their cousin were with us on our trip. Their uncle left the family farm at the beginning of the war — the family was upset with his decision. Fred Marych paid the ultimate sacrifice. He was among the men murdered on the outskirts of Putot en Bessin. It was an emotional moment for his nieces. Born after the war, none of them had ever met their uncle but grieved for him as though they'd known him their entire life, leaving me with a palpable sense of sadness for them and the man they never knew.

Headstone of F.H Marych. Murdered by the SS while held as a prisoner.

A local battlefield historian took us to the location of the battle where their uncle, Jack Hamilton, and other members of The Royal Winnipeg Rifles fought for their lives. During that encounter, many Canadians, including Fred Marych, were captured near the railway on the outskirts of Putot. There is evidence they were cared for by their German captors on the first evening. They were also given first aid in a farmyard not far from the battle. The following day, while the prisoners were being escorted back to the German lines, orders were given to shoot the Canadians.

We visited the Chateau d' Audrieu. Today it is a luxury accommodation boasting elegant rooms, suites, and fine dining. You can even experience history in their deluxe treehouse and follow the glory of William the Conqueror while enjoying a gourmet breakfast on the terrace that overlooks the gardens.[145]

After we had explained the purpose of our visit, they allowed us to walk the grounds freely. This is where captured Canadian soldiers were interrogated, then taken into the woods around the property and murdered. Those killed included Major Fred Hodge and other members of the RWRs.

In Putot-en-Bessin, over one hundred residents of the town, including young children and dignitaries, held a personal remembrance service for our small band of Canadians. A plaque bearing the names of those killed is mounted on a wall. The memorial was made from bricks of the Chateau, where they died. First, the names were read aloud. Following a moment of silence, six beautiful wreaths, including one from our group, were placed to honour Canada's fallen soldiers.

We visited museums paying homage to various battles and the men and women who fought in them while liberating France and Europe. We saw memorials, squares, streets, and gardens dedicated to Canada's various regiments in most towns where we stopped.

As we travelled throughout Normandy, Canadian flags were prominently hung alongside those of France and other nations who helped with the liberation. The street lamps of the coastal towns were strung with banners depicting Veterans' names and the countries they came from, proudly displayed. These gestures filled me with a sense of pride, not only for my father but for our country, as I have never felt before. One of the last surviving veterans of The Royal Winnipeg Rifles, Jim Parks was among those distinguished Canadians with his picture adorning a flag. I had the pleasure of meeting Jim while in Normandy. He read the manuscript for this book and honoured me by writing an endorsement.

Jim Parks Banner, Courseulles-sur-Mer.

To this day, Jim, who turned 97 years young in 2021, continues to contribute to society. In 2020, during the pandemic, he helped raise funds and awareness for the Juno Beach Centre, a museum in France that honours the contributions and sacrifices of Canadians on D-Day. Jim was only 19 when he approached the beaches with his mortar platoon. Unfortunately, his landing craft was damaged as they neared the beach, and his platoon lost all their equipment. Jim survived by jumping into the water and swimming to shore.

The memorial garden outside of the town of Arromanches was particularly poignant — the most touching memorial I have ever seen dedicated to the memories of our veterans. It could be used as a template for monuments across North America. In the garden, there is a statue of an elderly veteran.

Memorial Garden at Arromanches: a veteran re-membering the friends he lost.

With his hands on his knees, he appears lost in thought, gazing into his past. Yet, it is what he is looking at in the distance that was so moving: statues made from thousands of metal washers welded together, allowing you to see through them. These finished figures give the ghostly appearance of soldiers coming out of the sea onto the shore. The ability to see through the soldiers' images represents the fading memories of his friends and comrades who never made it home.

Memorial Garden at Arromanches showing a veteran's fading memory.

After returning to Canada, I reached out to John Everiss, the artist who built the memorial. He told me the statue's concept depicts a veteran with a myriad of memories that never diminish. Still, the passage of time is making it fade into history. Soon there will only be stories read in books and recollections of the few who were there.

I think Marie Brown said it best:

"We are the generation left who owe it to our family members to ensure we record who these brave, but in most cases, very ordinary men were. Not just statistics — they were flesh and blood, and let's face it, 'our dads.'"

Should you have an opportunity to walk in the footsteps of your father, grandfather, or great-grandfather, it will not be a wasted trip. On the contrary, I hope that when you take those steps, you discover the same sense of pride and understanding of all the sacrifices previous generations have made for us.

Conclusion

The importance of the contributions of the men in this book and thousands of others cannot be overstated.

Accountants, clerks, dockworkers, farmers, doctors, and nurses represented men and women from all walks of life. They assisted in their part of the war effort, putting their lives on hold. Joining the armed forces of countries throughout the world, they did their part to help rid the world of a fascist dictator who sought world domination.

In the end, they were victorious, but not before thousands of men and women gave their lives for what was a noble and just cause.

Those who survived seldom spoke about their experiences. They returned to their countries and tried valiantly to put the horrors they had witnessed behind them. Many succeeded, showing no outward signs of the physical and mental scars they carried. Others were not so fortunate and had difficulty holding a job. Many drank to excess in an attempt to chase away the demons that broke their spirit.

Men like Gerry, Harry, Jack, and Johnny were the lucky ones. They went on to live full and purposeful lives. Each of them did their part to shape the communities where they lived and raised good families. This wasn't possible for those who did not survive their "What If" moments.

During my trip to Normandy, I met author Ted Barris during the official ceremony at Juno Beach on June 6, 2019. Ted is an accomplished author of seven books about World War II, including *Juno: Canadians at D-Day, June 6, 1944*, and his newest, *Rush to Danger: Medics in the Line of Fire*.

That evening I was scheduled to do a live broadcast back to Edmonton from the town of Graye-sur-Mer. I was both nervous and overwhelmed. How could I tell the people back home about what I had seen and how the people of Normandy welcomed us everywhere we went? How could I explain what it felt like to be standing in the shadow of history? All I needed to do was talk about it, not live it as my father and so many others had done. I was overly emotional about the entire experience. Ted offered me some advice. I'm sure many officers were giving similar speeches to their men on their way to the beaches seventy-five years earlier. I think it was something simple like, "You better get a grip."

At ten o'clock on June 6, I stood in the middle of the streets of Graye-sur-Mer and stared back through the fading light toward the beach where my father had landed 75 years earlier. Thanks to Ted's encouragement, I managed to conduct several surreal interviews with Edmonton broadcasters. One was with CTV's Alberta Prime News program. The other was with Gord Steinke of Global News and J'lyn Nye on CHED radio. They had dedicated their program to the events that took place in Normandy that day.

I have stayed in touch with Ted. His books are the results of thousands of interviews with veterans. During one of his speaking engagements, Ted said one of the biggest compliments he ever received came from a veteran. He said: "My name isn't in your book Ted, but my story is. Thank you."

I asked Ted if I could tell a few stories from his books to conclude *Our Fathers' Footsteps* because they are also "What if" stories.

One of the men Ted writes about in his book *Juno: Canadians at D-Day June 6, 1944,* was Mark Lockyear, a member of the 1st Canadian Parachute Battalion. After landing in the flooded pastureland around the village of Robenhomme and wading his way forward alone, he made it to the rendezvous point. Their mission was to blow the bridge over the River Dives. This would protect the eastern flank of the invasion from a German counter-attack. Lockyear made it to his objective in the early hours of June 6. After setting all the charges at 0300, he pushed the plunger. The bridge was crippled but not destroyed. The demolition experts would finish the job when they arrived.

The next part of their operation was to engage the enemy in hit-and-run actions to keep the Germans off balance as to where the next attack might occur. Lockyear and the 1st Para members carried out their mission to harass the enemy throughout June 7. By June 8, he, like many paratroopers and those who landed on the beaches, had not slept in three days.

On June 8, Mark was in a pitched battle with a German Grenadier Regiment. The skirmish went back and forth, but the Germans were in the process of springing a trap. There was mortar fire landing on the German position, and when it appeared they were pulling back, Mark's commander ordered his men to charge.

It didn't take long for seven men to be killed or wounded, including Lockyear, who was knocked down with a burning pain in his chest: a bullet had punctured his right lung. The shelling stopped, and the battlefield went quiet, except for the moaning of those wounded. As he laid there, he kept as silent as possible and watched as two enemy soldiers approached. One was a private, and the other appeared to be an SS officer. The officer pulled out his pistol and shot one of the wounded men dead.

Lockyear reached into his tunic and rubbed blood from his chest wound over his face. The German private came over and kicked Mark three times while the officer executed another of the wounded men. Because he did not respond, the man told his superior, "Soldat kaput."

Mark stayed motionless, then heard one of his friends pleading with the Germans, "No! No! Don't!" The pleading did no good, and the SS officer executed the third wounded paratrooper.

After another pitched battle, under cover of darkness, Mark managed to make his way back to the Canadian lines. Several days later, he was evacuated to England on one of the LCTs.

While recovering, Mark learned that of the twenty-five men who battled with the Germans on June 8, thirteen were wounded, one was taken prisoner, and eight were killed.

I don't know much about Mark's life after the war. Based on his story as told by Ted Barris, he did return to Normandy on a couple of occasions. Once in 1969, for the 25th anniversary, accompanied by his daughter; and again when the Juno Beach Centre opened in 2003. His son spoke about being pulled along to remembrance ceremonies to watch the parades that were often led by his father.

For the opening of the Juno Beach Centre, Mark withdrew a portion of his savings. He wanted to take his entire family to Normandy. Mark wanted them to see the location where, if not for his quick thinking and rubbing the blood from his wound on his face, he might not have survived his "What If" moment. If he had moved or moaned when kicked by the enemy, Private Mark Lockyear would have been "Kaput," like his comrades.

If he hadn't survived his "What If" moment, the next two generations of Lockyears would not have been there to applaud and take pictures of the seventy-nine-year-old veteran as he marched with his comrades at the opening of the Juno Beach Centre on June 6, 2003.[146]

Another story from Ted Barris' book *Rush to Danger* reiterates the premise of "What If" in this book. It is a story about the sixtieth wedding anniversary of Bob Ross and his wife, Jean. There would not have been a first anniversary for Bob and Jean if he failed to survive his "What If" moment on August 10, 1944, in Grainville-Langannerie, France.

Bob was a private with the Lincoln and Welland Regiment (L & WR), another Canadian Regiment with a long history in Canada. The L & WR can trace their roots back to the War of 1812.

Bob's lifelong friend, Jim Brittain, was a medic with the same regiment. On the afternoon of August 10, during a Canadian operation before the Falaise Pocket battle, the L & WRs were conducting a recon mission on the outskirts of Grainville-Langannerie. The Canadians landed on the beaches two months earlier and were still only thirty-six kilometres inland. While doing their recce on that hot Normandy summer afternoon, the Germans began to shell the scouting patrol. According to Jim Brittain, the concentrated fire from the German mortars, machine guns, and 88mm artillery was deadly.

An incoming shell made a direct hit on the recon section's Bren-gun carrier. When the smoke cleared, four of the men from the vehicle were wounded. Off to one side, Jim saw his friend, Private Ross, next to the wall of a building. In the confusion of the moment, men were rushing by Bob. When Jim took a closer look, he realized Bob wasn't standing against a wall with one foot in a slit trench. He was supporting himself against the wall because one of his legs was missing below the knee.

Shrapnel made a mess of the canvas stretchers, but before he could think of moving his patient, Jim needed to stop Bob from bleeding out. He grabbed a stick to make a tourniquet and applied it as tightly as he could to Bob's groin to stem the flow of blood from the main artery.

With the blood flow slowed, Jim could concentrate on getting his patient out of the area. The stretchers were useless, so he got his patient onto a door that was off its hinges. One of the things Jim remembered was Bob wanting his detached leg. Jim got it and placed it on the makeshift stretcher with his injured patient.

The L & WR troops were under constant shelling for the next several days. By the end of it, Jim's unit lost eight men in action, and two of the men wounded earlier ended up dying from their wounds. One of those two was not Private Bob Ross.

At Bob and Jean's sixtieth wedding anniversary, Jim Brittain, the quick-thinking medic from that August afternoon, was one of the guests. He was not just a casual invitee. The Ross family wanted him there as a guest of honour. Any time a couple manages to stay married for this many years calls for a celebration, and there are always tributes paid to the couple who have seen so many changes in the world.

During one of the many tributes given, the Ross offspring stopped the celebration for their parents and addressed the gathering of friends and family: "If it weren't for Mr. Brittain, we wouldn't be here." It was true. The quick thinking and innovation on Jim's part saved Bob's life.

Did Bob think about his "What If" moment throughout his life? How he might not have survived if Jim had rushed past him to help some of the other wounded men when he thought he was leaning against the wall? Would anyone else have noticed Bob in the confusion of the battle? Would he have ended up falling over where he stood and bled to death?

That Bob's family invited Jim as a guest of honour to their sixtieth wedding anniversary. I think this is proof that Bob thought about that moment throughout his life and made sure his family knew about it.[147]

Like me, Bob's family understood and appreciated how tiny variables could have made a difference to any of us even existing. If those moments in time, those "What If's" experienced by my father, had been altered somehow, I would not have written the stories of these men.

For descendants of family members who fought in any war, I encourage you to take a moment to give thanks that they survived their "What If" moments. Their survival made it possible for you and me to be alive. I ask you to think of the men and women who didn't make it home from the field of battle, forever ending their hopes, dreams, and future generations. Let us not forget what these men and women did seventy-five years ago and what they contributed to their societies upon their return.

I remember what Anthony Wilson Smith of Historica Canada said to young people before I began this project. "World War II is not just black and white photos shown on the internet or in history books. For those who were there, the war played out in living colour and sound."

In his book *Seven Days in Hell: Canada's Battle for Normandy and the rise of the Black Watch Snipers*, David O'Keefe eloquently summed up my thoughts as I wrote this book. After the decimation of the Black Watch Regiment at Verrières Ridge, which ended with the second greatest loss of lives of Canadian soldiers in a single day, those who survived wondered about the capricious nature of fate or luck. One right or wrong move in any direction, one moment of boldness or hesitation could have spelled the difference between life and death, between a minor scratch and a maiming.[148]

Neither the Great War nor World War II ended up being the last war to be fought by young men and women from around the world. NATO soldiers have continued to die and survive in deployments around the globe. Soldiers fighting in conflicts in Korea, Vietnam, Kosovo, Iraq, and Afghanistan have all had their own "What If" moments.

We can be thankful that the numbers killed or wounded have never reached the staggering numbers of either of the wars in the first half of the twentieth century. How big the conflict is doesn't matter; if you are a family member of those serving, even one casualty is too many.

While writing these men's stories, I have had the opportunity to learn about each of them. I'm confident I would have been proud to call each of them my friend. Speaking with and meeting family members has given me an appreciation for what these men did throughout the war years. It helped me respect them for who they were and what they did following that period of their lives. "What If" there hadn't been another war after the war to end all wars? Would their lives have changed? Perhaps they may have gone on to different careers or met other women to marry. We will never know.

I have always been moved by the final scene of the movie *Saving Private Ryan*. As an older man, Ryan stares at row upon row of crosses in the Normandy American Cemetery and Memorial. He is shown speaking to the headstone of Captain John Miller, who helped keep him alive. When his wife joins him, he says to her, "Tell me I've led a good life. Tell me I'm a good man." His wife takes him gently by the chin and says, "You are."[149] Ryan then gives the headstone of Captain Miller a crisp salute, and the movie ends.

Each of the men whose stories I have told would qualify as good men. Each of them did live a good life and made their lives count for something. After the movie's premiere, many veterans seeing it for the first time were brought to tears by the memories the recreation elicited. I have also heard grown men say the final scene may have been more moving and caused more than one hardened vet to cry.

As one final "What If," consider the letter written by General Dwight D. Eisenhower. He took full responsibility for the failure of the invasion. He had doubts in the face of a "well trained, well equipped and battle-hardened" enemy. If the invasion of Normandy had failed, this is the message he would have relayed to the public. The only apparent hint of nerves on his part is his error in dating the note "July 5" instead of June 5.[150] Fortunately for the world, the invasion was successful, and he never did have to deliver his "What If" letter.

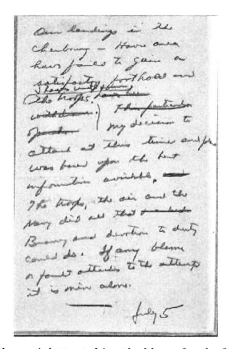

General Eisenhower's letter taking the blame for the failed invasion.

The writing is difficult to read. This is what the general wrote:

Our landings in the Cherbourg-Havre area have failed to gain a satisfactory foothold, and I have withdrawn the troops. My decision to attack at this time and place was based upon the best information available. The troops, the air and the Navy did all that bravery and devotion to duty could do. If any blame or fault attaches to the attempt, it is mine alone.

I hope this book's stories will help stop memories of veterans and their families from fading. I want people to understand and appreciate what they sacrificed, even if they never talked about it.

Another movie I have always loved is *It's a Wonderful Life*, starring Jimmy Stewart. After a series of setbacks, Stewart's character, George Bailey, decides to end his own life. After being saved by an angel in training, George gets the rare opportunity of seeing what life would have been like if he was never born. It makes me wonder how many lives would have changed if the "What If" moments in this story had been different.

In 1993, as the Canadian economy took a downturn, I was caught in a corporate shuffle and ended up out of a job. As black as the days ahead appeared, my wife told me, "There's a reason for everything."

As usual, she was right, and by March 1994, I owned my own company. Although business wasn't always blue sky and roses, we made the company successful. As they say, the rest is history. Did those who survived feel there was a reason for everything? Did they question why so many of their friends ended up not coming home?

As I was working on editing this book, I reached out to the family members of the men whose stories have been told on these pages. I wanted to know how many people are alive today because these men survived. Henry Hildyard's case is slightly different. He already had two children before the war began, and Marie was born after his "What If" moment. If Henry hadn't survived, life would undoubtedly have been much different for Marie's mother. She was thirty-nine years old, so not necessarily of second marriageable age, especially with two teenage children and a newborn. Men were returning from the war and had lots of young girlfriends and widows to choose from.

The "What If" moment for the Hildyard family's descendants was determined many years before because Henry survived the Spanish Flu. This meant in the years since, nineteen people had a direct connection to Henry. In the cases of the other three men – Levers, Nearingburg, and Hamilton – a total of thirty-two direct descendants are here today because their fathers survived.

The next time you are at a family or community gathering, take a look around. Think about how many might not be there if their mothers or fathers hadn't survived their "What If" so long ago.

Finally, in Putot-en-Bessin, something took place that put all our fathers' sacrifices into perspective. A car drove into the parking area as we prepared to leave the ceremony honouring the murdered Canadians. A young woman stepped out and came toward our group. She approached the two men in our party responsible for organizing the tour. Brian Batter and Gerry Woodman were both sharply dressed in their regimental green sports jackets. Their medals were pinned to those jackets. Both wore The Royal Winnipeg Rifles regimental ties and berets. It didn't seem to matter to the young woman that both were too young to have served in World War II. The combined service with the regiment of these two men was more than seventy years. Adorning their breast pocket was a patch with the Little Black Devil insignia. On their lapels were crocheted poppies, made for us by the people of Bethsonart.

We were fortunate to have a young man from Winnipeg, Louis-Phillipe Bujold, who spoke French. We all appreciated that Louis was with us throughout our trip to France and helped us with his interpretive skills.

The young lady handed Gerry a piece of glossy, golden, heavy bond paper. It was rolled up and bound with blue, white and red ribbon, the colours of the French flag. With Louis serving as interpreter, she told us she heard about the ceremony. She wanted to come by to thank the Canadians for what we did for their country. She said the young people of France have not forgotten what our nation did for them seventy-five years ago.

The sentiment was genuine. Once again, it made me feel that everything the Canadians did so long ago was worth the sacrifice. Our entire group was filled with pride as we left the ceremony at Putot-en-Bessin.

The following poem is what she left with us. When I returned home, I searched for the author. Unable to find anything about the poem, I concluded the young lady had written it.

I believe there is no better way to finish these stories.

Mr. Veteran,

I came to say thank you

And through me are thousands of children talking to thousands of veterans

How we have been young and careless

But at 20 years the FREEDOM was looking for you

She came to pick you up to tell you:

"I'm dying, come save me"

And you answered his call

You have risen full of courage and ardor,

You have been training day after day for D-Day

And one morning in June, you arrived by the sky and by the sea.

And you fought of all your soul free man for our freedom to us.

On our beaches and in our lands, and despite your wounds and sorrows,

You remained fighting alongside us.

So, I'm telling you, Mr. Veteran :

For yours whose sacrificed youth rest in peace in the sleep of the just :
    "WE ARE THE CHILDREN WHO HAVE NOT USED"

And to you, Mr. Veteran, who, here, offered your bravery and your best years, I say :
"WE ARE YOUR SONS, SONS AND GIRLS OF FREEDOM who today tell you THANKS "

                                    Jean GOUGEON

Sources and Pictures

War Diaries
*The official war diaries of the regiments for Levers,
Nearingburg, Hildyard and Hamilton were crucial in telling
each of these men's stories. Therefore, the war diaries
are highlighted throughout this book. In addition, their
personal accounts have been italicized.*

7th Brigade, 3rd Canadian Division
The Royal Winnipeg Rifles
*War Diary of the 1st Battalion, The Royal Winnipeg Rifles,
Lieutenant-Colonel John Meldrum. June 6 to August 1944.
Fonds Collection R.G. 24 D.N.D. Original Archive Reference
RG-24-C-3 Volume 15233 (3rd Canadian Division)*

The Highland Light Infantry of Canada
*War Diary of the Highland Light Infantry Lieutenant-
Colonel F.M. Griffiths (June) Lieutenant-Colonel Kingsmill
(July-Aug) Fonds Collection RG-24 C-3 15076. (3rd Canadian
Division)*

*Special thanks to The Laurier Military History Archives for
the preservation of these diaries. Their site also includes
the war diaries for other infantry and artillery regiments.
In addition, it lists other divisional troops involved in the
battle of Normandy. They can be viewed on their website:
www.lmharchive.ca/canadian-divisions-of-the-normandy-
campaign/3rd-canadian-infantry-division/.*

999 Port Operating Company

War Diary 999 Port Operating Company, Major J.K Abson (June-July 1944) Imperial War Museum

The Royal Engineers diaries were obtained from the Imperial War Museums. Supplied by Marie Brown, daughter of Harry Hildyard.

The following is a link to the CBC broadcast my dad made in June of 1944: www.cbc.ca/archives/entry/four-d-day-soldiers-tell-their-stories-from-london.

More stories about WW II veterans can be found by searching: War in Europe 1944 at www.CBC Archives - History.

Endnotes

Periodicals, News Features, Broadcasts, Journals, Videos, and Weblogs

1   History.com Editors."Germany surrenders unconditionally to the Allies at Reims." History.com, November 5, 2009, history.com/this-day-in-history/germany-surrenders-unconditionally-to-the-allies-at-reims.

2   Redekop, Bill. "Survival of the weakest." *The Winnipeg Free Press Above the fold,* February 15, 2019, www.winnipegfreepress.com/local/cover-at-deaths-door-inside-survival-of-the-weakest-505892622.

3   Suddath, Claire. "Brief History of the Crash of 1929." *Time.com,* October 19, 2008, www.content.time.com/time/nation/article.

4   Hillmer, Norman. "The Great Crash of 1929 in Canada." *The Canadian Encyclopedia,* July 27, 2017, *Historica Canada,* www.thecanadianencyclopedia.ca/en/article/the-great-crash-feature. Accessed March 14, 2021.

5   Klein, Christopher. "1929 Stock Market Crash: Did Panicked Investors Really Jump From Windows?" *History.com,* March 17, 2019, www.history.com/news/stock-market-crash-suicides-wall-street-1929-great-depression.

6   Klein, Christopher. "Chamberlain declares, 'Peace for our time.'" *History.com,* September 30, 2013, www.history.com /news/chamberlain-declares-peace-for-our-time-75-years-ago.

7   The Editors of Encyclopaedia Britannica. "German-Soviet Nonaggression Pact." *Encyclopedia Britannica,* August 16, 2020, www.britannica.com/event/German-Soviet-Nonaggression-Pact. Accessed March 15, 2021.

8   United States Holocaust Memorial Museum. "Invasion of Poland, Fall 1939" *Holocaust Encyclopedia,* Last edited: May 30, 2019, encyclopedia.ushmm.org/content/en/article/invasion-of-poland-fall-1939 Accessed March 15, 2021.

9   William Lyon Mackenzie King. September 3, 1939, *CBC Radio Special . . . .* "[Radio Broadcast]" CBC, www.cbc.ca/archives/entry/1939-canada-at-the-side-of-britain.

10   D'Aliesio, Renata. "Moment in time: Canada declared war on this day in. . . . 1939." *The Globe and Mail.* Sept 10, 2013, www.theglobeandmail.com/community/sept-10-1939-canada-declares-war/article14213144.

11   "1939 Mobilization." *The Fort Garry Horse Museum and Archives 1939- . . . 1945.* fortgarryhorse.ca fortgarryhorse.ca/wp/1939-1945.

12   Levers, Gerald Wallace. "Attestation Papers." (Don Levers)

13   Newman, Michael. "*Manitoba History*: February 19, 1942: If Day." *Manitoba Historical Society* no. 13, Spring 1987, www.mhs.mb.ca/cods/mb_history/13/ifday.

14   Cassidy, Christian. "This was Manitoba. When war came to Winnipeg."
        Winnipeg Free Press. Winnipegfreepress.com, February 19, 2017, www.
        winnipegfreepress.com/local/when-war-came-to-winnipeg-414169033.

15   Herd, Alex. "Dieppe Raid." *The Canadian Encyclopedia*, August 15, 2017,. .
        Historica Canada. www.thecanadianencyclopedia.ca/en/article/dieppe-raid.
        Accessed March 15, 2021.

16   Canada, Department of National Defence, "The Royal Winnipeg Rifles,"
        in *The Official Lineages of the Canadian Armed Forces, Volume 3 Part 1,
        Infantry Regiments,* 2019, www.canada.ca/en/department-national-defence/
        services/military-history/history-heritage/official-military-history-lineages/
        lineages/infantry-regiments/royal-winnipeg-rifles.

17   *War Diary of the 1ˢᵗ Battalion, The Royal Winnipeg Rifles.*

18   Caddick-Adams, Peter. "Pre-Invasion madness in England: The Final Days
        beforeD-Day."June 2019, historynet.com, www.historynet.com/pre-invasion-
        madness-in-england-the-final-days-before-d-day.

19   Two Brothers Productions. "WW2 British 24 hour rations pack." *You Tube.
        com.* June 30, 2018, youtube.com/watch?v=T_xFn8mp4YI.

20   Laurenceau, Marc. "Mark III helmet History." *D-Day Overlord
        Encyclopedia*, www.dday-overlord.com/en/material/uniforms/mark-3-turtle-
        helmet.

21   Laurenceau, Marc. "Landing Craft Assault." *D-Day Overlord Encyclopedia*,
        www.dday-overlord.com/en/material/warships/landing-craft/lca.

22   Horton, Capt. E.W. "Experiences of a D-Day Padre" *The Devils' Blast,
        Annual Chronicle of The Royal Winnipeg Rifles*, Brian Batter, editor. 2014 P.
        83-87.

23   Marischal, Murray. "Llangibby Castle. D-Day The Master's Story." *The
        Union-Castle Chronicle 1853-1953 The British & Commonwealth Shipping
        Co. Register.* Accessed March 16, 2021, www.bandcstaffregister.com/
        page72.

24   Ibid

25   Juno Beach Centre. "Canada in the Second World War, D-Day." March 16,
        2021, junobeach.org/canada-in-wwii/articles/d-day.

26   Operation Overlord/Neptune Force' J' Juno Beach "Landing tables." Mike
        Beach H+20, www.6juin1944.com.

27   *War Diary of the 1ˢᵗ Battalion, The Royal Winnipeg Rifles.*

28   Huard, Paul Richard. "Hitler's Buzz Saw: The MG42 Was (And Still Is)
        an Impressive Weapon."November 15, 2020, *The National Interest,* www.
        nationalinterest.org/blog/reboot/hitlers-buzz-saw-mg42-was-and-still-
        impressive-weapon.

29   Reid, Brian A. *Named by the Enemy A History of The Royal Winnipeg Rifles.*
        (Published by Robin Brass Studio, 2010)

30   *War Diary of the 1ˢᵗ Battalion, The Royal Winnipeg Rifles.*

31   Scott, Jack. June 16, 1944 *"Four D-Day soldiers tell their stories from
        London."* [Radio Broadcast] CBC, www.cbc.ca/search?q=Four%20Day%20
        soldiers%20tell%20their%20stories%20from%20London&section=all&sort
        Order=relevance&media=all.

32   Calais 1944. Canadiansoliers.com Accessed March 17, 2021, www.
        canadiansoldiers.com/history/battlehonours/northwesteurope/calais1944.

33   The Royal Winnipeg Rifles. *"Nominal Rolls, RWRs C/W updated P.O.W.
        information."*

34   Calais 1944. Canadiansoliers.com, Accessed March 17, 2021, www.
      canadiansoldiers.com/history/battlehonours/northwesteurope/calais1944.
35   "The end of Market Garden." *Operation Market Garden 17-27 1944.*
      Military History Encyclopedia on the web, www.historyofwar.org/articles/
      battles_arnhem.
36   Levers, Gerald Wallace. "Official Records of Service." (Don Levers)
37   Dewar, Taryn. "Banting and the First World War." *Banting House,*
      December 5, 2014, www.bantinghousenhsc.wordpress.com/2014/12/05/
      banting-and-world-war-i/ Accessed March 20, 2021.
38   Maavaral, Alexander. "Lester B. Pearson." *Through Veterans Eyes.* Laurier
      Centre for Military Strategic and Disarmament Studies September 14, 2017,
      www.throughveteranseyes.ca/2017/09/14/lester-b-pearson.
39   Monet, S.J. Jacques. "Georges Vanier." *The Canadian Encyclopedia,*
      February 14, 2018, *Historica Canada.* Accessed March 20, 2021, www.
      thecanadianencyclopedia.ca/en/article/georges-phileas-vanier.
40   Florence, Elinor. "Stocky Edwards: fighter ace, family man." *The Battleford
      News Optimist,* July 15, 2014, www.newsoptimist.ca/features/everybody-
      has-a-story/stocky-edwards-fighter-ace-family-man-1.1554938 Accessed
      March 20, 2021.
41   Pelletier, Joe. "Howie Meeker." *Greatest Hockey Legends.com,*www.
      mapleleafslegends.blogspot.com/2006/05/howie-meeker.
42   Crane, Emily. "Incredible D-Day heroics of Star Trek actor 'Scotty' revealed."
      Daily Mail, June 6, 2019, Accessed March 20, 2021, www.com.dailymail.
      co.uk/news/article-7113117/Incredible-D-Day-heroics-Star-Trek-actor-Scotty.
43   *War Diary of the 1st Battalion, The Royal Winnipeg Rifles.*
44   Herd, Alex. "Dieppe Raid." *The Canadian Encyclopedia,* August 15, 2017,
      HistoricaCanada, www.thecanadianencyclopedia.ca/en/article/dieppe-raid.
      Accessed March 15, 2021.
45   O'Keefe, David. *One Day in August. Ian Fleming, Enigma, and the Deadly
      Raid onDieppe.* (Published by Icon Books 2020)
46   *War Diary of the Highland Light Infantry.*
47   Ibid
48   Slee, Geoff. *U.S. Landing Craft Tank (Rocket)-D-Day.* combinedops.com.
      www.combinedops.com/us%20landing%20craft%20rocket Accessed
      March 17, 2021.
49   *War Diary of the Highland Light Infantry.*
50   Ibid
51   Juno Beach Centre "Beach Obstacles" junobeach.org/beach-obstacles.
52   Chen, Peter, C. *J.U. 88.* World War II database. *ww2db.com,* www.ww2db.
      com/aircraft_spec.php?aircraft_model_id=10.
53   Churchill, Winston. "The Few." *Churchill's speech to The House of
      Commons.* August 20, 1940, The Churchill Society London, www.churchill-
      society-london.org.uk/thefew.
54   March, William. "Battle of Britain." *The Canadian Encyclopedia,*January
      14, 2016, *Historica Canada.* www.thecanadianencyclopedia.ca/en/article/
      battle-britain. Accessed March 17,2021.
55   *War Diary of the Highland Light Infantry.*
56   Rose, Larry.Six Months. *Three Brothers. All dead during the SecondWorld
      War.* National Post, November 11, 2014, www.nationalpost.com/opinion/
      larry-rose-six-months-three-brothers-all-dead-during-the-second-world-war.
      Accessed March 17, 2021.

57   *War Diary of the Highland Light Infantry.*

58   47 Royal Marine Commando. 47commando.org.uk.

59   *War Diary of the Highland Light Infantry.*

60   The Orne (Buron) *canadiansoldiers.com* Accessed March 17, 2021, www.
      canadiansoldiers.com/history/battlehonours/northwesteurope/
      theorne.

61   Outhit, Jeff. "The farmhand at war: Remembering the greatest hero of
      bloody Buron." *The Record* November 11, 2010. www.therecord.com/news/
      waterloo-region/2010/11/11/the-farmhand-at-war-remembering-the-greatest-
      hero-of-bloody-buron.

62   *War Diary of the Highland Light Infantry.*

63   Ibid

64   Nearingburg, John Grant. "Official Records of Service." (Courtesy
      PattNearingburg)

65   Milivojevic, Dejan. "Crossword Alarm: The Puzzle That Nearly Stopped
      D-Day." *War History Online*, March 11, 2019, www.warhistoryonline.com/
      instant-articles/crosswords-alarm-d-day.

66   Johnson, Ben. "The Spanish Flu Pandemic of 1918". *Historic U.K.*, Accessed
      March 17, 2021, www.historic-uk.com/HistoryUK/HistoryofBritain/The-
      Spanish-Flu-pandemic-of-1918/#:~:text=During%20the%20pandemic%20
      of%201918,of%20those%20who%20were%20infected.

67   Klein, Christopher. September 30, 2013 Chamberlain declares, "Peace for
      our time." *History.com,* www.history.com/news/chamberlain-declares-
      peace-for-our-time-75-years-ago.

68   Goodall, Felicity. "Life during the Blackout." *The Guardian,* November 1,
      2009, www.theguardian.com/lifeandstyle/2009/nov/01/blackout-britain-
      wartime. Accessed March 17, 2021.

69   Ibid

70   Ibid

71   Nicholas, Herbert G. "Winston Churchill." *Encyclopedia Britannica*,
      January 24,2021, www.britannica.com/biography/Winston-Churchill.
      AccessedMarch 17, 2021.

72   Perry, BP. "The Compiégne Wagon: One train carriage two peace treaties"
      Histroy.co.uk, www.history.co.uk/article/the-compi%25C3%25A8gne-
      wagon-one-train-carriage-two-peace-treaties.

73   Atkinson, David, Trauma, resilience and utopianism in Second World
      War Hull. The sporadic but deadly bombing nature of the Hull Blitz. *Hull:
      Culture, History, Place.* D. Starkey, D. Atkinson, B. McDonagh, S McKeon,
      E. Salter, & S. McKeon). Liverpool University Press (2017) Pages 245-247.

74   "Hull marks the 75th anniversary of its heaviest bombing raids in
      WW2." *B.B.C. News* May 5, 2016, www.bbc.com/news/uk-england-
      humber-36212234.

75   Geraghty, Terry. *A North East Coast Town, Ordeal and Triumph.* (Hull
      Academic Press, 2002)

76   Ibid

77   Campbell, James. "Wartime Hull Like you've never seen it. Picture of
      HisMajesty King George VI and Queen Elizabeth during their visit to Hull".
      Hull Dailey Mail October 29, 2020, www.hulldailymail.co.uk/news/hull-east-
      yorkshire-news/gallery/wartime-hull-war-photographs-pictures-4650391.

78   Gibbons, Trevor. "Hull's WWII records put online." *BBC News Yorkshire*
      November15, 2012, bbc.news/news/uk-england-humber-20341765.

79   Atkinson, David, Hull: Culture, Place, History. Liverpool: Liverpool
      University Press(2017) Page 254.
80   Geraghty, Terry. *A North East Coast Town, Ordeal and Triumph.*
81   Atkinson, David, Hull: Culture, Place, History. Liverpool: Liverpool
      University Press(2017) Page 246.
82   Cartwright, Mark. "Battle of Stamford Bridge." *World History
      Encyclopedia.* World History Encyclopedia, January 7, 2019. Accessed
      March 17, 2021.
83   Wilson, Stephen. "Rationing in World War Two." *Historic U.K.,* Accessed
      March 17, 2021, www.historic-uk.com/CultureUK/Rationing-in-World-War-
      Two.
84   *999 Port Operating Company RE – Operation Order No. 1 May 27, 1944.*
85   Ibid
86   Ibid
87   Prime Minister Winston Churchill, Southampton dockside –1944 (YouTube)
88   The coasters provided…Marie Brown interview July 19, 2019 Information
      supplied by (ww2talk.com)
89   Laurenceau, Marc. History of Landing on Sword Beach on D-Day. *D-Day
      Overlord Encyclopedia.* www.dday-overlord.com/en/d-day/beaches/sword-
      beach.
90   The others included…Marie Brown interview. July 19, 2020 Information
      supplied by (ww2talk.com)
91   Foot, Richard. "D-Day and the Battle of Normandy." *The Canadian . . . .
      Encyclopedia,* May 3 2019, *Historica Canada,* . . . . www.
      thecanadianencyclopedia.ca/en/article/normandy-invasion. Accessed March
      18, 2021.
92   "Port and Inland Waterway Units Royal Engineers." ww2talk.com.
      August 29, 2010. www.ww 2talk.com/index.php?threads/royal-engineers-
      june-1944.76959.
93   Laurenceau, Marc. Gooseberries and Blockships-Battle of Normandy-
      1944.*D-DayOverlord Encyclopedia,* www.dday-overlord.com/en/d-day/
      armada/gooseberries-blockships.
94   The European Centre for Medium-Range Weather Forecasts. ECMWF
      simulates storm that destroyed Normandy invasion. 29 August, 2017, ecmwf.
      int/en/about/media-centre/news/2017/ecmwf-simulates-storm-destroyed-
      normandy-invasion-harbour. (ecmwf.int)
95   Destruction of Mulberry A in a fierce storm.WWII. *World War 2
      Headquarters.* www.worldwar2headquarters.com/HTML/normandy/
      mulberries/wreckedMulberry.
96   *War Diary 999 Port Operating Company.*
97   Ibid
98   Zimmer, Phil. Why the German 88mm Gun Was the Best Throughout
      WWII. *Warfare History Network,* www.warfarehistorynetwork.
      com/2017/07/10/why-german-88mm-gun-was-best-in-the-war.
99   *War Diary 999 Port Operating Company.*
100   Ibid
101   Coasters continued… Marie Brown interview July 19, 2019 Information
      supplied by (ww2talk.com)
102   "Hercules Cycle and Motor Co. History." *Hercules Cycle and Motor Co.
      Museum,* www.herculesmuseum.wordpress.com/hercules-cycle-motor-co-
      history.

103   Hull, Michael, D. "The Story of Bill Millin, Lord Lovat's Mad Piper of Sword Beach," *Warfare History Network,* www.warfarehistorynetwork. com/2020/11/06/the-story-of-bill-millin-lord-lovats-mad-piper-of-sword-beach.

104   "1940 – Dunkirk, St Valery en Caux" *The Duke of Wellington'sRegiment (West Riding) Regimental Association.* www.dwr.org.uk/history/1899-1949/.

105   The 2ⁿᵈ Battalion East Yorks 1939-1945. *East Yorkshire Living History Group.* www.eastyorkshiregiment.blogspot.com /p/history.

106   Peck, Michael. "What Happened at Dunkirk: Hitler's Halt Order (AndUltimate Failure)" *Warfare History Network,* www. warfarehistorynetwork.com/2019/01/05/what-happened-at-dunkirk-hitlers-halt-order-and-ultimate-failure.

107   "The East Yorkshire Regiment: From the West Indies to the Western Front." *Hull Museums Collection.* www.hullmuseumscollection.hullcc.gov.uk/ collections/storydetail.php?irn=193&master=199#:~:text=Raising%20a%20 Regiment&text=It%20was%20at%20the%20Battle,helping%20them%20 win%20the%20battle.

108   Stevens, Christopher. Heroes to the very end: The story of the 20,000 men left behind after Dunkirk to make one last, desperate stand is told in a new documentary. *Dailymail.com* July 6, 2018, www.dailymail.co.uk/femail/ article-5914183/The-story-20-000-men-left-Dunkirk.

109   Harbicht-Sczesny, "D-Day veteran remembers the cost of freedom."*Western Journal,* November 7, 2012, P15.

110   "Historical Chronology for the City of Brandon 1935, 1936, 1937."*HeritageBrandon,* www.heritagebrandon.ca/resources/chronology.

111   Granatstein, J.l. and Richard Jones. "Conscription in Canada". *The Canadian Encyclopedia*, March 19, 2020, *Historica Canada*, www. thecanadianencyclopedia.ca/en/article/conscription. Accessed March 19, 2021.

112   Manitoba – Canadian Military Bases. (militarybruce.com)

113   The Royal Winnipeg Rifles. The official lineage of The Royal Winnipeg Riflesinfantry regiment. *Government of Canada.* www.canada.ca /en/ department-national-defence/services/military-history/history-heritage/ official-military-history-lineages/lineages/infantry-regiments/royal-winnipeg-rifles.

114   Hamilton, Grant. "Down on the Titanic." *The Brandon Sun*, June 2, 2012, brandonsun.com, www.brandonsun.com/princeedwardhotel/Down-on-the-Titanic-156004365.

115   RMS Queen Mary ship specifications/facts. *RMS Queen Mary,* November 29, 2015, www.queenmarycruises/rms-queen-mary.

116   Ibid

117   Trueman, C.N. "U-Boats." *The History Learning Site.* May 18, 2015. Accessed March 19, 2021. historylearningsite.co.uk. www. historylearningsite.co.uk/world-war-two/war-in-the-atlantic/u-boats.

118   The Maritime Executive. "Cunard Releases Historic Queen Mary Picture." *The Maritime Executive*, July 3, 2016, www.maritime-executive.com/ features/cunard-releases-historic-queen-mary-picture.

119   Hamilton, Jack. *Souvenirs of overseas duty. 1942-1946.* Personal memoirs. (Courtesy Anne Hamilton)

120   Cherney, Kristeen. "What is Trench Foot" *Health Line.* March 29, 2019, www.healthline.com/health/trench-foot.

121 1937 Pattern Web Equipment. *canadiansoldiers.com* Accessed March 17, 2021, www.canadiansoldiers.com/equipment/loadbearing/1937pattern.

122 Olson, Donald. "Astronomy and D-Day: The Sun, Moon and Tides at Normandy*." Sky and Telescope The Essential Guide to Astronomy* 2 June 2019, www.skyandtelescope.org /astronomy-news/astronomy-d-day-sun-moon-tides.

123 Parker, Bruce. "The tide predictions D-Day." *Physics Today* September 1, 2011, P35. www.physicstoday.scitation.org/doi/10.1063/PT.3.1257.

124 McRae, John. "In Flanders Fields." *Poetry Foundation,* www. poetryfoundation.org/poems/47380/in-flanders-fields.

125 *War Diary of the 1st Battalion, The Royal Winnipeg Rifles.*

126 Ibid

127 "Chateau D'Audrieu massacre of 24 Canadians and 2 British P.O.W.s Normandy." *normandy warguide.com.* Accessed March 19 2021, www. normandywarguide.com/articles/the-massacre-of-24-canadian-and-2-british-pows-at-chateau-d-audrieu-normandy.

128 *War Diary of the 1st Battalion, The Royal Winnipeg Rifles.*

129 Laurenceau, Marc. History of the Sherman Firefly Tank-Battle of Normandy. *D-Day Overlord Encyclopedia*, www.dday-overlord.com/en/material/tank/sherman-firefly.

130 Dowling, Stephen, "The Strange Tanks that helped win D-Day." *B.B.C.* June 6, 2016, www.bbc.com/future/article/20160603-the-strange-tanks-that-helped-win-d-day.

131 Batter, Brian. Lt. Colonel (R) retired, The Royal Winnipeg Rifles, commentary during the Carpiquet tour, June 2019.

132 Carpiquet and Caen. "Normandy-1944" Veterans Affairs Canada, www. veterans gc.ca/eng/remembrance/history/second-world-war/normandy-1944#carpiquet.

133 Batter, Brian. Lt. Colonel (R) retired, The Royal Winnipeg Rifles, commentary during the Carpiquet tour, June 2019.

134 *War Diary of the 1st Battalion, The Royal Winnipeg Rifles.*

135 Batter, Brian. Lt. Colonel (R) retired, The Royal Winnipeg Rifles, commentary during the Carpiquet tour, June 2019.

136 *War Diary of the 1st Battalion, The Royal Winnipeg Rifles.*

137 Trueman, C. N. "V1" *The History Learning Site*, www.historylearningsite.co.uk /world-war-two/weapons-of-world-war-two/v1/. May 25, 2015. Accessed March 20, 2021.

138 Frame, Chris. "Queen Elizabeth History, Part 2: War Years." Chris' Cunard Page, www.chriscunard.com/queen-elizabeth.

139 Goosens, Reuben. "Cunard White Star Line. R.M.S. Queen Elizabeth." *SS Maritime.Com.*ssmaritime.com/RMS-Queen-Elizabeth.

140 Gower, P.E Captain. Repatriation Report and testimony of Commanding Officers' Company 1945, section 29. (*The Devils' Blast 2014: Annual Chronicle of The Royal Winnipeg Rifles*, Brian Batter, editor.)

141 Harbicht-Sczesny, "D-Day veteran remembers the cost of freedom." *Western Journal* November 7, 2012, P15.

142 Stewart, Lanny. "Memories of times gone by remain at the forefront for World War II veteran. *"Western Journal*, May 7, 2015.

143 Harbicht-Sczesny, "D-Day veteran remembers the cost of freedom." *Western Journal,* November 7, 2012, P18.

144 "Personal memoirs of Jack Hamilton." (Courtesy Anne Hamilton)

145   Chateau d'Audrieu, chateaudaudrieu.com/en/luxury-tree-house.html.

146   Barris, Ted, *Juno Canadians at D-Day June 6, 1944.* (Thomas
      AllanPublishers, 2004)

147   Barris, Ted. *Rush into Danger: Medics in the Line of Fire.* (Harper Collins
      Publishers, 2019)

148   O'Keefe, David. *Seven Days in Hell: Canada's Battle for Normandy and the
      rise of the Black Watch Snipers.* (HarperCollins Publishers 2019)

149   Rodat, Robert. Screenwriter. *Saving Private Ryan.* (ParamountPictures,
      1998)

150   Eisenhower, Dwight D. General Eisenhower's letter taking the blame for
      the failed invasion of Normandy. *The Collection DDE-EPRE: Eisenhower,
      Dwight D.: Papers,* Pre-Presidential. National Archives Identifier: 186470
      (Public Domain)

Photograph Credits

Gerry Levers

Johnny Nearingburg

About the Cover

Choosing the cover design for this book was an enjoyable process. With thousands of books about World War II on the market, we wanted something unique. Working with cover designer, Lea Kulmatycki to transform my vision into reality was a rewarding experience. Each picture was chosen to express my personal feelings about this historic event.

 It was imperative to use the iconic picture of my father's regiment, The Royal Winnipeg Rifles, in a landing craft as it headed to Juno Beach on June 6th, 1944.

Beneath the text on the back cover is a picture of footsteps in the sand. I took this photo while visiting Juno Beach in 2019 for the 75th Anniversary of D-Day. As I walked across the beach that first evening, I felt I was following the footsteps of my father as he crossed Juno Beach that famous day.

The photograph of the ageing veteran is an image I captured at Arromanches. It is part of the most incredible memorial dedicated to veterans that I have ever seen. I become emotional each time I attempt to describe this monument to people. Placing this veteran's image on the cover was important because he represents the fathers whose footsteps we walk in today. John Everiss, sculptor and award-winning garden designer, graciously gave me permission to use the images of his work on the cover and in the book.

The sea thrift would have been seen by the troops as they stormed the Normandy beaches. These flowers add colour, life, and authenticity to the cover.

You can find out more about this stunning memorial by searching D-Day Gardens Arromanches.

Cover design: Lea Kulmatycki Cover pictures: Library and Archives Canada / PA-132651 / PA 131889 Picture of Statue of Veteran Bill Pendle: Courtesy of John Everiss

Find out more about Our Fathers' Footsteps and other books by Don Levers at DonLeversBooks.com

Don Levers can be contacted at:
ourfathersfootsteps@gmail.com

To order more copies of this book, find books by other Canadian authors, or make inquiries about publishing your own book, contact PageMaster at:

PageMaster Publication Services Inc.
11340-120 Street, Edmonton, AB T5G 0W5
books@pagemaster.ca
780-425-9303

catalogue and e-commerce store
PageMasterPublishing.ca/Shop

About the Author

Don Levers was born and raised in the Fraserview area of Vancouver in 1954. This neighbourhood was filled with the children of veterans from World War II. After his daughters were born, Don would make stories for them. Then, in 1985 he self-published his children's book, "*Ogopogo the Misunderstood Lake Monster.*" It has since sold more than 30,000 copies.

In 1987 Don began work on *Loot for the Taking*, a novel inspired by actual events

Life got in the way, and in 2016, Don returned to his writing passion and completed *Loot for the Taking.* Don has been married for 45 years. He and his wife currently live in Sturgeon County, Alberta.

Don was honoured by the Vancouver Public Library as an upcoming Indie author and was featured in the library's 2017 annual report. "Self-publishing is a challenge, but a program like this (Vancouver Indie Authors collection) helps to give indie authors a feeling of legitimacy. It helps us realize that we are indeed real authors."

In June 2019, Don fulfilled a lifelong dream of going to Normandy, France, to see where his father had landed on Juno Beach on D-Day 1944.

Our Fathers' Footsteps results from conversations, interviews and research Don conducted during and after his trip to France. He hopes the stories in *Our Fathers' Footsteps* will inspire other families to take a walk in their Father's Footsteps. To help them realize how lucky they are to be alive today.